MW01146362

The Adventures of

Darby O'Gill

The Adventures of

Darby O'Gill

and Other Tales of
Supernatural Ireland

HERMINIE TEMPLETON KAVANAGH

Coachwhip Publications
Landisville, Pennsylvania

The Adventures of Darby O'Gill and Other Tales of Supernatural Ireland
Copyright © 2009 Coachwhip Publications

ISBN 1-930585-88-8
ISBN-13 978-1-930585-88-1

Cover: Shamrock design © Sherri Camp
Back Cover: Trim Castle © Arvydas Kniukšta

Coachwhipbooks.com

All Rights Reserved. No part of this publication may be reproduced, stored in a retrieval system or transmitted in any form or by any means—electronic, mechanical, photocopy, recording or any other—except for brief quotations in printed reviews, without the prior permission of the author or publisher.

Contents

FOREWORD

This history sets forth the only true account of the adventures of a daring Tipperary man named Darby O'Gill among the Fairies of Sleive-na-mon.

These adventures were first related to me by Mr. Jerry Murtaugh, a reliable car-driver, who goes between Kilcuny and Ballinderg. He is a first cousin of Darby O'Gill's own mother.

DARBY O'GILL AND THE GOOD PEOPLE

Although only one living man of his own free will ever went among them there, still, any well-learned person in Ireland can tell you that the abode of the Good People is in the hollow heart of the great mountain Sleive-na-mon. That same one man was Darby O'Gill, a cousin of my own mother.

Right and left, generation after generation, the fairies had stolen pigs, young childher, old women, young men, cows, churnings of butter from other people, but had never bothered any of our kith or kin until, for some mysterious rayson, they soured on Darby, and took the eldest of his three foine pigs.

The next week a second pig went the same way. The third week not a thing had Darby left for the Balinrobe fair. You may aisly think how sore and sorry the poor man was, an' how Bridget his wife an' the childher carried on. The rent was due, and all left was to sell his cow Rosie to pay it. Rosie was the apple of his eye; he admired and rayspected the pigs, but he loved Rosie.

Worst luck of all was yet to come. On the morning when Darby went for the cow to bring her into market, bad scrans to the hoof was there; but in her place only a wisp of dirty straw to mock him. Millia murther! What a howlin' and screechin' and cursin' did Darby bring back to the house!

Now Darby was a bould man, and a desperate man in his anger, as you soon will see. He shoved his feet into a pair of brogues, clapped his hat on his head, and gripped his stick in his hand.

"Fairy or no fairy, ghost or goblin, livin' or dead, who took Rosie'll rue this day," he says.

With those wild words he bolted in the direction of Sleive-na-mon. All day long he climbed like an ant over the hill, looking for a hole or cave through which he could get at the prison of Rosie. At times he struck the rocks with his blackthorn, cryin' out challenge.

"Come out, you that took her," he called. "If ye have the courage of a mouse, ye murtherin' thieves, come out!"

No one made answer—at laste, not just then. But at night, as he turned, hungry and footsore, toward home, who should he meet up with on the crossroads but the ould fairy doctor, Sheelah Maguire. Well known she was as a spy for the Good People. She spoke up:

"Oh, then, you're the foolish, blundherin'-headed man to be saying what you've said, and doing what you've done this day, Darby Gill," says she.

"What do I care!" says he fiercely. "I'd fight the divil to-night for my beautiful cow."

"Then go into Mrs. Hagan's meadow beyant," says Sheela, "and wait till the moon is up. By-an'-by ye'll see a herd of cows come down from the mountain, and yer own'll be among them."

"What'll I do then?" asked Darby, his voice thrembling with excitement.

"Sorra a hair I care what ye do! But there'll be lads there, and hundreds you won't see, that'll stand no ill words, Darby Gill."

"One question more, ma'am," says Darby, as Sheelah was moving away. "How late in the night will they stay without?"

Sheelah caught him by the collar and, pulling his head close, whuspered: "When the cock crows the Good People must be safe at home. After cock-crow they have no power to help or to hurt, and every mortal eye can see them plain."

"I thank you kindly," says Darby, "and I bid you good-evening, ma'am." He turned away, leaving her standing there alone, looking after him; but he was sure he heard voices talkin' to her, and laughin' and tittherin' behind him.

It was dark night when Darby stretched himself on the ground in Hagan's meadow; the yellow rim of the moon just tipped the edge of the hills.

As he lay there in the long grass amidst the silence there came a cowld shudder in the air, an' afther it had passed the deep cracked voice of a near-by bull-frog called loudly an' ballyraggin':

"The Omadhaun! Omadhaun! Omadhaun!" it said.

From a sloe three over near the hedge an owl cried, surprised and thremblin':

"Who-o-o? who-o-o?" it axed.

At that every frog in the meadow—an' there must have been tin thousand of them—took up the answer, an' shrieked shrill an' high together. "Darby O'Gill! Darby O'Gill! Darby O'Gill!" sang they.

"The Omadhaun! The Omadhaun!" cried the wheezy masther frog again. "Who-o? Who-o?" axed the owl. "Darby O'Gill! Darby O'Gill!" screamed the rollicking chorus; an' that way they were goin' over an' over agin until the bould man was just about to creep off to another spot whin, sudden, a hundred slow shadows, stirring up the mists, crept from the mountain way toward him. First he must find was Rosie among the herd. To creep quiet as a cat through the hedge and raich the first cow was only a minute's work. Then his plan, to wait till cock-crow, with all other sober, sensible thoughts, went clane out of the lad's head before his rage; for cropping eagerly the long, sweet grass, the first baste he met, was Rosie.

With a leap Darby was behind her, his stick falling sharply on her flanks. The ingratitude of that cow almost broke Darby's heart. Rosie turned fiercely on him, with a vicious lunge, her two horns aimed at his breast. There

was no suppler boy in the parish than Darby, and well for
him it was so, for the mad rush the cow gave would have
caught any man the laste thrifle heavy on his legs, and
ended his days right there.

As it was, our hayro sprang to one side. As Rosie
passed, his left hand gripped her tail. When one of the Gills
takes hould of a thing, he hangs on like a bull-terrier.
Away he went, rushing with her.

Now began a race the like of which was never heard of
before or since. Ten jumps to the second, and a hundred
feet to the jump. Rosie's tail standing straight up in the
air, firm as an iron bar, and Darby floating straight out
behind; a thousand furious fairies flying a short distance
after, filling the air with wild commands and threatenings.

Suddenly the sky opened for a crash of lightning that
shivered the hills, and a roar of thunder that turned out
of their beds every man, woman, and child in four counties. Flash after flash came the lightning, hitting on every
side of Darby. If it wasn't for fear of hurting Rosie, the
fairies would sartenly have killed Darby. As it was, he
was stiff with fear, afraid to hould on and afraid to lave
go, but flew, waving in the air at Rosie's tail like a flag.

As the cow turned into the long, narrow valley which
cuts into the east side of the mountain, the Good People
caught up with the pair, and what they didn't do to Darby,
in the line of sticking pins, pulling whiskers, and pinch-
ing wouldn't take long to tell. In troth, he was just about
to let go his hould, and take the chances of a fall, when
the hillside opened and—whisk! The cow turned into the
mountain. Darby found himself flying down a wide, high
passage which grew lighter as he went along. He heard
the opening behind shut like a trap, and his heart almost
stopped beating, for this was the fairies' home in the heart
of Sleive-na-mon. He was captured by them!

When Rosie stopped, so stiff were all Darby's joints,
that he had great trouble loosening himself to come down.
He landed among a lot of angry-faced little people, each

no higher than your hand, everyone wearing a green velvet cloak and a red cap, and in every cap was stuck a white owl's feather.

"We'll take him to the king," says a red-whuskered wee chap. "What he'll do to the murtherin' spalpeen'll be good and plenty!"

With that they marched our bould Darby, a prisoner, down the long passage, which every second grew wider and lighter, and fuller of little people.

Sometimes, though, he met with human beings like himself, only the black charm was on them, they having been stolen at some time by the Good People. He saw Lost People there from every parish in Ireland, both commoners and gentry. Each was laughing, talking, and divarting himself with another. Off to the sides he could see small cobblers making brogues, tinkers mending pans, tailors sewing cloth, smiths hammering horseshoes, everyone merrily to his trade, making a diversion out of work.

To this day Darby can't tell where the beautiful red light he now saw came from. It was like a soft glow, only it filled the place, making things brighter than day.

Down near the center of the mountain, was a room twenty times higher and broader than the biggest church in the world. As they drew near this room, there arose the sound of a reel played on bagpipes. The music was so bewitching that Darby, who was the gracefullest reel dancer in all Ireland, could hardly make his feet behave themselves.

At the room's edge Darby stopped short and caught his breath, the sight was so entrancing. Set over the broad floor were thousands and thousands of the Good People, facing this way and that, and dancing to a reel; while on a throne in the middle of the room sat ould Brian Conners, King of the Fairies, blowing on the bagpipes. The little king, with a goold crown on his head, wearing a beautiful green velvet coat and red knee-breeches, sat with his legs crossed, beating time with his foot to the music.

There were many from Darby's own parish; and what was his surprise to see there Maureen McGibney, his own wife's sister, whom he had supposed resting dacintly in her grave in holy ground these three years. She had flowers in her brown hair, a fine colour in her cheeks, a gown of white silk and goold, and her green mantle raiched to the heels of her purty red slippers.

There she was, gliding back and forth, ferninst a little gray-whiskered, round-stomached fairy man, as though there was never a care nor a sorrow in the worruld.

As I told you before, I tell you again, Darby was the finest reel dancer in all Ireland; and he came from a family of dancers, though I say it who shouldn't, as he was my mother's own cousin. Three things in the world banish sorrow—love and whisky and music. So, when the surprise of it all melted a little, Darby's feet led him in to the thick of the throng, right under the throne of the king, where he flung care to the winds, and put his heart and mind into his two nimble feet. Darby's dancing was such that purty soon those around stood still to admire.

There's a saying come down in our family through generations which I still hould to be true, that the better the music the aisier the step. Sure never did mortal men dance to so fine a chune and never so supple a dancer did such a chune meet up with.

Fair and graceful he began. Backward and forward, sidestep and turn; cross over, then forward; a hand on his hip and his stick twirling free; sidestep and forward; cross over again; bow to his partner, and hammer the floor.

It wasn't long till half the dancers crowded around admiring, clapping their hands, and shouting encouragement. The ould king grew so excited that he laid down the pipes, took up his fiddle, came down from the throne, and standing ferninst Darby, began a finer chune than the first.

The dancing lasted a whole hour, no one speaking a word except to cry out, "Foot it, ye divil!" "Aisy now, he's threading on flowers!" "Hooroo! Hooroo! Hooray!" Then the king stopped and said:

"Well, that bates Banagher, and Banagher bates the world! Who are you, and how came you here?"

Then Darby up and tould the whole story.

When he had finished, the king looked sayrious. "I'm glad you came, an' I'm sorry you came," he says. "If we had put our charm on you outside to bring you in, you'd never die till the end of the world, when we here must all go to hell. But," he added quickly, "there's no use in worrying about that now. That's nayther here nor there! Those willing to come with us can't come at all, at all; and here you are of your own free act and will. Howsomever, you're here, and we daren't let you go outside to tell others of what you have seen, and so give us a bad name about— about taking things, you know. We'll make you as comfortable as we can; and so you won't worry about Bridget and the childher, I'll have a goold sovereign left with them every day of their lives. But I wish we had the comeither on you," he says, with a sigh, "for it's aisy to see you're great company. Now come up to my place and have a noggin of punch for friendship's sake," says he.

That's how Darby Gill began his six months' stay with the Good People. Not a thing was left undone to make Darby contented and happy. A civiler people than the Good People he never met. At first he couldn't get over saying, "God keep all here," and "God save you kindly," and things like that, which was like burning them with a hot iron.

If it weren't for Maureen McGibney, Darby would be in Sleive-na-mon at this hour. Sure she was always the wise girl, ready with her crafty plans and warnings. On a day when they two were sitting alone together, she says to him:

"Darby, dear," says she, "it isn't right for a dacint man of family to be spending his days cavortin', and idlin', and fillin' the hours with sport and nonsense. We must get you out of here; for what is a sovereign a day to compare with the care and protection of a father?" she says.

"Thrue for ye!" moaned Darby, "and my heart is just splittin' for a sight of Bridget an' the childher. Bad luck to the day I set so much store on a dirty, ongrateful, threacherous cow!"

"I know well how you feel," says Maureen, "for I'd give the whole world to say three words to Bob Broderick, that ye tell me that out of grief for me he has never kept company with any other girl till this day. But that'll never be," she says, "because I must stop here till the Day of Judgment, and then I must go to—" says she, beginning to cry, "but if you get out, you'll bear a message to Bob for me, maybe?" she says.

"It's aisy to talk about going out, but how can it be done?" asked Darby.

"There's a way," says Maureen, wiping her big gray eyes, "but it may take years. First, you must know that the Good People can never put their charm on any one who is willing to come with them. That's why you came safe. Then, again, they can't work harm in the daylight, and after cock-crow any mortal eye can see them plain; nor can they harm anyone who has a sprig of holly, nor pass over a leaf or twig of holly, because that's Christmas bloom. Well, there's a certain evil word for a charm that opens the side of the mountain, and I will try to find it out for you. Without that word, the armies of the world couldn't get out or in. But you must be patient and wise, and wait."

"I will so, with the help of God," says Darby.

At these words, Maureen gave a terrible screech.

"Cruel man!" she cried, "don't you know that to say pious words to one of the Good People, or to one under their black charm, is like cutting him with a knife?"

The next night she came to Darby again. "Watch yerself now," she says, "for to-night they're goin' to lave the door of the mountain open, to thry you; and if you stir two steps outside they'll put the comeither on you," she says.

Sure enough, when Darby took his walk down the passage, after supper, as he did every night, there the side of

the mountain lay wide open and no one in sight. The temptation to make one rush was great; but he only looked out
a minute, and went whistling back down the passage,
knowing well that a hundred hidden eyes were on him the
while. For a dozen nights after it was the same.

At another time Maureen said:

"The king himself is going to thry you hard the day, so
beware!" She had no sooner said the words than Darby
was called for, and went up to the king.

"Darby, my sowl," says the king, in a sootherin' way,
"have this noggin of punch. A betther never was brewed;
it's the last we'll have for many a day. I'm going to set you
free, Darby O'Gill, that's what I am."

"Why, king," says Darby, putting on a mournful face,
"how have I offended ye?"

"No offense at all," says the king, "only we're depriving
you."

"No depravity in life!" says Darby. "I have lashins and
lavings to ate and to drink, and nothing but fun an'
divarsion all day long. Out in the world it was nothing but
work and throuble and sickness, disappointment and
care."

"But Bridget and the childher?" says the king, giving
him a sharp look out of half-shut eyes.

"Oh, as for that, King," says Darby, "it's aisier for a
widow to get a husband, or for orphans to find a father,
than it is for them to pick up a sovereign a day."

The king looked mighty satisfied and smoked for a while
without a word.

"Would you mind going out an evenin' now and then,
helpin' the boys to mind the cows?" he asked at last.

Darby feared to thrust himself outside in their company.

"Well, I'll tell ye how it is," replied my brave Darby.
"Some of the neighbors might see me, and spread the re-
port on me that I'm with the fairies, and that'd disgrace
Bridget and the childher," he says.

The king knocked the ashes from his pipe.

"You're a wise man besides being the hoight of good company," says he, "and it's sorry I am you didn't take me at my word; for then we would have you always, at laste till the Day of Judgment, when—but that's nayther here nor there! Howsomever, we'll bother you about it no more."

From that day they thrated him as one of their own.

It was one day five months after that Maureen plucked Darby by the coat and led him off to a lonely spot.

"I've got the word," she says.

"Have you, faith! What is it!" says Darby, all of a thremble.

Then she whispered a word so blasphaymous, so irrayligious, that Darby blessed himself. When Maureen saw him making the sign, she fell down in a fit, the holy emblem hurt her so, poor child.

Three hours after this me bould Darby was sitting at his own fireside talking to Bridget and the childher. The neighbors were hurrying to him, down every road and through every field, carrying armfuls of holly bushes, as he had sent word for them to do. He knew well he'd have fierce and savage visitors before morning.

After they had come with the holly, he had them make a circle of it so thick around the house that a fly couldn't walk through without touching a twig or a leaf. But that was not all.

You'll know what a wise girl and what a crafty girl that Maureen was when you hear what the neighbors did next. They made a second ring of holly outside the first, so that the house sat in two great wreaths, one wreath around the other. The outside ring was much the bigger, and left a good space between it and the first, with room for ever so many people to stand there. It was like the inner ring, except for a little gate, left open as though by accident, where the fairies could walk in.

But it wasn't an accident at all, only the wise plan of Maureen's; for nearby this little gap, in the outside wreath, lay a sprig of holly with a bit of twine tied to it. Then the twine ran along up to Darby's house, and in through the window, where its ind lay convaynient to his hand. A little pull on the twine would drag the stray piece of holly into the gap, and close tight the outside ring.

It was a trap, you see. When the fairies walked in through the gap, the twine was to be pulled, and so they were to be made prisoners between the two rings of holly. They couldn't get into Darby's house, because the circle of holly nearest the house was so tight that a fly couldn't get through without touching the blessed tree or its wood. Likewise, when the gap in the outer wreath was closed, they couldn't get out again. Well, anyway, these things were hardly finished and fixed, when the dusky brown of the hills warned the neighbors of twilight, and they scurried like frightened rabbits to their homes.

Only one amongst them all had courage to sit inside Darby's house waiting the dreadful visitors, and that one was Bob Broderick. What vengeance was in store couldn't be guessed at all, at all, only it was sure that it was to be more terrible than any yet wreaked on mortal man.

Not in Darby's house alone was the terror, for in their anger the Good People might lay waste the whole parish. The roads and fields were empty and silent in the darkness. Not a window glimmered with light for miles around. Many a blaggard who hadn't said a prayer for years was now down on his marrow bones among the dacint members of his family, thumping his craw, and roaring his Pather and Aves.

In Darby's quiet house, against which the cunning, the power, and the fury of the Good People would first break, you can't think of half the suffering of Bridget and the childher, as they lay huddled together on the settle bed; nor of the strain on Bob and Darby, who sat smoking their dudeens and whispering anxiously together.

For some rayson or other the Good People were long in coming. Ten o'clock struck, thin eleven, afther that twelve,

and not a sound from the outside. The silence and the no
sign of any kind had them all just about crazy, when suddenly there fell a sharp rap on the door.

"Millia murther," whispered Darby, "we're in for it.
They've crossed the two rings of holly, and are at the door
itself."

The childher begun to cry and Bridget said her prayers
out loud; but no one answered the knock.

"Rap, rap, rap," on the door, then a pause.

"God save all here!" cried a queer voice from the outside.

Now no fairy would say, "God save all here," so Darby
took heart and opened the door. Who should be standing
there but Sheelah Maguire, a spy for the Good People. So
angry were Darby and Bob that they snatched her within
the threshold, and before she knew it they had her tied
hand and foot, wound a cloth around her mouth, and rolled
her under the bed. Within the minute a thousand rus-
tling voices sprung from outside. Through the window, in
the clear moonlight, Darby marked weeds and grass being trampled by invisible feet, beyond the farthest ring of
holly.

Suddenly broke a great cry. The gap in the first ring
was found. Signs were plainly seen of uncountable feet
rushing through, and spreading about the nearer wreath.
Afther that a howl of.madness from the little men and
women. Darby had pulled his twine and the trap was
closed, with five thousand of the Good People entirely at
his mercy.

Princes, princesses, dukes, dukesses, earls, earlesses,
and all the quality of Sleive-na-mon were prisoners. Not
more than a dozen of the last to come escaped, and they
flew back to tell the King.

For an hour they raged. All the bad names ever called
to mortal man were given free, but Darby said never a
word. "Pickpocket," "sheep-stayler," "murtherin' thafe of
a blaggard," were the softest words trun at him.

By an' by, howsomever, as it begun to grow near to cock-crow, their talk grew a great dale civiler. Then came beggin', pladin', promisin', and enthratin', but the doors of the house still stayed shut an' its windows down.

Purty soon Darby's old rooster, Terry, came down from his perch, yawned, an' flapped his wings a few times. At that the terror and the screechin' of the Good people would have melted the heart of a stone.

All of a sudden a fine, clear voice rose from beyant the crowd. The King had come. The other fairies grew still, listening. "Ye murtherin' thafe of the world," says the king grandly, "what are ye doin' wid my people?"

"Keep a civil tongue in yer head, Brian Connor," says Darby, sticking his head out the window, "for I'm as good a man as you, any day," says Darby.

At that minute Terry, the cock, flapped his wings and crowed. In a flash there sprang into full view the crowd of Good People—dukes, earls, princes, quality, and commoners, with their ladies, jammed thick together about the house; every one of them with his head thrown back bawling and crying, and tears as big as pigeons' eggs rouling down his cheeks.

A few feet away, on a straw-pile in the barnyard, stood the king, his goold crown tilted on the side of his head, his long green cloak about him, and his rod in his hand, but thremblin' allover.

In the middle of the crowd, but towering high above them all, stood Maureen McGibney in her cloak of green an' goold, her purty brown hair fallin' down on her shoulders, an' she—the crafty villain—cryin, an' bawlin', an' abusin' Darby, with the best of them.

"What'll you have an' let them go?" says the king.

"First an' foremost," says Darby, "take yer spell off that slip of a girl there, an' send her into the house."

In a second Maureen was standing inside the door, her both arms about Bob's neck, and her head on his collar-bone.

What they said to aich other, an' what they done in the way of embracin' an' kissin' an' cryin' I won't take time in telling you.

"Next," says Darby, "send back Rosie and the pigs."

"I expected that," says the King. And at those words they saw a black bunch coming through the air; in a few seconds Rosie and the three pigs walked into the stable.

"Now," says Darby, "promise in the name of Ould Nick" ('tis by him the Good People swear) "never to moil nor meddle agin with anyone or anything from this parish."

The King was fair put out by this. Howsomever, he said at last, "You ongrateful scoundrel, in the name of Ould Nick, I promise."

"So far, so good," says Darby, "but the worst is yet to come. Now you must ralayse from your spell every sowl you've stole from this parish; and besides, you must send me two hundhred pounds in goold."

Well, the King gave a roar of anger that was heard in the next barony.

"Ye high-handed, hard-hearted robber," he says, "I'll never consent!" says he.

"Plase yerself," says Darby. "I see Father Cassidy comin' down the hedge," he says, "an' he has a prayer for ye all in his book that'll burn ye up like wisps of sthraw if he ever catches ye here," says Darby.

With that the roaring and bawling was pitiful to hear, and in a few minutes a bag with two hundhred goold sovereigns in it was trun at Darby's threshold; and fifty people, young an' some of them ould, flew over an' stood beside the King. Some of them had spent years with the fairies. Their relatives thought them dead an' buried. They were the lost ones from that parish.

With that Darby pulled the bit of twine again, opening the trap, and it wasn't long until every fairy was gone.

The green coat of the last one was hardly out of sight when, sure enough, who should come up but Father Cassidy, his book in his hand. He looked at the fifty people who had been with the fairies standin' there—the poor crathures—thremblin' an' wondherin', an' afeared to go to their homes.

Darby tould him what had happened.

"Ye foolish man," says the priest, "you could have got out every poor presoner that's locked in Sleive-na-mon, let alone those from this parish."

One could have scraped with a knife the surprise off Darby's face.

"Would yer Reverence have me let out the Corkonians, the Connaught men, and the Fardowns, I ask ye?" he says hotly. "When Mrs. Malowney there goes home and finds that Tim has married the Widow Hogan, ye'll say I let out too many, even of this parish, I'm thinkin'."

"But," says the priest, "ye might have got two hundred pounds for aich of us."

"If aich had two hundhred pounds, what comfort would I have in being rich?" axed Darby agin. "To enjoy well being rich, there should be plenty of poor," says Darby.

"God forgive ye, ye selfish man!" says Father Cassidy.

"There's another rayson besides," says Darby. "I never got betther nor friendlier thratement than I had from the Good People. An' the divil a hair of their heads I'd hurt more than need be," he says.

Some way or other the king heard of this saying, an' was so mightily pleased that next night a jug of the finest poteen was left at Darby's door.

After that, indade, many's the winter night, when the snow lay so heavy that no neighbor was stirrin', and when Bridget and the childher were in bed, Darby sat by the fire, a noggin of hot punch in his hand, argying an' getting news of the whole worruld. A little man, with a goold crown on his head, a green cloak on his back, and one foot trun over the other, sat ferninst him by the hearth.

DARBY O'GILL AND THE LEPRECHAUN

The news that Darby O'Gill had spint six months with the Good People spread fast and far and wide.

At fair or hurlin' or market he would be backed be a crowd agin some convaynient wall, and there for hours men, women, and childher, with jaws dhroppin', and eyes bulgin'd stand ferninst him listening to half frightened questions or to bould mystarious answers.

Alway, though, one bit of wise adwise inded his discoorse: "Nayther make nor moil nor meddle with the fairies," Darby'd say. "If you're going along the lonely boreen at night, and you hear, from some fairy fort, a sound of fiddles, or of piping, or of sweet woices singing, or of little feet pattering in the dance, don't turn your head, but say your prayers an' hould on your way. The pleasures the Good People'll share with you have a sore sorrow hid in them, an' the gifts they'll offer are only made to break hearts with."

Things went this a-way till one day in the market, over among the cows, Maurteen Cavanaugh, the school masther—a cross-faced, argifying ould man he was—contradicted Darby pint blank. "Stay a bit," says Maurteen, catching Darby by the coat collar. "You forget about the little fairy cobbler, the Leprechaun," he says. "You can't deny that to catch the Leprechaun is great luck entirely. If one only fix the glance of his eye on the cobbler, that look makes the fairy a presner—one can do anything with him as long as a human look covers the little lad—and he'll give the favors of three wishes to buy his freedom," says Maurteen.

At that Darby, smiling high and knowledgeable, made answer over the heads of the crowd.

"God help your sinse, honest man!" he says. "Around the favors of thim same three wishes is a bog of thricks an' cajoleries and conditions that'll defayt the wisest.

"First of all, if the look be taken from the little cobbler for as much as the wink of an eye, he's gone forever," he says. "Man alive, even when he does grant the favors of the three wishes, you're not safe, for, if you tell anyone you've seen the Leprechaun, the favors melt like snow, or if you make a fourth wish that day, whiff! They turn to smoke. Take my adwice, nayther make nor moil nor meddle with the fairies."

"Thrue for ye," spoke up long Pether McCarthy, siding in with Darby. "Didn't Barney McBride, on his way to early mass one May morning, catch the fairy cobbler sewing an' workin' away under a hedge. 'Have a pinch of snuff, Barney agra,' says the Leprechaun, handing up the little snuff-box. But, mind ye, when my poor Barney bint to take a thumb an' finger full what did the little villain do but fling the box, snuff and all, into Barney's face. An' thin, whilst the poor lad was winkin' and blinkin', the Leprechaun gave one leap and was lost in the reeds.

"Thin again, there was Peggy O'Rourke, who captured him fair an' square in a hawthorn-bush. In spite of his wiles she wrung from him the favors of the three wishes. Knowing, of course, that if she towld anyone of what happened to her the spell was broken, and the wishes wouldn't come thrue, she hurried home, aching and longing to in some way find from her husband, Andy, what wishes she'd make.

"Throwing open her door, she said, 'What would ye wish for most in the world, Andy dear. Tell me an' your wish'll come true,' says she. A peddler was crying his wares out in the lane. 'Lanterns, tin lanterns!' cried the peddler. 'I wish I had one of thim lanterns,' says Andy, careless and bendin' over to get a coal for his pipe, when, lo and behold, there was a lantern in his hand.

"Well, so vexed was Peggy that one of her fine wishes should be wasted on a palthry tin lantern that she lost all patience with him. 'Why, thin, bad scran to you,' says she—not mindin' her own words, 'I wish the lantern was fastened to the ind of your nose.'

"The word wasn't well out of her mouth till the lantern *was* hung swinging from the ind of Andy's nose in a way that the wit of man couldn't loosen. It took the third and last of Peggy's wishes to relayse Andy."

"Look at that now," cried a dozen voices from the admiring crowd. "Darby said so from the first."

Well, after a time people used to come from miles around to see Darby, and sit under the sthraw-stack beside the stable to adwise with our hayro about their most important business—what was the best time for the settin' of hins and what was good to cure colic in childher, an' things like that.

Any man so parsecuted with admiration an' hayrofication might aisily feel his chest swell out a bit, so it's no wondher that Darby set himself up for a knowledge-able man.

He took to talking slow an' shuttin' one eye whin he listened, and he walked with a knowledgeable twist to his chowldhers. He grew monsthrously fond of fairs and public gatherings, where people made much of him; and he lost every ounce of liking he ever had for hard worruk.

Things wint on with him in this way from bad to worse, and where it would have inded no man knows, if one unlucky morning he hadn't rayfused to bring in a creel of turf his wife Bridget had axed him to fetch her. The unfortunit man said it was no work for the likes of him.

The last word was still on Darby's lips whin he rayalized his mistake, an' he'd have given the worruld to have the sayin' back agin.

For a minute you could have heard a pin dhrop. Bridget, instead of being in a hurry to begin at him, was crool dayliberate. She planted herself at the door, her two fists on her hips an' her lips shut.

The look Julius Sayser'd trow at a servant-girl he'd caught stealing sugar from the rile cupboard was the glance she waved up and down from Darby's toes to his head and from his head to his brogues agin.

Thin she began an' talked steady as a fall of hail that has now an' then a bit of lightning an' tunder mixed in it.

The knowledgeable man stood purtendin' to brush his hat and tryin' to look brave, but the heart inside of him was meltin' like butther.

Bridget began aisily be carelessly mentioning a few of Darby's best known wakenesses. Afther that she took up some of them not so well known, being ones Darby himself had sayrious doubts about having at all. But on these last she was more savare than on the first. Through it all he daren't say a word—he only smiled lofty and bitther.

'Twas but natural next for Bridget to explain what a poor crachure her husband was on the day she got him, an' what she might have been if she had married aither one of the six others who had axed her. The step for her was a little one, thin, to the shortcomings and misfortunes of his blood relaytions, which she follyed back to the blaggardisms of his fourth cousin, Phelim McFadden.

Even in his misery poor Darby couldn't but marvel at her wondherful memory.

By the time she began talking of her own family, and especially about her Aunt Honoria O'Shaughnessy, who had once shook hands with a bishop, and who in the rebellion of '98 had trun a brick at a Lord Liftenant, whin he was riding by, Darby was as wilted and as forlorn-looking as a roosther caught out in the winther rain.

He lost more pride in those few minutes than it had taken months to gather an' hoard. It kept falling in great drops from his forehead.

Just as Bridget was lading up to what Father Cassidy calls a pur-roar-ration—that being the part of your wife's discoorse whin, afther telling you all that she's done for you, and all she's stood from your relaytions, she breaks down and cries, and so smothers you entirely—just as she was coming to that, I say, Darby scrooged his caubeen down on his head, stuck his fingers in his two ears, and making one grand rush through the door, bolted as fast as his legs could carry him down the road toward the Sleive-na-mon Mountains.

Bridget stood on the step looking after him too surprised for a word. With his fingers still in his ears, so that he couldn't hear her commands to turn back, he ran without stopping till he came to the willow-tree near Joey Doolan's forge. There he slowed down to fill his lungs with the fresh, sweet air.

'Twas one of those warm-hearted, laughing autumn days which steals for a while the bonnet and shawl of the May. The sun, from a sky of feathery whiteness, laned over, telling jokes to the worruld an' the goold harvest-fields and purple hills, lazy and continted, laughed back at the sun. Even the black-bird flying over the haw-tree looked down an' sang to those below, "God save all here," an' the linnet from her bough answered back quick an' sweet, "God save you kindly, sir."

With such pleasant sights and sounds an' twitterings at every side, our hayro didn't feel the time passing till he was on top of the first hill of the Sleive-na-mon Mountains, which, as every one knows, is called the Pig's Head.

It wasn't quite lonesome enough on the Pig's Head, so our hayro plunged into the valley an' climbed the second mountain—the Divil's Pillow—where 'twas lonesome and desarted enough to shuit anyone.

Beneath the shade of a three, for the day was warm, he sat himself down in the long, sweet grass, lit his pipe, and let his mind go free. But, as he did, his thoughts rose together, like a flock of frightened, angry pheasants, an' whirred back to the owdacious things Bridget had said about his relations.

Wasn't she the mendageous, humbrageous woman, he thought, to say such things about as illigant stock as the O'Gills and the O'Gradys?

Why, Wullum O'Gill, Darby's uncle, at that minute was head butler at Castle Brophy, and was known far an' wide as being one of the foinest scholars an' as having the most beautiful pair of legs in all Ireland!

This same Wullum O'Gill had tould Bridget in Darby's own hearing, on a day when the three were going through the great picture gallery at Castle Brophy, that the O'Gills at one time had been kings in Ireland.

Darby never since could raymember whether this time was before the flood or after the flood. Bridget said it was durin' the flood, but surely that sayin' was nonsinse.

Howsumever, Darby knew his Uncle Wullum was right, for he often felt in himself the signs of greatness.

And now, as he sat alone on the grass, he said out loud:

"If I had me rights I'd be doing nothing all day long but sittin' on a throne, an' playin' games of forty-five with me Lord Liftenant an' some of me generals. There never was a lord that liked good ateing or dhrinking better nor I, or who hates worse to get up airly in the morning. That last disloike, I'm tould, is a great sign entirely of gentle blood the worruld over," says he.

As for his wife's people, the O'Hagans and the O'Shaughnessys, well—they were no great shakes, he said to himself, at laste so far as looks were consarned. All the handsomeness in Darby's childher came from his own side of the family. Even Father Cassidy said the childher took afther the O'Gills.

"If I were rich," says Darby to a lazy ould bumble bee who was droning an' tumbling in front of him, "I'd have a castle like Castle Brophy, with a great picture gallery in it. On one wall I'd put the pictures of the O'Gills and the

O'Gradys, and on the wall ferninst thim I'd have the
O'Hagans an' the O'Shaughnessys."

At that ideah his heart bubbled in a new and fierce
deloight. "Bridget's people," he says agin, scowling at the
bee, "would look four times as common as they raylly are,
whin they were compared in that way with my own relations. An' whenever Bridget got rampageous, I'd take her
in and show her the difference betwixt the two clans, just
to punish her, so I would."

How long the lad sat that way warming the cowld
thoughts of his heart with drowsy pleasant dhrames an'
misty longings he don't rightly know, whin—tack, tack,
tack, tack, came the busy sound of a little hammer from
the other side of a fallen oak.

"Be jingo!" he says to himself with a start, "'tis the
Leprechaun that's in it."

In a second he was on his hands an' knees, the tails of
his coat flung across his back, an' he crawling softly toward the sound of the hammer. Quiet as a mouse he lifted
himself up on the mossy log to look over, and there, before his two popping eyes, was a sight of wondheration.

Sitting on a white stone, an' working away like fury,
hammering pegs into a little red shoe, half the size of your
thumb, was a bald-headed ould cobbler of about twice
the height of your hand. On the top of a round, snub nose
was perched a pair of horn-rimmed spectacles, an' a narrow fringe of iron-grey whiskers grew under his stubby
chin. The brown leather apron he wore was so long that it
covered his green knee-breeches an' almost hid the knitted grey stockings.

The Leprechaun—for 'twas he indade—as he worked,
mumbled an' mutthered in great discontent.

"Oh, haven't I the hard, hard luck!" he said. "I'll never
have thim done in time for her to dance in to-night. So
thin, I'll be kilt intirely," says he. "Was there ever another
quane of the fairies as wearing on shoes an' brogues an'
dancin' slippers? Haven't I the—" Looking up, he saw Darby.

"The top of the day to you, dacint man," says the cobbler, jumpin' up. Giving a sharp cry, he pinted quick at Darby's stomach. "But, wirra, wirra, what's that woolly ugly thing you have crawlin' an' creepin' on your weskit?" he said, purtendin' to be all excited.

"Sorra thing on my weskit," answered Darby, cool as ice, "or anywhere else, that'll make me take my two bright eyes off'n you—not for a second," says he.

"Well! Well! Will you look at that, now!" laughed the cobbler. "Mark how quick an' handy he took me up. Will you have a pinch of snuff, clever man?" he axed, houlding up the little box.

"Is it the same snuff you gave Barney McBride awhile ago?" axed Darby, sarcastic. "Lave off your foolishness," says our hayro, growin' fierce, "and grant me at once the favors of the three wishes, or I'll have you smoking like a herring in my own chimney before nightfall," says he.

At that the Leprechaun, seeing that he but wasted time on so knowledgeable a man as Darby O'Gill, surrendhered and granted the favours of the three wishes.

"What is it you ask?" says the cobbler, himself turning on a sudden very sour an' sullen.

"First an' foremost," says Darby, "I want a home of my ansisthers, an' it must be a castle like Castle Brophy, with pictures of my kith an' kin on the wall, and then facing them pictures of my wife Bridget's kith an' kin on the other wall."

"That favor I give you; that wish I grant ye," says the fairy, making the shape of a castle on the ground with his awl. "What next?" he grunted.

"I want goold enough for me an' my generations to enjoy in grandeur the place forever."

"Always the goold," sneered the little man, bending to dhraw with his awl on the turf the shape of a purse.

"Now for your third and last wish. Have a care!"

"I want the castle set on this hill—the Divil's Pillow—where we two stand," says Darby. Then sweeping with his arm, he says, "I want the land about to be my demesne."

The Leprechaun struck his awl on the ground. "That wish I give you; that wish I grant you," he says. With that he straightened himself up, and, grinning most aggravatin' the while, he looked Darby over from top to toe. "You're a foine knowledgeable man, but have a care of the fourth wish," says he.

Bekase there was more of a challenge than friendly warning in what the small lad said, Darby snapped his fingers at him an' cried:

"Have no fear, little man! If I got all Ireland ground for making a fourth wish, however small, before midnight, I'd not make it. I'm going home now to fetch Bridget an' the childher, and the only fear or unaisiness I have is that you'll not keep your word, so as to have the castle here ready before us when I come back."

"Oho! I'm not to be thrusted, amn't I?" screeched the little lad, flaring into a blazing passion. He jumped upon the log that was betwixt them an' with one fist behind his back, shook the other at Darby.

"You ignorant, auspicious-minded blaggard," says he. "How dare the likes of you say the likes of that to the likes of me?" cried the cobbler. "I'd have you to know," he says, "that I had a repitation for truth an' voracity ayquil, if not shuperior to the best, before you were born," he shouted. "I'll take no high talk from a man that's afraid to give words to his own wife whin she's in a tantrum," says the Leprechaun.

"It's aisy to know you're not a married man," says Darby, mighty scornful, "bekase if you—"

The lad stopped short, forgetting what he was going to say in his surprise an' aggaytation, for the far side of the mountain was waving up an' down before his eyes like a great green blanket that is being shook by two women; while at the same time high spots of turf on the hillside toppled sidewise to level themselves up with the low places. The enchantment had already begun to make things ready for the castle. A dozen foine threes that stood in a little groove bent their heads quickly together, and thin by some inwisible hand they were plucked up by the roots an' dhropped aside, much the same as a man might grasp a handful of weeds an' fling them from his garden.

The ground under the knowledgeable man's feet began to rumble an' heave. He waited for no more. With a cry that was half of gladness an' half of fear, he turned on his heel an' started on a run down into the walley, leaving the little cobbler standing on the log, shouting abuse after him an' ballyraggin' him as he ran.

So excited was Darby that, going up the Pig's Head, he was nearly run over by a crowd of great brown building stones which were moving down slow an' ordherly like a flock of driven sheep—but they moved without so much as bruising a blade of grass or bendin' a twig, as they came.

Only once, and that at the top of the Pig's Head, he trew a look back.

The Divil's Pillow was in a great commotion; a whirl-wind was sweeping over it, whether of dust or of mist he couldn't tell.

After this, Darby never looked back agin, or to the right or the left of him, but kept straight on till he found him-self, panting and puffing, at his own kitchen door. 'Twas tin minutes before he could spake, but at last, whin he tould Bridget to make ready herself and the childher to go up to the Divil's Pillow with him, for once in her life that raymarkable woman, without axing, How comes it so, What rayson have you, or Why should I do it, set to work wash-ing the childher's faces.

Maybe she dabbed a little more soap in their eyes than was needful, for 'twas a habit she had; though this time, if she did, not a whimper broke from the little hayros. For the matther of that, not one word, good, bad, or indiffer-ent, did herself spake till the whole family were trudging down the lane two by two, marching like sojers.

As they came near the first hill, along its sides, the evening twilight turned from purple to brown, and at the top of the Pig's Head the darkness of a black night swooped suddenly down on them. Darby hurried on a step or two ahead, an' resting his hand upon the large rock that crowns the hill, looked anxiously over to the Divil's Pillow. Although he was ready for something foine, yet the greatness of the foineness that met his gaze knocked the breath out of him.

Across the deep walley, and on top of the second mountain, he saw lined against the evening sky the roof of an imminse castle, with towers an' parrypets an' battlements. Undher the towers a thousand sullen windows glowed red in the black walls. Castle Brophy couldn't hould a candle to it.

"Behold!" says Darby, flinging out his arms and turning to his wife, who had just come up, "Behold the castle of my ansisthers, who were my forefathers!"

"How," says Bridget, quick and scornful— "How could your aunt's sisters be your four fathers?"

What Darby was going to say to her he don't just raymember, for at that instant, from the right hand side of the mountain, came a cracking of whips, a rattling of wheels, an' the rush of horses, and, lo and behold! a great dark coach with flashing lamps, and drawn by four coal-black horses, dashed up the hill and stopped beside them. Two shadowy men were on the driver's box.

"Is this Lord Darby O'Gill?" axed one of them in a deep, muffled voice. Before Darby could reply, Bridget took the words out of his mouth.

"It is," she cried, in a kind of a half cheer, "an' Lady O'Gill an' the childher."

"Then hurry up," says the coachman, "your supper's gettin' cowld."

Without waiting for anyone, Bridget flung open the carriage door, an' pushin' Darby aside, jumped in among the cushins. Darby, his heart sizzlin' with vexation at her audaciousness, lifted in one after another the childher, and then got in himself.

He couldn't understand at all the change in his wife, for she had always been the odherliest, modestist woman in the parish.

Well, he'd no sooner shut the door than crack went the whip, the horses gave a spring, the carriage jumped, and down the hill they went. For fastness there was never another carriage ride like that before nor since. Darby hildt tight with both hands to the window, his face pressed against the glass. He couldn't tell whether the horses were only flying, or whether the coach was falling down the hill into the walley. By the hollow feel in his stomach he thought they were falling. He was striving to think of some prayers when there came a terrible joult, which sint his two heels against the roof, an' his head betwixt the cushins. As he righted himself the wheels began to grate on a graveled road, an' plainly they were dashing up the side of the second mountain.

Even so, they couldn't have gone far whin the carriage dhrew up in a flurry, an' he saw through the gloom a high iron gate being slowly opened.

"Pass on," said a woice from somewhere in the shadows, "their supper's getting cowld."

As they flew undher the great archway Darby had a glimpse of the thing which had opened the gate, and had said their supper was getting cowld. It was standing on its hind legs; in the darkness he couldn't be quite sure as to its shape, but it was ayther a Bear or a Loin.

His mind was in a pondher about this when, with a swirl an' a bump, the carriage stopped another time; an' now it stood before a broad flight of stone steps which led up to the main door of the castle.

Darby, half afraid, peering out through the darkness, saw a square of light high above him which came from the open hall door. Three sarvents in livery stood waiting on the thrashol.

"Make haste, make haste," says one in a doleful voice, "their supper's gettin' cowld."

Hearing these words, Bridget imagetly bounced out an' was half way up the steps before Darby could ketch her an' hould her till the childher came up.

"I never in all my life saw her so audacious," he says, half cryin' and linkin' her arm to keep her back; an' thin, with the childher follying, two by two, according to size, the whole family payraded up the steps till Darby, with a gasp of deloight, stopped on the thrashol of a splendid hall. From a high ceiling hung great flags from every nation an' domination, which swung an' swayed in the dazzlin' light.

Two lines of men and maid servants, dhressed in silks an' satins an' brocades, stood facing aich other, bowing an' smiling an' wavin' their hands in welcome. The two lines stretched down to the go old stairway at the far ind of the hall.

For half of one minute, Darby, every eye in his head as big as a tay-cup, stood hesitaytin'. Thin he said, "Why should it flutther me? Arrah, ain't it all mine? Aren't all these people in me pay? I'll engage it's a pretty penny all this grandeur is costing me to keep up this minute." He trew out his chest. "Come on Bridget!" he says, "let's go into the home of my ansisthers."

Howandever, scarcely had he stepped into the beautiful place, whin two pipers with their pipes, two fiddlers with their fiddles, two flute-players with their flutes, an' they dhressed in scarlet an' goold, stepped out in front of him, and thus to maylodious music the family proudly marched down the hall, climbed up the goolden stairway at its ind, an' thin turned to enter the biggest room Darby had ever seen.

Something in his sowl whuspered that this was the picture-gallery.

"Be the powers of Pewther," says the knowledgeable man to himself, "I wouldn't be in Bridget's place this minute for a hatful of money. Wait, oh just wait, till she has to compare her own relations with my own foine people! I know how she'll feel, but I wondher what she'll say," he says.

The thought that all the unjust things, all the unraysonable things Bridget had said about his kith an' kin were just going to be disproved and turned against herself made him proud an' almost happy.

But wirrasthrue! He should have raymembered his own adwise not to make nor moil nor meddle with the fairies, for here he was to get the first hard welt from the little Leprechaun.

It was the picture-gallery sure enough, but how terribly different everything was from what the poor lad expected. There on the left wall, grand an' noble, shone the pictures of Bridget's people. Of all the well-dhressed, handsome, proud-appearing persons in the whole worruld the O'Hagans an' the O'Shaughnessys would compare with the best. This was a hard enough crack, though a crushinger knock was to come. Ferninst them, on the right wall, glowered the O'Gills and the O'Gradys, and of all the ragged, sheep-stealing, hangdog-looking villains one ever saw, in jail or out of jail, it was Darby's kindred.

The place of honor on the right wall was given to Darby's fourth cousin, Phelem McFadden, an' he was painted with a pair of handcuffs on him. Wullum O'Gill had a squint in his right eye, and his thin legs bowed like hoops on a barrel.

If you have ever at night been groping your way through a dark room, and got a sudden hard bump on the forehead from the edge of the door, you can understand the feelings of the knowledgeable man.

"Take that picture out!" he said hoarsely, as soon as he could speak. "An' will some one kindly inthrojuice me to the man who med it. Bekase," he says, "I intend to take his life. There was never a crass-eyed O'Gill since the world began," says he.

Think of his horror an' surprise whin he saw the left eye of Wullum Gill twist itself slowly over toward his nose and squint worse than the right eye.

Purtending not to see this, an' hoping no one else did, Darby fiercely led the way over to the other wall.

Fronting him stood the handsome picture of Honoria O'Shaughnessy, an' she dhressed in a shuit of tin clothes, like the knights of ould used to wear—armor I think they calls it.

She hildt a spear in her hand, with a little flag on the blade, an' her smile was proud and high.

"Take that likeness out too," says Darby, very spiteful. "That's not a dacint shuit of clothes for any woman to wear."

The next minute you might have knocked him down with a feather, for the picture of Honoria O'Shaughnessy opened its mouth and stuck out its tongue at him.

"The supper's getting cowld, the supper's getting cowld," some one cried at the other ind of the picture gallery. Two big doors were swung open, an' glad enough was our poor hayro to folly the musicianers down to the room where the ateing an' drinking were to be thransacted.

This was a little room with lots of looking glasses, and it was bright with a thousand candles, and white with the shiningest marble. On the table was biled beef an' reddishes an' carrots an' roast mutton an' all kinds of important ateing an' drinking. Beside these stood fruits an' sweets an'—but sure what is the use in talkin'?

A high-backed chair stood ready for aich of the familly, an' 'twas a lovely sight to see them all whin they were sitting there—Darby at the head, Bridget at the foot, the childher—the poor little paythriarchs—sitting bolt upright on aich side, with a bewigged and befrilled serving man standing haughty behind every chair.

The ateing and dhrinkin' would have begun at once—in troth there was already a bit of biled beef on Darby's plate—only that he spied a little silver bell beside him. Sure, 'twas one like those the quality keep to ring whin they want more hot wather for their punch, but it puzzled the knowledeable man, and 'twas the beginning of his misfortune.

"I wondher," he thought, "if 'tis here for the same raison as the bell is at the Curragh races—do they ring this one so that all at the table will start ateing an' drinking fair, an' no one will have the advantage; or is it," he says to himself agin, "to ring whin the head of the house thinks every one has had enough? Haven't the quality quare ways! I'll be a long time learning them," he says.

He sat silent and puzzling an' staring at the biled beef on his plate, afeared to start in without ringing the bell, an' dhreading to risk ringing it. The grand servants towered cowldly on every side, their chins tilted, but they kep' throwing over their chowlders glances so scornful and haughty that Darby shivered at the thought of showing any uncultivaytion.

While our hayro sat thus in unaisy contimplaytion an' smouldhering mortification an' flurried hesitaytion, a powdhered head was poked over his chowlder, and a soft beguiling voice said, "Is there anything else you'd wish for?"

The foolish lad twisted in his chair, opened his mouth to spake, and gave a look at the bell; shame rushed to his cheeks, he picked up a bit of the biled beef on his fork, an' to consale his turpitaytion gave the misfortunit answer,

"I'd wish for a pinch of salt, if you plaze," says he.

'Twas no sooner said than came the crash. Oh, tunderation an' murdheration, what a roaring crash it was! The lights winked out together at a breath, an' left a pitchy, throbbing darkness. Overhead and to the sides was a roaring, smashing, crunching noise, like the ocean's madness when the winthry storm breaks agin the Kerry shore; an' in that roar was mingled the tearing and the splitting of the walls and the falling of the chimneys. But through all this confusion could be heard the shrill laughing voice of the Leprechaun. "The clever man med his fourth grand wish," it howled.

Darby—a thousand wild woices screaming an' mocking above him—was on his back, kicking and squirming and striving to get up, but some load hilt him down an' something bound his eyes shut.

"Are you kilt, Bridget asthore?" he cried. "Where are the childher?" he says.

Instead of answer, there suddenly flashed a fierce an' angry silence, an' its quickness frightened the lad more than all the wild confusion before.

'Twas a full minute before he dared to open his eyes to face the horrors which he felt were standing about him; but when courage enough to look came, all he saw was the night-covered mountain, a purple sky, and a thin new moon, with one trembling goold star a hand's space above its bosom.

Darby struggled to his feet. Not a stone of the castle was left, not a sod of turf but what was in its ould place; every sign of the little cobbler's work had melted like April snow. The very threes Darby had seen pulled up by the roots that same afternoon now stood a waving blur below the new moon, an' a nightingale was singing in their branches. A cricket chirped lonesomely on the same fallen log which had hidden the Leprechaun.

"Bridget! Bridget!" Darby called agin an' agin. Only a sleepy owl on a distant hill answered.

A shivering thought jumped into the boy's bewildered sowl—maybe the Leprechaun had stolen Bridget an' the childher. The poor man turned, and for the last time darted down into the night-filled walley.

Not a pool in the road he waited to go around, not a ditch in his path he didn't leap over, but ran as he never ran before, till he raiched his own front door.

His heart stood still as he peeped through the window. There were the childher croodled around Bridget, who sat with the youngest asleep in her lap before the fire, rocking back an' forth, an' she crooning a happy, continted baby song.

Tears of gladness crept into Darby's eyes as he looked in upon her. "God bless her," he says to himself. "She's the flower of the O'Hagans and the O'Shaughnessys, and she's a proud feather in the caps of the O'Gills an' the O'Gradys."

'Twas well he had this happy thought to cheer him as he lifted the door latch, for the manest of all the little cobbler's spiteful thricks waited in the house to meet Darby—nayther Bridget nor the childher raymembered a single thing of all that had happened to them during the day. They were willing to make their happydavitts that they had been no farther than their own petatie-patch since morning.

The Convarsion of Father Cassidy

I tould you how on cowld winther nights whin Bridget and the childher were in bed, ould Brian Connors, King of the Fairies, used to sit visitin' at Darby O'Gill's own fireside. But I never tould you of the wild night whin the King faced Father Cassidy there.

Darby O'Gill sat at his own kitchen fire the night afther Mrs. Morrisey's burying, studyin' over a gr-r-reat daybate that was heldt at her wake.

Half-witted Red Durgan begun it be asking loud an' sudden of the whole company, "Who was the greatest man that ever lived in the whole worruld? I want to know purtic'lar, an' I'd like to know at once," he says.

At that the dayliberations started.

Big Joey Hooligan, the smith, hildt out for Julius Sayser, bekase Sayser had throunced the widdy woman Clayopathra.

Maurteen Cavanaugh, the little schoolmaster, stood up for Bonyparte, an' wanted to fight Dinnis Moriarity for disputin' agin the Frenchman.

Howsumever, the starter of the rale excitement was ould Mrs. Clancy. She was not what you'd call a great histhorian, but the parish thought her a foine, sinsible woman. She said that the greatest man was Nebbycodnazer, the King of the Jews, who ate grass like a cow and grew fat on it.

"Could Julius Sayser or Napoleon Bonyparte do as much?" she axed.

Well, purty soon everyone was talking at once, hurling at aich other, as they would pavin'-stones, the names of poets an' warriors an' scholars.

But afther all was said an' done, the mourners wint away in the morning with nothing settled.

So the night afther, while Darby was warming his shins before his own turf fire in deep meditaytion and wise cogitaytion and ca'm contemplaytion over these high conversations, the Master of the Good People flew ragin' into the kitchen.

"Darby O'Gill, what do you think of your wife Bridget?" says he, fiercely.

"Faix, I don't know what particular thing she's done," says Darby, rubbing his shins and lookin' troubled, "but I can guess it's something mighty disagrayable. She wore her blue petticoat and her brown shawl whin she went away this morning, and I always expect ructions whin she puts on that shuit of clothes. Thin agin, she looked so sour and so satisfied whin she came back that I'm worried bad in my mind; you don't know how uncomfortable she can make things sometimes, quiet as she looks," says he.

"And well you may be worried, dacint man!" says the ruler of Sleive-na-mon; "you'll rage and you'll roar whin ye hear me. She wint this day to Father Cassidy and slandhered me outrageous," he says. "She tould him that you and Maureen were colloguing with a little ould, wicked, thieving fairy-man, and that if something wasn't done at once agin him the sowls of both of ye would be desthroyed entirely."

Whin Darby found 'twas not himself that was being bothered, but only the King, he grew aisier in his feelings. "Sure you wouldn't mind women's talk," says he, waving his hand in a lofty way. "Many a good man has been given a bad name by them before this, and will be agin—you're not the first by any manes," says he. "If Bridget makes you a bad repitation, think how many years you have to live it down in. Be sinsible, King!" he says.

"But I do mind, and I must mind!" bawled the little fairy-man, every hair and whusker bristling, "for this minute Father Cassidy is putting the bridle and saddle on his black hunter, Terror; he has a prayer-book in his pocket, and he's coming to read prayers over me and to banish me into the say. Hark! listen to that," he says.

As he spoke, a shrill little voice broke into singing outside the window.

> "Oh, what'll you do if the kittle biles over,
> Sure, what'll you do but fill it agin;
> Ah, what'll you do if you marry a sojer,
> But pack up your clothes and go marchin'
>   with him."

"That's the signal!" says the King, all excited; "he's coming and I'll face him here at this hearth, but sorrow foot he'll put over that threshol' till I give him lave. Then we'll have it out face to face like men ferninst this fire!"

Whin Darby heard those words great fright struck him.

"If a hair of his Riverence's head be harmed," he says, "'tis not you but me and my generation'll be blamed for it. Plaze go back to Sleive-na-mon this night, for pace and quietness sake!" he begged.

While Darby spoke, the fairy-man was fixing one stool on top of another undher the window.

"I'll sit at this window," says the Master of the Good People, wagging his head threateningly, "and from there I'll give me ordhers. The throuble he's thrying to bring on others is the throuble I'll throuble him with. If he comes dacint, he'll go dacint; if he comes bothering, he'll go bothered," says he.

Faith, thin, your Honour, the King spoke no less than the truth, for at that very minute Terror, as foine a horse as ever followed hounds, was galloping down the starlit road to Darby's house, and over Terror's mane bent as foine a horseman as ever took a six-bar gate—Father Cassidy.

On and on through the moonlight they clattered, till they came in sight of Darby's gate, where, unseen and onwisible, a score of the Good People, with thorns in their fists, lay sniggering and laughing, waiting for the horse. Of course the fairies couldn't harm the good man himself, but Terror was complately at their marcy.

"We'll not stop to open the gate, Terror," says his Riverence, patting the baste's neck. "I'll give you a bit of a lift with the bridle-rein, and a touch like that on the flank, and do you clear it, my swallow-bird."

Well, sir, the priest riz in his stirrups, lifted the rein, and Terror crouched for the spring, whin, with a sudden snort of pain, the baste whirled round and started like the wind back up the road.

His Riverence pulled the horse to its haunches and swung him round once more facing the cottage. Up on his hind feet went Terror and stood crazy for a second, pawing the air, then with a cry of rage and pain in his throat, the baste turned, made a rush for the hedge at the roadside, and cleared it like an arrow.

Now, just beyant the hedge was a bog so thin that the geese wouldn't walk on it, and so thick that the ducks couldn't swim in it. Into the middle of that cowld pond Terror fell with a splash and a crash.

That minute the King climbed down from the window splitting with laughter. "Darby," he says, slapping his knees, "Father Cassidy is floundhering about in the bog outside. He's not hurt, but he's mighty cowld and uncomfortable. Do you go and make him promise not to read any prayers this night, then bring him in. Tell him that if he don't promise, by the piper that played before Moses, he may stay reading his prayers in the bog till morning, for he can't get out unless some of my people go in and help him!" says the King.

Darby's heart began hammerin' agin his ribs as though it were making heavy horseshoes.

"If that's so, I'm a ruined man!" he says. "I'd give tunty pounds rather than face him now!" says he.

The disthracted lad put his hat on to go out, an' thin he took it off to stay in. He let a groan out of him that shook all his bones.

"You may save him or lave him," says the King, turning to the window. "I'm going to lave the priest see in a minute what's bothering him. If he's not out of the bog be that time, I'd adwise you to lave the counthry. Maybe you'll only have a pair of cow's horns put on ye, but I think ye'll be kilt," he says. "My own mind's aisy. I wash my hands of him!

"That's the great comfort and adwantage of having your sowl's salwation fixed and sartin one way or the other," says the King, peering out. "Whin you do a thing, bad as it is or good as it may be, your mind is still aisy, bekase—" he turned from the window to look at Darby, but the lad was gone out into the moonlight, and was shrinkin' an' cringin' up toward the bog, as though he were going to meet and talk with the ghost of a man he'd murdhered. 'Twas a harsher an' angrier woice than that of any ghost that came out of a great flopping and splashin' in the bog.

Father Cassidy sat with his feet dhrawn up on Terror, and the horse was half sunk in the mire. At times he urged Terror over to the bank, an' just as the baste was raising to step out, with a snort, it'd whirl back agin.

He'd thry another side, but spur as he might, and whip as he would, the horse'd turn shivering back to the middle of the bog.

"Is that you, Darby O'Gill, you vagebone?" cried his Riverence. "Help me out of this to the dhry land so as I can take the life of you!" he cried.

"What right has anyone to go trespassin' in my bog, mussing it all up an' spiling it?" says Darby, purtendin' not to raycognise the priest; "I keep it private for my ducks

and geese, and I'll have the law on you, so I will—Oh, be
the powers of pewther, 'tis me own dear Father Cassidy!"
he cried.

Father Cassidy, as an answer, raiched for a handful of
mud, which he aimed and flung so fair an' thrue that three
days afther Darby was still pulling bits of it from his hair.

"I have a whip I'll keep private for your own two foine
legs!" cried his Riverence; "I'll taich you to tell lies to the
counthry-side about your being with the fairies, and for
deludherin' your own poor wife. I came down this night to
eggspose you. But now that's the laste I'll do to you!"

"Faith," says Darby, "if I was with the fairies, 'tis no
less than you are this minute, an' if you eggspose me, I'll
eggspose you!" With that Darby up and tould what was
the cause of the whole botheration.

His Riverence, afther the telling, waited not a minute,
but kicked the spurs into Terror, and the brave horse
headed once more for shore. 'Twas no use. The poor baste
turned at last with a cry and floundhered back agin into
the mire.

"You'll not be able to get out, Father acushla," says
Darby, "till you promise fair an' firm not to read any
prayers over the Good People this night, and never to hurt
or molest meself on any account. About this last promise
the King is very particular entirely."

"You dundherheaded Booligadhaun!" says Father
Cassidy, turning all the blame on Darby; "you mayandherin' Mayrauder of the Sivin Says!" he says. "You big-
headed scorpion of the worruld, with bow-legs!" cried he,—
an' things like that.

"Oh, my! Oh, my! Oh, my!" says Darby, purtendin' to
be shocked, "to think that me own pasture should use
sich terrible langwidge! That me own dear Father Cassidy
could spake blaggard words like thim! Every dhrop of blood
in me is biling with scandalation. Let me beg of you and
implore your Riverence never agin to make use of talk like
that. It breaks my heart to hear you!" says the villain.

For a few minutes afther that Darby was doin' nothing but dodging handfuls of mud.

While this was going on, a soft red glow, like that which hangs above the lonely raths an' forts at night when the fairies are dancin' in thim, came over the fields. So whin Father Cassidy riz in his stirrups the soft glow was resting on the bog, and there he saw two score of little men in green jackets and brown caps waiting about the pond's edge, and everyone houlding a switch in his hands.

The little lads knew well 'twas too dark for the clergyman to read from his book any banishing prayers, and barring having too much fun, the divil a thing they had to fear!

'Twas fresh anger that came to Father Cassidy afther the first rush of surprise and wondher. He thried now to get at the Good People, to lay his hands on thim. A dozen charges at the bank his Riverence made, and as many times a score of the Little People flew up to meet him and sthruck the poor baste over the soft nose with their wands till the horse was welted back.

Long afther the struggle was proved hopeless it wint on till at last the poor baste, thrembling and disheartened, rayfused to mind the spur.

At that Father Cassidy gave up. "I surrender," he said, "an' I promise for the sake of my horse," said he.

The baste himself undherstood the worruds, for with that he waded ca'm an' quiet to the dhry land and stood shaking himself there among the pack of fairies.

Mighty few words were passed betwixt Darby and Terror's rider as the whole party went up to Darby's stable, the little people follying behind quiet and ordherly.

It was not long till Terror was nibbling comfortably in a stall, Father Cassidy was dhrying himself before the kitchen fire, the King and Darby were sitting by the side of the hearth, and two score of the green-cloaked Little People were scatthered about the kitchen waiting for the great debate which was sure to come betwixt his Riverence and the head man of the Good People, now that the two had met.

So full was the room that some of the Good People sat on the shelves of the dhresser, others lay on the table, their chins in their fists, whilst little Phelim Beg was perching himself on a picture above the hearth. He'd no sooner touched the picture-frame than he let a howl out of him and jumped to the floor. "I'm burned to the bone!" says he.

"No wondher," says the King, looking up; "'twas a picture of St. Patrick you were sitting on."

Phadrig Oge, swinging his heels, balanced himself on the edge of a churn filled with buttermilk, but everyone of them kept wondhering eyes fastened on the priest.

And to tell the truth, Father Cassidy at first was more scornful and unpolite than he need be.

"I suppose," says his Riverence, "you do be worrying a good deal about the place you're going to afther the Day of Judgment?" he says, kind of mocking.

"Arrah, now," says the King, taking the pipe from his mouth and staring hard at the clargyman, "there's more than me ought to be studying that question. There's a parish priest I knew, and he's not far from here, who ate mate on a fast day, three years ago come next Michaelmas, who should be a good lot intherested in that same place," says the King.

The laughing and tittering that follyed this hit lasted a minute.

Father Cassidy turned scarlet. "When I ate it I forgot the day!" he cried.

"That's what you tould," says the King, smiling sweet, "but that saying don't help your chanst much. Maybe you failed to say your prayers a year ago last Ayster Monday night for the same rayson?" axed the King, very cool.

At this the laughing broke out agin, uproarious, some of the little men houlding their sides and tears rowling down their cheeks; two lads begun dancing together before the chiny dishes upon the dhresser. But at the height of the merriment there was a cry and a splash, for Phadrig Oge had fallen into the churn.

Before anyone could help him Phadrig had climbed bravely up the churn-dash, hand over hand like a sailor man, and clambered out all white and dripping. "Don't mind me," he says; "go on wid the discoorse!" he cried, shaking himself. The Ruler of the Good People looked vexed.

"I marvel at yez, an' I am ashamed of yez!" he says. "If I'm not able alone for this dayludhered man, yer shoutin' and your gallivantin'll do me no good. Besides, fair play's a jewel, even two agin one ain't fair," says the King. "If I hear another word from one of yez, back to Sleive-na-mon he'll go, an' lay there on the broad of his back, with his heels in the air, for a year and tin days!

"You were about to obsarve, Father Cassidy," says his Majesty, bowing low "your most obaydient sir!"

"I was about to say," cried his Riverence, "that you're a friend of Sattin!"

"I'll not deny that," says the King; "what have you to say agin him?"

"He's a rogue and a rapscallion and the inemy of mankind!" tundered Father Cassidy.

"Prove he's a rogue!" cries the King, slapping one hand on the other; "and why shouldn't he be the inemy of mankind? What has mankind iver done for him except to lay the blame of every mane, cowardly thrick of its own on his chowlders. Wasn't it on their account he was put inside of the swine and dhrove into the say? Wasn't it bekase of them he spint sivin days and sivin nights in the belly of a whale, wasn't it—"

"Stop there, now!" says Father Cassidy, pinting his finger; "hould where you are—that was Jonah."

"You're working meracles to make me forget!" shouted the King.

"I'm not!" cried the priest, "and what's more, if you'll agree not to use charms of the black art to help yourself, I'll promise not to work meracles agin you."

"Done! I'll agree," says the King, "and with that bargain I'll go on first, and I'll prove that mankind is the inemy of Sattin."

"Who begun the inmity?" intherrupted his Riverence; "who started in be tempting our first parents?"

"Not wishing to make little of a man's relaytions in his own house or to his own face, but your first parents were a poor lot," said the King. "Didn't your first parent turn quane's evidence agin his own wife? Answer me that!"

"Undher the sarcumstances, would ye have him tell a lie whin he was asked?" says the priest right back.

Well, the argyment got hotter and hotter until Darby's mind was in splinthers. Sometimes he sided with Ould Nick, sometimes he was agin him. Half of what they said he didn't undherstand. They talked Tayology, Conchology, and Distrology, they hammered aich other with Jayography, Orthography, and Misnography, they welted aich other with Hylosophy, Philosophy, and Thrimosophy. They bounced up and down in their sates, they shouted and got purple in the face. But every argyment brought out another nearly as good and twict as loud.

Through all this time the follyers of the King sat upon their perches or lay upon the table motionless, like little wooden images with painted green cloaks and brown caps.

Darby, looking from one to the other of them for help to undherstand the thraymendous argyment that was goin' on, felt his brain growin' numb. At last it balked like Shamus Free's donkey, and urge as he would, the divil a foot his mind'd stir afther the two hayros. It turned at last and galloped back to Mrs. Morrisey's wake.

Now, thin, the thought that came into Darby's head as he sat there ferninst Father Cassidy an' the King was this:

"The two wisest persons in Ireland are this minute shouting and disputing before me own turf fire. If I ax them those questions, I'll be wiser than Maurteen Cavanaugh, the schoolmaster, an' twict as wise as any other man in this parish. I'll do it," he says to himself.

He raised the tongs and struck them so loud and quick against the hearth that the two daybaters stopped short in their talk to look at him.

"Tell me," he says— "lave off and tell me who was the greatest man that ever lived?" says he.

At that a surprising thing happened. Brian Connors and Father Cassidy, aich striving to speak first, answered in the same breath and gave the same name.

"Dan'le O'Connell," says they.

There was at that the instant's silence an' stillness which follys a great explosion of gunpowdher.

Thin every subject of the King started to his feet.

"Three cheers for Dan'le O'Connell!" cried little Roderick Dhue. Every brown cap was swung in the air. "Hooray! Hooray! Hooroo!" rang the cheers.

His Riverence and the fairy-chief turned sharp about and stared at each other, delighted and wondhering.

Darby shtruck agin with the tongs. "Who was the greatest poet?" says he.

Agin the two spoke together. "Tom Moore," says they. The King rubbed his hands and gave a glad side look at the priest. Darby marked the friendly light that was stealing into Father Cassidy's brown eyes. There was great excitement among the Good People up on the cupboard shelves.

On the table little Nial, the wise, was thrying to start three cheers for Father Cassidy, when Darby said agin: "Who was the greatest warrior?" he says.

The kitchen grew still as death, aich of the two hayros waiting for the other.

The King spoke first. "Brian Boru," says he.

"No," says Father Cassidy, half laughing; "Owen Roe O'Nale."

Phadrig Oge jumped from the churn. "Owen Roe forever! I always said it!" cries he. "Look at this man, boys," he says, pinting up to the priest. "There's the making of the foinest bishop in Ireland!"

"The divil a much differ betwixt Owen Roe an' Brian Boru! 'Tis one of them two, an' I don't care which!" says the King.

The priest and the King sank back in their chairs, eyeing aich other with admayration.

Darby powered something out of a jug into three brown stone noggins, and then turned hot wather from the kittle, on top of that agin.

Says the King to the clargyman, "You're the cleverest and the knowingest man I've met in five thousand years. That joult you gave me about Jonah was a terror!"

"I never saw your ayquil! If we could only send you to Parliament, you'd free Ireland!" says Father Cassidy. "To think," says he, "that once I used to believe there was no such thing as fairies!"

"That was bekase you were shuperstitious," says the King. "Everyone is so, more or less. I am meself—a little," says he.

Darby was stirrin' spoons in the three steaming noggins and Father Cassidy was looking throubled.

What would his flock say to see him dhrinking punch with a little ould pagin, who was the friend of Ould Nick?

"Your health!" says the King, houlding up the cup.

His Riverence took a bowl of the punch, for daycency's sake, and stood quiet a minute. At last he says, "Happiness to you and forgiveness to you, and my heart's pity folly you!" says he, raising the noggin to his lips.

He dhrained the cup thoughtful and solemn, for he didn't know rightly whether 'twas a vaynial sin or a mortial sin he'd committed by the bad example he was giving Darby.

"I wisht I could do something for yez," he says, putting on his cloak, "but I have only pity and kind wishes to give you!"

He turned agin when his hand was on the door-knob, and was going to say something else, but changed his mind, and wint out to where Darby was houlding the horse.

Manewhile, the Little People were consultin' eager in a knot beside the fireplace, until the King broke away an' follyed Father Cassidy out.

"Wait a minute!" the fairy says. "There's somethin' important your Riverence should know about," he says. "There's two speckled hins that sthrayed away from your own door over to the black pond, an' they've been there this twelvemonth. I'm loathe to say it, but in yer own mind your honour a-ccused Bothered Bill Donahue, the tinker, with takin' thim. Well, they've raised two great clutches of chickens an' they're all yours. We thought we'd tell ye," he says.

"An' last Chewsday night Nancy Burke bate her husband Dicky for being 'toxicated. I think she bate him too scan'lous," says little Nial, the fiddler, comin' out. "An' Dicky is too proud to complain of her to your honour. He says 'twould be makin' a kind of informer out of himself. But maybe she'll bate him agin, so I thought to mintion it," he says. With that Phadrig Oge broke in from where he stood on the thrashol':

"Tom Healy's family, up the mountainy way, is all down with the faver; they have no one to send worrud!" cried Phadrig; "your honour ought to know about it," he says.

Be this time the Good People were all outside, crowded about the horse, an' aich one excited, shouting up some friendly informaytion. Father Cassidy, from Terror's back, sat smilin' down kind, first on this one, then on that, an' then on the other.

"Wisha!" says he, "ain't ye the kindly crachures! I've heard more news of me own parish in the last foive minutes than I'd have learned in a twelvemonth. But there's one thing I'd liked mighty well to know. Maybe yez could tell me," says he, "who committed the mystarious crime in this parish a year ago last Christmas? Who stole the six shillin's from ould Mrs. Frawley? She counted them at Mrs. McGee's, an' she felt them in her pocket at Mrs. Donovan's; the crowd jostled her at the chapel door, an' afther that they were gone," he says.

Well, the fairies were splittin' with laughter as he spoke.

"No one stole thim at all," says Shaun Rhue, the tears of merriment rollin' down his face. "The disraymemberin' woman only aymagins she counted thim at Mrs. McGee's an' felt thim at Mrs. Donovan's. She was only thinkin' about the money at thim places, an' that's how she got the ideeh. She hid the shillin's in the blue taypot with the broken spout, that stands in the left-han' corner of the mayhogany dhresser, an' thin forgot it entirely," he says.

"Well, look at that, now," says the priest, "an' all the turmile there's been about that same six shillin's, an' she afther hidin' them in the taypot herself. Now isn't there something I can do in rayturn for all your kindness?" he says.

"There's one thing," says King Brian Connors, lookin' a good dale confuged. "If your Riverence could just as well—if it'd be no positive inconvaynience—we'd like mightilly for ye not to be singin' pious hymns as you go riding along the highway afther dark. If you'd sing ballads, now, or Tom Moore's melodies. You mane no harrum, of course, as it is, but last week you broke up a dance we were having at Murray's rath, an' Saturday night you put a scatther on a crowd of us as we were coming by McGrath's meadow," he says, anxious.

'Twas a quare bargain for a clargyman to make, an' faix it wint agin his conscience, but he hadn't the heart to rayfuse. So he bint down an' shook the King's hand. "I promise," he says. A wild, shrill cheer broke from the throng of Little People.

"Now I'll go home an' lave yez in peace," says Father Cassidy, grippin' his bridle-rein. "I came yer inemy, but I'm convarted. I'll go back yer friend," he says.

"Ye won't go home alone, we'll escorch ye!" shouted Phadrig Oge.

Wullum Fagin, the poacher, was sneakin' home that night about one o'clock, with a bag full of rabbits undher his arrum, whin hearing behind him the bate of horse's hoofs and the sound of maylodious music, he jumped into the ditch and lay close within the shadow.

Who should come canthering up the starlit road but Father Cassidy, on his big black hunter, Terror.

Wullum looked for the musicianers who were singing and playing the enthrancing music, but sorra one could he see, and what was more, the sounds came from the air high above Father Cassidy's head.

"'Tis the angels guarding the good man," says Wullum.

Sure 'twas only the Good People escorching his Riverence from Darby O'Gill's house, and to cheer him on his way, singing the while, "Believe me, if all those endearing young charms."

How the Fairies Came to Ireland

The most lonesome bridle-path in all Ireland leads from Tom Healy's cottage down the sides of the hills, along the edge of the valley, till it raiches the high-road that skirts the great mountain, Sleive-na-mon.

One blusthering, unaisy night, Father Cassidy, on his way home from a sick call, rode over that same path. It wasn't strange that the priest, as his horse ambled along, should be thinking of that other night in Darby O'Gill's kitchen—the night when he met with the Good People; for there, off to the left, towered and threatened Sleive-na-mon, the home of the fairies.

The dismal ould mountain glowered toward his Riverence, its dark look saying, plain as spoken words:

"How dare ye come here; how dare ye?"

"I wondher," says Father Cassidy to himself, looking up at the black hill, "if the Good People are fallen angels, as some do be saying.

"Why were they banished from heaven? It must have been a great sin entirely they committed, at any rate, for at the same time they were banished the power to make a prayer was taken from them. That's why to say a pious word to a fairy is like trowing scalding wather on him. 'Tis a hard pinnance that's put on the poor crachures. I wisht I knew what 'twas for," he says.

He was goin' on pondherin' in that way, while Terror was picking his steps, narvous, among the stones of the road, whin suddenly a frowning, ugly rock seemed to jump up and stand ferninst them at a turn of the path.

Terror shied at it, stumbled wild, and thin the most aggrewating of all bothersome things happened—the horse cast a shoe and wint stone lame.

In a second the priest had leaped to the ground and picked up the horseshoe.

"Wirra! Wirra!" says he, lifting the lame foot, "why did you do it, allannah? 'Tis five miles to a smith an' seven miles to your own warm stable."

The horse, for answer, raiched down an' touched with his soft nose the priest's cheek; but the good man looked rayproachful into the big brown eyes that turned sorrowful to his own.

With the shoe in his hand the priest was standin' fretting and helpless on the lonesome hillside, wondhering what he'd do at all at all, whin a sudden voice spoke up from somewhere near Terror's knees.

"The top of the avinin' to your Riverence," it said, "I'm sorry for your bad luck," says the voice.

Looking down, Father Cassidy saw a little cloaked figure, and caught the glint of a goold crown. 'Twas Brian Connors, the king of the fairies, himself, that was in it.

His words had so friendly a ring in them that the clargyman smiled in answering, "Why, thin, good fortune to you, King Brian Connors," says the good man, "an' save you kindly. What wind brought you here?" he says.

The king spoke back free an' pleasant. "The boys told me you were comin' down the mountainy way, and I came up just in time to see your misfortune. I've sent for Shaun Rhue, our own farrier—there's no betther in Ireland; he'll be here in a minute, so don't worry," says the king.

The priest came so near saying "God bless ye!" that the king's hair riz on his head. But Father Cassidy stopped in the nick of time, changed his coorse, an' steered as near a blessing as he could without hurting the Master of the Good People.

"Well, may you never hear of throuble," he says, "till you're wanted to its wake," says he. "There's no throuble to-night at any rate," says the king, "for while Shaun is fixing the baste we'll sit in the shelter of that rock yonder; there we'll light our pipes and divart our minds with pleasant discoorsin' and wise convarsaytion."

While the king spoke, two green-cloaked little men were making a fire for the smith out of twigs. So quick did they work, that by the time the priest and the fairy man could walk over to the stone and sit themselves in the shelther, a thousand goold sparks were dancin' in the wind, and the glimmer of a foine blaze fought with the darkness.

Almost as soon, clear and purty, rang the cheerful sound of an anvil, and through the swaying shadows a dozen busy little figures were working about the horse. Some wore leather aprons and hilt up the horse's hoof whilst Shaun fitted the red hot shoe; others blew the bellows or piled fresh sticks on the fire; all joking, laughing, singing, or thrickin'; one couldn't tell whether 'twas playing or workin' they were.

Afther lighting their pipes and paying aich other an armful of complayments, the Master of Sleive-na-mon and the clargyman began a sayrious discoorse about the deloights of fox hunting, which led to the considheration of the wondherful wisdom of racing horses and the disgraceful day-ter-ray-roar-ation of the Skibberbeg hounds.

Father Cassidy related how whin Ned Blaze's steeplechasin' horse had been entered for the Connemarra Cup, an' found out at the last minute that Ned feared to lay a bet on him, the horse felt himself so stabbed to the heart with shame by his master's disthrust, that he trew his jockey, jumped the wall, an', head in the air, galloped home.

The king then tould how at a great hunting meet, whin three magisthrates an' two head excises officers were in the chase, that thief of the worruld, Let-Erin-Raymimber, the chief hound of the Skibberbeg pack, instead of follying

the fox, led the whole hunt up over the mountain to Patrick
McCaffrey's private still. The entire counthryside were dhry
for a fortnit afther.

Their talk in that way dhrifted from one pleasant subject to another, till Father Cassidy, the sly man, says aisy
an' careless "I've been tould," says he, "that before the
Good People were banished from heaven yez were all angels," he says.

The king blew a long thin cloud from betwixt his lips,
felt his whuskers thoughtful for a minute, and said:

"No," he says, "we were not exactly what you might
call angels. A rale angel is taller nor your chapel."

"Will you tell me what they're like?" axed Father
Cassidy, very curious.

"I'll give you an idee be comparison what they're like,"
the king says. "They're not like a chapel, and they're not
like a three, an' they're not like the ocean," says he.
"They're different from a goint—a great dale different—
and they're dissembler to an aygle; in fact you'd not mistake one of them for anything you'd ever seen before in
your whole life. Now you have a purty good ideeah what
they're like," says he.

"While I think of it," says the fairy man, a vexed frown
wrinkling over his forehead, "there's three young bach-
elors in your own parish that have a foolish habit of callin'
their colleens angels whin they's not the laste likeness—
not the laste. If I were you, I'd preach ag'in it," says he.

"Oh, I dunno about that!" says Father Cassidy, fitting
a live coal on his pipe. "The crachures *must* say thim
things. If a young bachelor only talks sensible to a sensible colleen he has a good chanst to stay a bachelor. An
thin agin, a gossoon who'll talk to his sweetheart about
the size of the petatie crop'll maybe bate her whin they're
both married. But this has nothing to do with your his-
torical obserwaytions. Go on, King," he says.

"Well, I hate foolishness, wherever it is," says the fairy.
"Howsumever, as I was saying, up there in heaven they

called us the Little People," he says; "millions of us flocked together, and I was the king of them all. We were happy with one another as birds of the same nest, till the ruction came on betwixt the black and the white angels.

"How it all started I never rightly knew, nor wouldn't ask for fear of getting implicayted. I bade all the Little People keep to themselves thin, because we had plenty of friends in both parties, and wanted throuble with nayther of them.

"I knew ould Nick well; a civiler, pleasanter spoken sowl you couldn't wish to meet—a little too sweet in his ways, maybe. He gave a thousand favors and civilities to my subjects, and now that he's down, the devil a word I'll say agin him."

"I'm agin him," says Father Cassidy, looking very stern; "I'm agin him an' all his pumps an' worruks. I'll go bail that in the ind he hurt yez more than he helped yez!"

"Only one thing I blame him for," says the king; "he sajooced from the Little People my comrade and best friend, one Thaddeus Flynn be name. And the way that it was, was this. Thaddeus was a warm-hearted little man, but monsthrous high-spirited as well as quick-tempered. I can shut me eyes now, and in me mind see him thripping along, his head bent, his pipe in his mouth, his hands behind his back. He never wore a waistcoat, but kept always his green body-coat buttoned. A tall caubeen was set on the back of his head, with a sprig of green shamrock in the band. There was a thin rim of black whiskers undher his chin."

Father Cassidy, liftin' both hands in wondher, said: "If I hadn't baptized him, and buried his good father before him, I'd swear 'twas Michael Pether McGilligan of this parish you were dayscribin'," says he.

"The McGilligans ain't dacint enough, nor rayfined enough, nor proud enough to be fairies," says the king, wavin' his pipe scornful. "But to raysume and to continue," he says.

"Thaddeus and I used to frayquint a place they called the battlements or parypets—which was a great goold wall about the edge of heaven, and which had wide steps down on the outside face, where one could sit, pleasant avenings, and hang his feet over, or where one'd stand before going to take a fly in the fresh air for himself. Well, agra, the night before the great battle, Thady and I were sitting on the lowest step, looking down into league upon league of nothing, and talking about the world, which was suxty thousand miles below, and hell, which was tunty thousand miles below that agin, when who should come blusthering over us, his black wings hiding the sky, and a long streak of lightning for a spear in his fist, but Ould Nick.

"'Brian Connors, how long are you going to be downthrodden and thrajooced and looked down upon—you and your subjects?' says he.

"'Faix, thin, who's doing that to us?' asks Thady, standing up and growing excited.

"'Why,' says Ould Nick, 'were you made little pigmies to be the laugh and the scorn and the mock of the whole world?' he says, very mad; 'why weren't you made into angels, like the rest of us?' he says.

"'Musha,' cries Thady, 'I never thought of that.'

"'Are you a man or a mouse; will you fight for your rights?' says Sattin. 'If so, come with me and be one of us. For we'll bate them black and blue to-morrow,' he says. Thady needed no second axing.

"'I'll go with ye, Sattin, me dacent man,' cried he. 'Wirra! Wirra! To think of how down-throdden we are!' And with one spring Thady was on Ould Nick's chowlders, and the two flew away like a humming-bird riding on the back of an aygle. 'Take care of yerself, Brian,' says Thady, 'and come over to see the fight; I'm to be in it. And I extind you the inwitation,' he says.

"In the morning the battle opened; one line of black angels stretched clear across heaven, and faced another line of white angels, with a walley between.

"Everyone had a spaking trumpet in his hand, like you see in the pictures, and they called aich other hard names across the walley. As the white angels couldn't swear or use bad langwidge, Ould Nick's army had at first in that way a great adwantage. But when it came to hurling hills and shying tunderbolts at aich other, the black angels were bate from the first.

"Poor little Thaddeus Flynn stood amongst his own, in the dust and the crash and the roar, brave as a lion. He couldn't hurl mountains, nor was he much at flinging lightning bolts, but at calling hard names he was ayquil to the best.

"I saw him take off his coat, trow it on the ground, and shake his pipe at a thraymendous angel. 'You owdacious villain,' he cried. 'I dare you to come half way over,' he says.

"My, oh my, whin the armies met together in the rale handy grips, it must have been an illigent sight," says Father Cassidy. "'Tis a wondher you kep' out of it," says he.

"I always belayved," says the king, "that if he can help it, no one should fight whin he's sure to get hurted, onless it's his juty to fight. To fight for the mere sport of it, when a throuncin' is sartin, is wasting your time and hurtin' your repitation. I know there's plenty thinks different," he says, p'inting his pipe. "I may be wrong, an' I won't argyfy the matther. 'Twould have been betther for myself that day if I had acted on the other principle.

"Howsumever, be the time that everybody was sidestepping mountains and dodging tunderbolts, I says to myself, says I, 'This is no place fer you or the likes of you.' So I took all me own people out to the battlements and hid them out of the way on the lower steps. We'd no sooner got placed whin—whish! A black angel shot through the air over our heads, and began falling down, down, and down, till he was out of sight. Then a score of his friends came tumbling over the battlements; imagetly hundreds of others came whirling, and purty soon it was raining black wings down into the gulf.

"In the midst of the turmile, who should come jumping down to me, all out of breath, but Thady.

"'It's all over, Brian; we're bate scandalous,' he says, swinging his arms for a spring and balancing himself up and down on the edge of the steps. 'Maybe you wouldn't think it of me, Brian Connors; but I'm a fallen angel,' says he.

"'Wait a bit, Thaddeus Flynn!' says I. 'Don't jump,' I says.

"'I must jump,' he says, 'or I'll be trun,' says he.

"The next thing I knew he was swirling and darting and shooting a mile below me.

"And I know," says the king, wiping his eyes with his cloak, "that when the Day of Judgment comes I'll have at laste one friend waiting for me below to show me the coolest spots and the pleasant places.

"The next minute up came the white army with presners—angels, black and white, who had taken no side in the battle, but had stood apart like ourselves.

"'A man,' says the Angel Gabriel, 'who, for fear of his skin, won't stand for the right when the right is in danger, may not desarve hell, but he's not fit for heaven. Fill up the stars with these cowards and throw the lavin's into the say,' he ordhered.

"With that he swung a lad in the air, and gave him a fling that sent him ten miles out intil the sky. Every other good angel follyed shuit, and I watched thousands go, till they faded like a stretch of black smoke a hundred miles below.

"The Angel Gabriel turned and saw me, and must confess I shivered.

"'Well, King Brian Connors,' says he, 'I hope you see that there's such a thing as being too wise and too cute and too ticklish of yourself. I can't send you to the stars, bekase they're full, and I won't send you to the bottomless pit so long as I can help it. I'll send yez all down to the world. We're going to put human beans on it purty soon, though they're going to turn out to be blaggards, and at last we'll have to burn the place up. Afther that, if you're still there, you and yours must go to purdition, for it's the only place left for you.

"'You're too hard on the little man,' says the Angel Michael, coming up—St. Michael was ever the outspoken, friendly person— 'sure what harm, or what hurt, or what good could he have done us? And can you blame the poor little crachures for not interfering?'

"'Maybe I was too harsh,' says the Angel Gabriel, 'but being saints, when we say a thing we must stick to it. Howsumever, I'll let him settle in any part of the world he likes, and I'll send there the kind of human beans he'd wish most for. Now, give your ordher,' he says to me, taking out his book and pencil, 'and I'll make for you the kind of people you'd like to live among.'

"'Well,' says I, 'I'd like the men honest and brave, and the women good.'

"'Very well,' he says, writing it down; 'I've got that—go on.'

"'And I'd like them full of jollity and sport, fond of racing and singing and hunting and fighting, and all such innocent divarsions.'

"'You'll have no complaint about that,' says he.

"'And,' says I, 'I'd like them poor and parsecuted, bekase when a man gets rich, there's no more fun in him.'

"'Yes, I'll fix that. Thrue for you,' says the Angel Gabriel, writing.

"'And I don't want them to be Christians,' says I; 'make them Haythens or Pagans, for Christians are too much worried about the Day of Judgment.'

"'Stop there! Say no more!' says the saint. 'If I make as fine a race of people as that I won't send them to hell to plaze you, Brian Connors.'

"'At laste,' says I, 'make them Jews.'

"'If I made them Jews,' he says, slowly screwing up one eye to think, 'how could you keep them poor? No, no!' he said, shutting up the book; 'go your ways; you have enough.'

"I clapped me hands, and an the Little People stood up and bent over the edge, their fingers pointed like swimmers going to dive. 'One, two, three,' I shouted; and with that we took the leap.

"We were two years and tunty-six days falling before we raiched the world. On the morning of the next day we began our sarch for a place to live. We thraveled from north to south and from ayst to west. Some grew tired and dhropped off in Spain, some in France, and others agin in different parts of the world. But the most of us thraveled ever and ever till we came to a lovely island that glimmered and laughed and sparkled in the middle of the say.

"'We'll stop here,' I says; 'we needn't sarch farther, and we needn't go back to Italy or Swizzerland, for of all places on the earth, this island is the nearest like heaven; and in it the County Clare and the County Tipperary are the purtiest spots of all.' So we hollowed out the great mountain Sleive-na-mon for our home, and there we are till this day."

The king stopped a while, and sat houldin' his chin in his hands. "That's the thrue story," he says, sighing pitiful. "We took sides with nobody, we minded our own business, and we got trun out for it," says he.

So intherested was Father Cassidy in the talk of the king that the singing and hammering had died out without his knowing, and he hadn't noticed at all how the darkness had thickened in the valley and how the stillness had spread over the hillside. But now, whin the chief of the fairies stopped, the good man, half frightened at the silence, jumped to his feet and turned to look for his horse.

Beyond the dull glow of the dying fire a crowd of Little People stood waiting, patient and quiet, houlding Terror, who champed restless at his bit, and bate impatient with his hoof on the hard ground.

As the priest looked toward them, two of the little men wearing leather aprons moved out from the others, leading the baste slow and careful over to where the good man stood beside the rock.

"You've done me a favyer this night," says the clargyman, gripping with his bridle hand the horse's mane, "an' all I have to pay it back with'd only harry you, an' make you oncomfortable, so I'll not say the words," he says.

"No favyer at all," says the king, "but before an hour there'll be lyin' on your own threshold a favyer in the shape of a bit of as fine bacon as ever laughed happy in the middle of biling turnips. We borryed it last night from a magisthrate named Blake; who lives up in the County Wexford," he says.

The clargyman had swung himself into the saddle.

"I'd be loath to say anything disrayspectful," he says quick, "or to hurt sensitive feelings, but on account of my soul's sake I couldn't ate anything that was come by dishonest," he says.

"Bother and botheration, look at that now!" says the king. "Every thrade has its drawbacks, but I never rayalized before the hardship of being a parish priest. Can't we manage it some way? Couldn't I put it some place where you might find it, or give it to a friend who'd send it to you?"

"Stop a minute," says Father Cassidy. "Up at Tim Healy's I think there's more hunger than sickness, more nade for petaties than for physic. Now, if you sent that same bit of bacon—"

"Oh, ho!" says the king, with a dhry cough, "the Healy's have no sowls to save, the same as parish priests have."

"I'm a poor, wake, miserable sinner," says the priest, hanging his head; "I fall at the first temptation. Don't send it," says he.

"Since you forbid me, I'll send it," says the king, chucklin'. "I'll not be ruled by you. To-morrow the Healy's'll have five tinder-hearted heads of cabbage, makin' love in a pot to the finest bit of bacon in Tipperary—that is, unless you do your juty an' ride back to warn them.

Raymember their poor sowls," says he, "an' don't forget
your own," he says.

The priest sat unaisy in the saddle. "I'll put all the
raysponsibility on Terror," he says. "The baste has no sowl
to lose. I'll just drop the reins on his neck; if he turns and
goes back to Healy's I'll warn them; if he goes home let it
be on his own conscience." He dhropped the reins, and
the dishonest baste started for home imagetly.

But afther a few steps Father Cassidy dhrew up an'
turned in the saddle. Not a sowl was in sight; there was
only the lonely road and the lonesome hillside; the last
glimmer of the fairy fire was gone, and a curtain of soft
blackness had fallen betwixt him an' where the blaze had
been.

"I bid you good night, Brian Connors," the priest cried.
From somewhere out of the darkness a woice called back
to him, "Good night, your Riverence!"

THE ADVENTURES OF KING BRIAN CONNORS

Chapter I
The King and the Omadhaun*

Did your honour ever hear how Anthony Sullivan's goat came to join the fairies?

Well, it's a quare story and a wandhering, quarrelsome story, as a tale about a goat is sure to be. Howsumever, in the home of the Good People which, as you know, is the hollow heart of the great mountain Sleive-na-mon Anthony Sullivan's goat lives and prospers to this day, a pet and a hayro among the fairies.

And this is the way it came about:

All the world knows how for months Darby O'Gill an' his purty sister-in-law, Maureen McGibney, were kept presners by the Good People; an' how, afther they were relaysed by the King, that same little fairy, King Brian Connors, used often to visit thim an' sit with thim colloguin' and debaytin' an' considherin' in Darby O'Gill's kitchen.

One lonesome Decimber night, when Bridget and the childher were away visiting Bridget's father at Ballingher, and the angry blast was screaming and dhrifting the first white flakes of winther around Darby's house, thin it was

* Omadhaun, a foolish fellow.

69

that Darby O'Gill, Brian Connors, the King of the Good People, and Maureen McGibney sat with their heads together before the blazing hearth. The King, being not much higher than your two hands, sat on the child's stool betwixt the other two, his green cloak flung back from his chowlders, and the goold crown on his head glistening in the firelight.

It was a pleasant sight to watch them there in the flickering hearth glow. From time to time, as he talked, the ould King patted Maureen's hands and looked smiling up into her purty gray eyes. They had been discoursing on the subject of Throubles and Thribulations.

"Arrah! You ought to be the happy man, King," Darby says, sipping his noggin of punch, "with no silly woman to ordher you or to cross you or to belittle you. Look at meself. Afther all the rayspect I've climbed into from being with the fairies, and afther all the knowledge I've got from them, there's one person in this parish who has no more riverence for me now than she had the first day she met me—sometimes not so much, I'm thinking," he says, hurt-like.

"I've seen the workings of families during more than five thousand years," says the little King, "so you needn't tell me who that one person is, me poor man—'tis your own wife, Bridget."

"Thrue for you! Whin it's the proud woman she ought to be this day to have the likes of me for a husband," says Darby. "Ah, then, you ought to be the happy man, whatever wind blows," he sighed again; "when you see a fat pig you like, you take it without so much as saying by your lave; if you come upon a fine cow or a good horse, in a twinkling you have it in Sleive-na-mon. A girl has a good song with her, a boy has a nimble foot for a jig, or an ould woman a smooth tongue for a tale, and, whisk! they're gone into the heart of the mountain to sing or dance for you, or to beguile you with ould tales until the Day of Judgment."

The King shook his head slowly, and drew a long face.

"Maybe we ought to be happy," says he. "'Tis thrue there's no sickness in Sleive-na-mon, nor worry for to-morrow, nor fret for one's childher, nor parting from friends, or things like that, but throuble is like the dhrifting snow outside, Darby; it falls on the cottage and it covers the castle with the same touch, and once in a while it sifts into Sleive-na-mon."

"In the name of goodness!" cries Darby, surprised, "is there anything in the whole world you can't have for the wishing it?"

The King took off his goold crown and began polishing it with his sleeve to hide his narvousness. "I'll tell you a saycret," he whuspered, bending over toward Darby, and speaking slow. "In Sleive-na-mon our hearts are just breaking for something we can't get; but that's one thing we'd give the worruld for."

"Oh, King, what in the livin' worruld can it be?" cried Maureen.

"I'd give the teeth out of me head if I could only own a goat," says the King, looking as though he were going to cry.

"Man alive!" says Darby, dhropping the poker, "the counthry-side is full of goats, and all you have to do is to take your pick and help yourself. You're making game of us, King."

The King shook his head. "The Good People have been thrying for years to capture one," says he. "I've been bunted into ditches by the villains; I've been trun over hedges by them; I had to leap on the back of Anthony Sullivan's goat, and with two hundred of me subjects in full cry behind, ride him all night long, houlding by his horns to kape him from getting at me and disthroying me entirely. The jumps he took with me that night were thraymendous. It was from the cow-shed to the sthraw-stack, from the sthraw-stack to the house-top, and from there down to the ground agin, and then hooraying an'

hoorooing, a race up the mountain-side. But," says the
King, kind o' sniffling an' turning to the fire, "we love the
ground he walks upon," says he.

"Tare an' ouns!" says Darby, "why don't you put your
spell on one of them?"

"You don't know them," says the King. "We can't put
the black spell on thim—they're not Christian bastes, like
pigs or cows. Whin it comes to animals, we can only put
our come 'ither on cattle and horses, and such as are
Christian animals, ye know. In his mind and in his heart
a goat is a pagen. He wouldn't ask any betther diversion
than for me to thry and lay me hands on him," says the
King, wiping his eyes.

"But," says he agin, standing up on the stool and
houlding his pipe over his head, "Anthony Sullivan's goat
is the gallusest baste that roams the fields! There's more
fun in him, and no more fear in him, than in a yellow
lion. He'd do anything for sport; he'd bunt the King of
Russia, he'd ba-a at a parish priest, out of pure, rollicking divilment," says the King. "If the Good People had a
friend, a rale friend," says he, looking hard at Darby, "that
wouldn't be afeard to go into our home within the mountain once more, just once, and bring with him that goat—"

"Say no more," says Darby, hoarsely, and turning white
with fear— "say no more, Brian Connors! Not all the goold
in Sleive-na-mon would tempt me there agin! It's make a
presner of me for ever you would. I know your thricks."

The look of scorn the little man flung at Darby would
have withered the threes.

"I might have known it," he says, sitting down disgusted. "I was a fool for hoping you would," says he.
"There's no more spirit in ye nor sinse of gratichude than
in a hin. Wait till!—" and he shook his fist.

"Don't blame the lad," cried Maureen, patting the King's
head, sootheringly; "sure, why should the like of a
wondherful man, such as you, who has lived five thousand years, and knows everything, compare your wit or

your spirit or your sinse with the likes of us poor crachures that only stay here a few hours and thin are gone for ever?" This she cried, craftily, flatthering the ould man. "Be aisy on him, King, acushla!" says she, coaxing.

Well, the little man, being soothered, sat down agin. "Maybe I was too hard," he says, "but to tell the truth, the life is just bothered out of me, and my temper is runed these days with an omadhaun we've taken lately; I don't know what to do with him. Talk of throuble! He mopes and mourns and moothers in spite of all we can do. I've even tould him where the crocks of goold are hid—"

"You haven't tould me that," cries Darby, quickly.

"No," says the King, looking at him sideways.

"At laste not yit," says Darby, looking sideways at the King.

"Not yit, nor will I fer a long time yitter, you covetous, ungrateful spalpeen!" snapped the fairy.

"Well," said he, paying no more attention to Darby, "this young omadhaun is six feet high in his stockings, and as foine a looking lad as you'll see in a day's walk. Now what do you think he's mourning and crooning for?"

"Faix, I dunno," answered Darby. "Maybe it's a horse or a dog or a cow, or maybe a pair of pigs."

"You've not hit it," said the Ruler of the Good People; "it's a colleen. And him having a college education, too."

"Troth, thin," said Darby, with a knowledgeable wag of his head, "some of them larned students are as foolish in that way as ignorant people. I once met a tinker named Larry McManus, who knew the jography from cover to cover, and still he had been married three times."

"Poor gossoon! Who is the omadhaun?" asked Maureen, not minding Darby.

"He's no less," said the King, "than Roger O'Brien, a son of ould Bob O'Brien, who was the richest and proudest man in the County Tipperary. Ould Bob thraces his ancestors for five hundhred years, and he owns a mile of land and has forty tenants. He had no child but this omadhaun."

"And who is the colleen? Some grand Princess, I suppose," said Maureen.

"There was the whole throuble," answered the little man. "Why, she's no one at all, but a little white-cheeked, brown-eyed, black-haired girl named Norah Costello, belonging to one of his own tenants on the domain. It all came from eddicatin' people above their station."

"Faix," Darby says, "there's Phelem Brady, the stone-cutter, a fine, dacint man he was till he made up his mind to larn the history of Ireland from ind to ind. When he got so far as where the Danes killed Brian Boru he took to dhrink, and the divil a ha'porth's good he's been ever since. But lade on with your discoorse, King," says he, waving his noggin of punch.

At this the King filled his pipe, Maureen threw fresh turf on the fire, and the wind dhrew the sparks dancing up the chimney. Now and thin while the King talked, some of the fairies outside rapped on the window-panes and pressed their little faces against the glass to smile and nod at those within, thin scurried busily off agin intil the darkness. Once the wail of a child rose above the cry of the storm, and Maureen caught the flash of a white robe against the window-pane.

"It's a child we've taken this night from one Jude Casey down in Mayo," says King Brian Connors. "But fill my noggin with fresh punch, Maureen, and dhraw closter till I tell you about the omadhaun." And the Master of the Good People crossed his legs and settled into telling the story, comfortable as comfortable could be.

"The way the throuble began was foine and innocent as the day is long," said the King. "Five or six years ago it was on the day Roger was first sent to college at Dublin Misther and Misthress O'Brien, mighty lonesome an' down-hearted, were dhriving over the estate whin who should they spy standing, modest and timid, at her own gate, but purty little Norah Costello. Though the child was only fourteen years old, Misthress O'Brien was so taken with

her wise, gentle ways that Norah next day was sint for to
come up to the big house to spind an hour amusing the
Misthress. There was the rock they all split on.

"Every day afther for a month the little girl went visiting there. At the end of that time Misthress O'Brien grew
so fond of her that Norah was brought to the big house to
live. Ould Bob liked the little girl monsthrous well, so they
put fine clothes on her until in a couple of years one
couldn't tell her from a rale lady, whether he met her in
the house or at the cross- road.

"Only every Saturday night she'd put on a little brown
poplin dhress and go to her father's cottage, and stay there
helping her mother till Monday or maybe Chewsday. 'For
I mustn't get proud-hearted,' she'd say, 'or lose the love I
was born to, for who can tell whin I'll need it,' says she."

"A wise girl," says Darby.

"A dear colleen," says Maureen.

"Well, every summer me brave Roger came home from
college, and the two rode together afther the hounds, or
sailed his boat or roved the woods, and the longest summer days were too short entirely to suit the both of them.

"Although she had a dozen young fellows courting her—
some of them gentlemen's sons—the divil an eye she had
for anyone except Roger; and although he might pick from
twinty of the bluest-blooded ladies in Ireland any day he
liked, Norah was his one delight.

"Every servant on the place knew how things were going, but the ould man was so blind with pride that he saw
nothing at all; stranger than all, the two childher believed
that ould Bob guessed the way things were with them an'
was plazed with them. A worse mistake was never made.
He never dhramed that his son Roger would think of any
girl without a fortune or a title.

"Misthress O'Brien must have known, but, being
tendher-hearted and loving and, like all women, a trifle
weak-minded, hoped, in spite of rayson, that her husband
would consint to let the childher marry. Knowing ould Bob

as she knew him, that was a wild thought for Misthress O'Brien to have; for if ever there was a stiffer, bittherer, prouder, more unforgiving, boistherous man I haven't seen him, and I've lived five thousand years."

Darby, scowling mighty important, raised his hand. "Whist a bit," he says; "you raymind me of the ballad about Lord Skipperbeg's lovely daughter and the farmer's only son." Stretching his legs an; wagging his head, he sang:

> "Her cheeks were like the lily white,
>   Her neck was like the rose."

"Oh, my! oh, my!" said the King, surprised, "was her neck as red as that?"

"By no manes," said Darby. "I med a mistake; 'twas this away:

> "Her neck was like the lily white,
>   Her cheeks were like the rose,
> She quickly doffed her silk attire
>   And donned a yeoman's clothes.
>
> "'Rise up, rise up, my farmer's son,
>   Rise up thrue love,' says she,
> 'We'll fly acrost the ragin' main
>   Unto Amer-i—'"

"Have done you're fooling, Darby," says Maureen; "you have the King bothered."

"I wisht you hadn't shtopped him, agra," says the King. "I niver heard that song before, an' it promised well. I'm fond of love songs," he says.

"But the omadhaun," coaxed the colleen.

"I forgot where I was," the King says, scratching his head. "But, spaking of ould Bob," he wint on, "no one ever thought how evil and bitther he could be, until his son, the foolish lad, a few days before the ind of his schooling, wrote to the father that he wanted to marry Norah whin he came home, and that he would be home in a few days, he thought. He was breaking the news aisy to the family, d'ye see!

"'Whew! Hullabaloo! Out of the house with her—the sly, conniving hussy!' shouted ould Bob, whin he read the letter. 'Into the road with all we've given her! Pull the roof off Costello's house and dhrive off the place his whole brood of outraygeous villains!'

"So they packed Norah's boxes—faix, an' many a fine dhress was in them, too—and bade her begone. The Misthress slipped a bag of goold sovereigns with a letther into one of the chests. Norah took the letther, but she forbade them sending so much as a handkerchief afther her.

"She wouldn't even ride in the coach that the Misthress had waiting for her outside the grand gate; and all alone, in her brown poplin dhress, she marched down the gravel path, proud, like a queen going to be crowned. Nor did she turn her head when the servants called blessings afther her; but oh, asthore, her face was marble white; and whin she was on her way down the lonely high-road how she cried!

"'Twas a bitther time entirely, the night young Roger came home, and, hearing of all this, rushed up the stairs to face his father. What happened betwixt them there no one knows, only they never passed aich other a friendly look nor gave one to the other a pleasant word from that good hour to this.

"To make matthers worse, that same night young Roger wint and axed Norah Costello to marry him. But all the counthry-side knows how the girl rayfused him, saying she wouldn't beggar and rune the man she loved.

"Well, he took her at her word, but disbelieved and mocked at the raysons she gave—the omadhaun!

"He wasn't much good afther that, only for galloping his horse over the counthry like a madman, so I said to

meself, says I, that we might as well take him with us into
the Sleive-na-mon. I gave the ordhers, and there he is."

"Oh, the poor lad!" says Maureen; "does ould Bob sus-
pect the boy is with the fairies?"

"Not in the laste," says the King. "You know how it is with
us; whinever we take a person we lave one of our own in
his place, who looks and acts and talks in a way that the
presner's own mother can't tell the differ. By-and-by the
fairy sickens and purtends to die, and has his wake and his
burial. When the funeral's over he comes back to us hale
and spiling for more sport. So the lad the O'Briens put
into their tomb was one of our own—Phadrig Oge be name.

"Many a time Phadrig has taken the place of the genthry
and quality in every county of Ireland, and has been buried more than a hundhred times, but he swears he never
before had a dacinter funeral nor a rattliner wake."

"And the girl!" cried Maureen— "Norah, where is she?"

"Faith, that's strange, too," says the King. "She was
the first person ould Bob axed for afther the funeral. He
begged her to come back to them and forgive him, and the
poor girl went agin to live at the big house."

"He'll get her another good husband yet," said Darby.

"Oh, never!" says Maureen, crying like a child. "She'll
die of a broken heart."

"I've seen in me time," says the King, "people die from
being pushed off houses, from falling in wells, and every
manner of death you can mention, and I saw one ould
woman die from ating too much treacle," he says, "but
never a person die from a broken heart."

This he said to make light of what he had been telling,
because he saw by Maureen's face that she was growing
sick with pity. For Maureen was thinking of the black days
when she herself was a presner in Sleive-na-mon.

For an answer to the jest, the girl, with her clasped
hands held up to the King, moaned, "Oh, King, King, lave
the poor lad go! lave him go. Take the black spell off him
and send him home. I beg you lave him go!"

"Don't bother him," says Darby; "what right have we to interfere with the Good People?" Though at the same time he took the pipe from his mouth and looked kind of wistful at the little man.

But Maureen's tears only fell faster and faster.

"I can't do what you ask, avick," says the King, very kindly. "That day I let you and Darby go from us the power to free anyone was taken away from me by my people. Now every fairy in Sleive-na-mon must give his consent before the spell can be taken away entirely from anyone; and, well, you know they'll never consent to that," he says.

"But what I *can* do, I will do. I can lift the spell from the omadhaun for one hour, and that hour must be just before cock-crow."

"Is that the law now?" asked Darby, curiously. Maureen was sobbing, so she couldn't spake.

"It is," says the Master of the Good People. "And to-night I'll sind our spy, Sheelah Maguire, to Norah Costello with the message that if Norah has love enough and courage enough in her heart to stand alone at her thrue lover's grave in Kilmartin church-yard, to-morrow night an hour before cock-crow, she'll see him plain and talk with him. And let you two be there," he says, "to know that I keep me word."

At that he vanished and they saw him no more that night, nor until two hours afther the next midnight, whin as they were tying the ould horse and cart to the fence outside Kilmartin church, thin they heard him singing. He was sitting on the wall, chanting at the top of his woice a sthrange, wild song, and houlding in his hand a silver-covered noggin. On a fallen tombstone near by lay a white cloth, glimmering in the moonlight, and on the cloth was spread as fine a supper as heart could wish.

So beside the white rows of silent tombs, under the elm-trees and willows, they ate their fill, and Darby would have ate more if close to them they hadn't heard a long, deep sigh, and caught a glimpse of a tall man, gliding like a shadow into the shadows that hung around the O'Briens' family vault.

At the same time, standing on the top of the stile which led into the graveyard, a woman's form was seen wavering in the moonlight.

They watched her coming down the walk betwixt the tombs, her hand on her breast, clutching tight the cloak. Now and thin she'd stand, looking about the while, and shivering in mortal terror at the cry of the owls, and thin she'd flit on and be lost in the shadows; and thin they'd see her run out into the moonlight, where she'd wait agin, gathering courage. At last she came to a strip of soft light before the tomb she knew. Her strength failed her there, and she went down on her knees.

Out of the darkness before her a low, pleading woice called, "Norah! Norah! Don't be frightened, acushla machree!"

Slowly, slowly, with its arm spread, the dim shape of a man glided out of the shadows. At the same instant the girl rose and gave one cry, as she flung herself on his breast. They could see him bending over her, thin, pouring words like rain into her ears, but what he said they couldn't hear Darby thinks he whuspered.

"I wondher, oh, I wondher what he's telling her in this last hour!" says Maureen.

"It's aisy to know that," says Darby; "what should he be telling her but where the crocks of goold are hid."

"Don't be watching them, it ain't dacint," says the King; "uncultayvation or unpoliteness is ojus; come over here; I've a pack of cayrds, Darby," says he, "and as we have nearly an hour to wait, I challenge you to a game of forty-five."

"Sure we may as well," says Darby. "What can't be cured must be endured."

With that, me two bould hayroes sat asthride the fallen stone, and hammering the rock hard with their knuckles, played the game. Maureen went and, houlding on to the ivy, knelt at the church wall—it's praying an' cryin', too, I think she was. Small blame to her if she was. All through that hour she imagined the wild promisings of the two poor crachures over be the tomb, and this kept burning the heart out of her.

Just as the first glow of gray broke behind the hills the King stood up and said: "It's your game, Darby, more be good luck than be good shooting; 'tis time to lave. You know if I'm caught out afther cock-crow I lose all me spells for the day, and besides I'm wisible to any mortal eye. I'm helpless as a baby then. So I think I'll take the omadhaun and go. The roosthers may crow now any minute," says he.

The omadhaun, although he couldn't hear, he felt the charm dhrawing him. He trew a frightened look at the east and held the girl closer. 'Twas their last minute.

"King! King!" says Maureen, running up, "if I brought Sullivan's goat into Sleive-na-mon, would ye swear to let me out safe agin?"

"Troth, I would indade, I swear be Ould Nick!" ('Tis be him the Good People swear.) "I'll do that same."

"Then let the omadhaun go home. Get the Good People's consent and I'll bring you the goat," says Maureen,

The King thrembled all over with anxiety and excitement. "Why didn't you spake sooner? I'm afeard I haven't time to go to Sleive-na-mon and back before cock-crow," he stutthered, "and at cock-crow, if the lad was undher the say or in the stars, that spell'd bring him to us, and then he could never agin come out till the Day of Judgment. Howsumever, I'll go and thry," he says, houlding tight on to his crown with both hands; and with thim words he vanished.

Be this and be that, it wasn't two minutes till he was back and wid not a second to spare, ayther.

"Phadrig Oge wants Mrs. Nancy Clancy's nanny-goat, too. Will ye bring the both of them, Maureen?" he screamed.

"You're dhriving a hard bargain, King," cried Darby. "Don't promise him, Maureen."

"I will!" cried she.

"Then it's a bargain!" the fairy shouted, jumping to the top of a headstone. "We all consent," he says, waving the noggin.

He yelled to the omadhaun. "Go home, Roger O'Brien! Go back to your father's house and live your life out to its natural ind. The curse is lifted from you, the black spell is spint and gone. Pick up the girl, ye spalpeen; don't ye see she's fainted?"

When O'Brien looked up and saw the Master of the Fairies he staggered like a man that had been sthruck a powerful blow. Thin he caught up the girl in his arms and ran with her down the gravelled path and over the stile.

At that minute the sorest misfortune that can happen to one of the Good People came to pass. As the lad left the churchyard every cock in the parish crowed, and, tare and 'ounds! there on a tombstone, caught by the cock-crow, stood the poor, frightened little King! His goold crown was far back on his head, and his green cloak was twisted behind his back.

All the power for spells and charms was gone from him until the next sunset.

"I'm runed entirely, Darby!" he says. "Trow your shawl about me, Maureen alannah, and carry me in your arms, purtending I'm an infant. What'll I do at all at all?" says he, weakly.

Taking him at his word, Maureen wrapped the King in her shawl, and carrying him in her arms to the cart, laid him in the sthraw at the bottom, where he curled up, still and frightened, till they were on their way home.

Chapter II
The Couple Without Childher

Five miles down the road from Kilmartin churchyard, and thin two miles across, lived Barney Casey with Judy,

his wife—known far and wide as the Couple without
Childher.

Some foolish people whuspered that this lack of family
was a punishment for an ould saycret crime. But that
saying was nonsense, for an honester couple the sun didn't
shine on. It was only a pinance sint from Heaven as any
other pinance is sint; 'twas like poverty, sickness, or as
being born a Connaught man—just to keep them humble-
hearted.

But, oh, it was the sore pinance!

Many an envious look they gave their neighbour, Tom
Mulligan, the one-legged ballad-maker, who lived half a
mile up the road, for, twelve purty, red-haired innocents
sported and fought before Tom's door. The couple took to
going through the fields to avoid passing the house, for
the sight of the childher gave them the heartache.

By-and-by the two began conniving how on-be-knownst
they might buy a child, or beg or even steal one—they
were that lonesome-hearted.

Howsumever, the plan at last they settled on was for
Judy to slip away to a far part—Mayo, I think—where she
would go through the alms-houses till she found a gossoon
that suited her. And they had the cute plan laid by which
it was to pass before the neighbours as their own—a Casey
of the Caseys. "Lave it to me, Barney darling," said Judy,
with tears in her eyes, "and if the neighbours wondher
where I am, tell them I've gone to spind a few months
with my ould mother," says she.

Well, Judy stole off sly enough, and 'twas well intil the
cowld weather when Barney got word that she had found
a parfect angel, that it was the picture of himself, and
that she would be home in a few days.

With a mind like thistle-down he ran to Father Scanlan
to arrange for the christening. On his way to the priest's
house he inwited the first woman he met, Ann Mulligan,
the ballad-maker's wife, to be godmother; he picked bashful Ted Murphy, the bachelor, to be godfather; and on his

way home he was that excited and elayted that he also inwited big Mrs. Brophy, the proud woman, to be the boy's godmother, forgetting altogether there was sich a parson in the world as Ann Mulligan. The next day the neighbours made ready a great bonfire to celebrayte the dispositious occasion.

But ochone! Midnight before the day of the christening poor Judy came home with empty arms and a breaking heart. The little lad had died suddenly and was buried. Maybe the Good People had taken him—'twas hard to tell which.

Tare and ages, there was the throuble! For two hours the couple sat in their desolate kitchen houlding hands and crying and bawling together till Barney could stand it no longer. Snatching his caubeen, he fled from the coming disgrace and eggsposure out into the fields, where he wandhered aimless till after dawn, stamping his feet at times and wagging his head, or shaking his fist at the stars.

At that same unlucky hour who should be joulting in their cart along the high-road, two miles across, on their way home from Kilmartin churchyard, but our three hayroes, Maureen, the King, and Darby O'Gill!

Their ould white horse bobbed up and down through the sticky morning fog, Darby and Maureen shivering on the front sate. The Ruler of the Fairies, Maureen's shawl folded about him, was lying cuddled below in the sthraw. When they saw anyone coming, the fairy-chief would climb into Maureen's lap, and she'd hould him as though he were a baby.

Small blame to him to be sour and sullen!

"Here I am," he says to himself, "his Majesty, Brian Connors, King of all the Good People in Ireland, the Master of the Night Time, and having been King for more than five thousand years, with more power after sunset than the Emperor of Greeze or the Grand Turkey of barbayrious parts—here am I," he says, "disguised as a baby, wrapped in a woman's shawl, and depending for my safety on two

simple counthry people—" Then he groaned aloud, "Bad
luck to the day I first saw the omadhaun!"

Those were the first words he spoke. But it wasn't in
the little man to stay long ill-natured. At the first shebeen
house that they found open Maureen bought for him a
bottle of spirits, and this cheered him greatly. The first
dhrink warmed him, the second softened him, the third
put a chune to the ind of his tongue, and by the time they
raiched Tom Grogan's public-house, which was straight
two miles across from Barney Casey's, the liquor set him
singing like a nightingale.

Maureen and Darby slipped into Grogan's for a bit of
warmth and a mouthful to ate, laving the Master of Sleive-
na-mon well wrapped up at the bottom of the cart—his
head on a sack of oats and his feet against the cart-side—
and as I said, him singing.

He had the finest, liftenest way for a ballad you ever
heard! At the end of every verse he eleywated the last word
and hildt it high, and put a lonesome wobble into his woice
that would make you cry.

Peggy Collins, the tall, thieving ould beggar-woman who
used to wear the dirty red cloak, an' looked like a sojer in
it, was sleeping inside the hedge as the cart came along;
but when it stopped she peeped out to see who had the
good song with him.

When she saw it was an infant not much longer than
your two hands, "God presarve us and save us!" she
gasped, and began to say her prayers. The King went on
singing, clear and doleful and beautiful, the ballad of
Donnelly and Cooper.

> "Come all ye thrue-bom Irishmen wherever
> you may be,
> I hope you'll pay attintion and listen unto me-
> e-e,
> And if you'll pay attintion the truth I will de-
> clare

How Donnelly fought Cooper on the Curragh
of Kildare."

Prayers were never from Peggy's heart, so as she listened to the enthrancing song she turned from praying to
plotting. "If I had that child," she says, "I could go from
fair to fair and from pathron to pathron, and his singing'd
fill my apron with silver."

The King turned to another ditty, and you'd think he
was a thrush.

"They'll kiss you, they'll car-r-ress you," he
    sang.
"They'll spind your money free,
But of all the towns in Ire-eland Kilkenny for
    me-e-e-e."

The gray-haired ould rascal, Peggy, by this was creeping ever and ever till she raiched the cart. Up then she
popped, and the first thing me poor Captain knew the
shawl was slapped fast on his face, and two long, thin
arms were dragging him out over the wheel. He thried to
cry out, but the shawl choked him, and scrambling and
kicking did him no good.

Over the nearest stile bounced Peggy, and into the nearest field she flew, her petticoat lifted, her white hair
streaming, and her red cloak fluttering behind. She
crunched the chief man of the fairies undher her left elbow,
his head hanging behind, with as little riverence as if,
saving your presence, he were a sthray gander.

Well, your honour, Peggy ran till there wasn't a breath
in her before she slowed down to a walk, and then she
flung the King over her right chowldher, his face on her
back in that way some careless women carry childher.
This set his head free.

When he saw who it was had stolen him, oh, but he
was vexed; for all that he didn't say a word as they went,

but lay there on her collar-bone, bobbing up and down, blinking his eyes, and thinking what he should do to her. At last he quietly raiched over with his teeth and took a bite at the back of her neck that she felt to her toes. Wow! Your honour should have heard the screech Peggy let out of her!

Well, as she gave that screech she gave a jerk at the King's legs, pulling him down. As he flopped intil her arms he took a wisp of her hair with him. For a second's time the spiteful little eyes in the ould weazened face, looking up at her own from undher the goold crown, froze her stiff with terror, and then, giving a yell that was ten times louder than the first screech, she flung his Majesty from her down upon the hard ground. Leaping a ditch, she went galloping wildly across the meadow. The King fell flat on his back with an unraysonable joult.

That wasn't the worst of his bad luck. If Peggy had dhropped him at any other place in the field he might have crawled off into the ditch and hid till sunset, but oh, asthore, there not ten rods away, with eyes bulging and mouth gaping, stood Barney Casey, the Man without Childher!

Barney looked from the little bundle on the ground to Peggy as she went skimming, like a big red bird, over the low-lying morning fog. Through his surprise a foine hope slowly dawned for him.

He said: "Good fortune folly you, and my blessing rest on you wherever you go, Peggy Bawn, for the throuble you've lifted this day; you've given me a Moses in the bull rushers or a Pharyoah's daughter, but I disremember which, God forgive me for forgetting my rayligion!"

He stood for a minute slyly looking to the north, and the south and the ayst and the west. But what he saw, when he turned to look again for the baby, would have made any other man than one in Barney Casey's mind say his prayers and go on his way.

The baby was gone, but in its place was a little ould man with a goold crown on his head, a silver-covered noggin in his hand, and the most vexed expression in the world on his face, and he thrailing a shawl and throtting toward the ditch.

'Twas a hard fall for the Man without Childher, and hard he took it.

When Barney was done with bad langwidge, he says: "A second ago, me ould lad, you were, or you purtended to be, an innocent child. Well, then, you'll turn back again every hair and every look of you; you'll be a smiling, harmless, purty baby agin, or I'll know the rayson why," he says, gritting his teeth. With that he crept over and scooped up the King. There was the struggling and wiggling!

"Lave me down! Lave me down! You murthering spalpeen!" shouted the King, kicking vicious at Barney's chist. "I'm Brian Connors, the King of the Good People, and I'll make you sup sorrow in tay-cups for this!" cries he.

Well, Casey, his lips shut tight and his eyes grim and cowld, hildt in his two hands, out at arm's-length, the little man, who was kicking furious. For a minute Barney studied him.

"I believe in my sowl," says the Man without Childher, mighty rayproachful, "you're only a fairy! But if that's what you are, you must have charms and spells. Now, turn yourself into a purty, harmless infant this minute—have red hair, like the Mulligan childher at that—or I'll break every bone in your body!"

There was blazing anger in the King's eye and withering scorn in his woice.

"Ignorant man," he cried, "don't you know that betwixt cock-crow in the morning and sunset the Good People can work no spell or charm. If you don't lave me down I'll have a mark on you and on all your relaytions the world'll wondher at!"

But the divil a bit frightened was Casey.

He started in to help the charm along as one would thry to make a watch go. He shook the King slowly from side to side, thin joggled him softly up and down, mutthering earnestly betwixt his teeth, "Go on, now, you little haythen, change this minute, you scorpion of the world; come, come, twisht yourself!"

What the little King was saying all this time you must guess at, for I'm not bitther-tongued enough to repayt it.

Seeing that not a hair changed for all his work, Barney wrapped Maureen's shawl about the King and started for home, saying: "Hould your whist! It's a child I must have to be baptised this day. It'll be hard to manage, but I have a plan! You came as a child, and you'll be thrated as such and look, if you don't quit kicking me in the stomach, I'll strangle you!"

As you know, to say pious words to one of the Good People is worse than cutting him with a knife, to show him pious pictures is like burning him, but to baptise a fairy is the most turrible punishment in the whole worruld.

As they went along, the King argyed, besought and threatened, but he talked to stone.

At last, although he had but the strength of a six-year-old child, the Captain of the Good People showed what high spirit was in him.

"Set me down, you thief," he says. "I challenge you! If you have a dhrop of your mother's blood in you, set me ferninst you with sticks in our hands, so we can fight it out like men!"

"No, it's not needful," says Barney, cool as ice; "but in a few minutes I'll shave every hair from your head, and afther that make a fine Christian out of you. It's glad and thankful for it you ought to be, you wicious, ugly little pagan scoundhrel!"

Well, the King let a roar out of him: "You bandy-legged villain!" he cried and then whirled in to abuse the Man without Childher. He insulted him in English, he jeered him in Irish, he thrajooced him in Latin and Roosian, but the most awful crash of blaggarding that was known in Ireland since the world began was when the King used the Chinayse.

Casey looked wonder and admiraytion, but made no answer till the little man was out of breath, when he spoke up like a judge.

"Well, if there's any crather within the earth's four corners that needs baptising it's you, little man. But I'll not thrajooce you any more, for you're me own little Romulus or Raymus," he says, scratching his head. Then of a sudden he broke out excitedly, "Now may four kinds of bad luck fall on your proud head this day, Mrs. Brophy, and four times heavier ones on you, Ann Mulligan, and may the curse of Cromwell light on you now and for ever, Ted Murphy, the bachelor, for pushing yerselves here at this early hour in the morning!"

For the sight that met his eyes knocked every plan out of his head.

Long before the time she was expected, sailing down the road to his own house, happy and slow, came Ann Mulligan, carrying in her arms her two-weeks-old baby, Patsy Mulligan. With motion like a two-masted schooner, tacking in her pride from side to side, *up* the road came big Mrs. Brophy, the proud woman, carrying her little Cornaylius; behind Mrs. Brophy marched bashful Ted Murphy, the bachelor, his hands behind his back, his head bent like a captive, but stepping high. Not with the sheep-stealing air men are used to wear at christenings and weddings did Ted Murphy hop along, but with the look on his face of a man who had just been thried, convicted, sentenced, and who expects in few minutes to be hung for sheep-stealing.

They were come an hour before the time to bring the child to the church.

Beside the door stood Judy, straining her eyes to know what Barney had hiding in the bundle, and with an awful fear in her heart that he had robbed some near neighbour's cradle.

Well, Barney at once broke into a run so as to get inside the house with the King, and to close the door before the others got there, but as luck would have it, the whole party met upon the threshold and crowded in with him.

"Oh, the little darling; give us a sight of the poor crachure," says Mrs. Mulligan, laying Patsy on the bed.

"He's mine first, if you *plaze*," says Mrs. Brophy, the proud woman.

"He's sick," says Barney— "too sick to be uncovered."

"Is he too sick to go to church?" broke in Ted Murphy, eagerly, hoping to get rid of his job.

"He is," says Barney, catching at a chance for delay.

"Then," says Ted, with joy in his woice, "I'll run and bring Father Scanlan to the house. I'll be back with him in tunty minutes," says he.

Before anyone could stop the gawk, he was flying down the road to the village. Casey felt his bundle shiver.

"I'll have your life's blood for this!" the King whuspered, as Barney laid him on the bed betwixt the two childher.

"Come out! come out!" cries Casey, spreading his arms and pushing the three women over the threshold before they knew it.

Then he stood outside, holding the door shut against the three women, thrying to think of a plan, and listening to more blisthering talk than he ever heard on any day before that day, for the three women talked at the same time, aich striving to be more disagreeable than the other. What dhrove him crazy was that his own wife, Judy, was the worst. They threatened him, they wheedled, and they stormed. The priest might ride up at any minute. The sweat rained from Barney's forehead.

Once in desperaytion he opened the door to let the women pass, but shut it quick agin whin he saw the King standin' up on the bed and him changing his own clothes for those of little Patsy Mulligan.

Well, the women coaxed till Mrs. Mulligan lost all patience and went and sat sullen on the bench. At that Mrs. Brophy suddenly caught Barney around the waist, and whirling him aside, she and Judy rushed in. Barney, with the fierceness of a tiger, swung shut the door to keep Mrs. Mulligan at bay.

The other women inside were hopping with joy. Dhressed in Maureen's shawl, but divil a thing else, lay on the outside edge of the bed poor little Patsy Mulligan. The King, almost smothered, dhressed in Patsy's clothes, was scrooged in to the wall with a cloth about his head wrapped round and round.

"Oh, the little jewel," says Mrs. Brophy, picking up little Patsy Mulligan, and setting herself on the bed; "he's the dead cut of his father."

In that quare way women have Judy already had half a feeling that the child by some kind of magic was her own. So she spoke up sharp and said that the child was the image of her brother Mike.

While they were disputing, Mrs. Brophy turned her head and saw the legs of the King below the edge of little Patsy's dhress—the dhress that he'd stole an' put on.

"For the love of God, Mrs. Casey!" says she, laying her hand on Judy's chowlder, "did you ever before see feet on a child of two weeks old like them on Patsy Mulligan?"

Well, at this they laughed and titthered and doubled backward and forward on the bed, sniggering at the King and saying funny things about him, till, mad with the shame of the women looking at his bare knees, and stung be the provoking things they said, he did a very foolish thing;— he took a pin from his clothes and gave Mrs. Brophy so cruel a prod that, big as she was, and proud as she was, it lifted her in three leaps across the floor. "Whoop! whoop!" she says, as she was going. Now, though heavy and haughty, Mrs. Brophy was purty nimble on her feet, for, red and indignant, she whirled in a twinkling. "Judy Casey," says she, glowering and squaring off, "if that's your ideeah of a good, funny joke, I'll taiche you a betther!" she says.

When Barney, outside listening with his heart in his mouth, heard the angry woices within, a great wakeness came into his chist, for he thought everything was over.

Mrs. Mulligan pushed past him—he lost the power to prevent her—and he follyed her into the house with quaking knees. There was the uproar!

While the three was persuading the furious Mrs. Brophy that it must have been a pin in the bed-clothes, Ted Murphy, breathless, flung open the door.

"Father Scanlan wants to know," he cried, "what ails the baby that you can't bring it to church," he says.

All turned questioning eyes to Barney, till his mind flutthered like a wounded parthridge. Only two disayses could the unfortunate man on the suddint raymember.

"It's half maysles and a thrifle of scarlet faver," he says. He couldn't aisily have said anything worse. Seeing a turrible look on Mrs. Mulligan's face, he says agin, "But I don't think it's ketching, ma'am."

The fright was on. With a great cry, Mrs. Brophy dived for and picked up little Cornaylius and rushed with him out of the door and down the road; Mrs. Mulligan, thinking she had little Patsy, bekase of the clothes, snatched up the King—his head still rowled in the cloth—and darted up the road. She was clucking curses like an angry hen as she went, and hugging the King and coddling him, and crying over him and saying foolish baby langwidge, till he was so disgusted that he daytermined to give her a shock.

"Oh, me poor little darling!" she sobbed, pressing the King's head to her bosom— "oh, Patsy, me jewel, have they kilt you entirely?"

At that the King spoke up in a clear, cowld woice.

Misdoubting her ears, Mrs. Mulligan stopped and bent her head, listening to her baby.

"Don't worry for me, ma'am, thank you kindly," says the baby, polite and sthrong. "Don't throuble yourself about the general state of my robustness," it says, "it's thraymendous," says the child— "in fact, I never was betther."

As cautiously as if she was unwrapping a rowl of butther Mrs. Mulligan began to unwind the cloth from about the King's head.

When this was done she flung up her face an' yelled, "Ow! ow! ow!" and then came right up from the ground the second hard joult the King got that day.

As he lay on his back fastening his strange clothes and thinking what he would do next, he could hear Mrs. Mulligan going down the road. She was making a noise something like a steam whustle.

"Be-gorr," says the King, sitting up and feeling of his back, "to-day, with the women, I'm playing the divil entirely!"

Chapter III
The Luck of the Mulligans

The wee King of the Fairies sat in the dust of the road where Ann Mulligan had dhropped him. There were dents in his goold crown, and the baby's dhress he still wore was soiled and tore.

Ow! Ow! Ow! What a terrible joult agin the ground Ann Mulligan gave him when she took the covering from his head and found his own face gazing up at her instead of her baby Patsy's. He turned to shake his fist up the road, and twishted once more to shake his fist down the road.

"Be the bones of Pether White," he says, "what me and me subjects'll do to-night to this parish'll make the big wind seem like a cock's breath!"

"But," he says, again, "how'll I hide meself till dark? Wirra! Wirra! if it were only sunset—the sun has melted every power and charm and spell out of me—the power has left my four bones. I can be seen and molested by any spalpeen that comes along; what'll I do at all at all! I think I had best be getting through the fields back to Barney Casey's. It's little welcome they have for me there, but they must keep me saycret now for their own sakes."

With that he got upon his legs, and houldin' up his white dhress, climbed through the stile into Casey's field.

The first thing he saw there was a thin but jolly-minded looking pig, pushing up roots with her nose and tossing them into the air through sheer divilment.

Dark-eyed Susan was she called, and she belonged to Tom Mulligan, the one-legged ballad-maker, who had named her after the famous ballad.

Mulligan was too tindher-hearted to sell her to be kilt, and too poor to keep her in victuals, so she roamed the fields, a shameless marauder and a nimble-footed freebooter.

"Be-gorr, here's luck!" said the little King; "since 'tis in Casey's field, this must be Casey's baste. I couldn't ask betther; whinever a pig is frightened it runs to its own house; so I'll just get on her back and ride down to Casey's cabin."

The King looked inquirin' at Susan, and Susan looked impident suspicion at the King.

"Oh, ho, ye beauty, you know what's in me mind!" says he, whistlin' and coaxin' and sidlin' up to her. A pig likes a compliment if it's well tould, so Susan hung her head, grunted coquettish, and looked away. Taking adwantage of her head being turned, without another word, his Rile Highness ran over, laid hould of her ear, and with one graceful jump took an aisy saddle-sate on her back.

This was the last thing the pig expected, so with one frightened squeal from Susan both of them were off like the wind through the fields toward Mulligan's house, taking stones, ridges, and ditches like hurdle jumpers till they came in sight of a mud-plasthered cabin which stood on the hillside. A second afther the King's hair stood straight up and his heart grew cowld, for there, sitting on the thrashold, with her family in a little crowd about her, was the woman who, misconsthruing him for her own child, had fled with him from Barney Casey's, and, finding her mistake, had trun him into the high-road.

About the ballad-maker's door was gathered his whole family, listening to the wondherful tale being tould by Ann Mulligan. A frightened woman she was.

Indade, whin Ann Mulligan, afther dhropping the King
in the road, raiched home she fell unconscionable in the
door before her husband and her frightened childher, an'
she never come to till little Pether sprinkled a noggin of
wather on her; thin she opened her eyes and began telling
how Ould Nick had stole the baby and had taken little
Patsy's place in her own two arms.

There she sat wringing her hands and waving back and
forth. The fairy-man could aisily guess the story she was
telling, and his flying steed was hurrying straight toward
the house and nothing could stop it. They'd both be there
in tin seconds.

"Well, this time, anyhow, I'll be kilt intirely," says the
King.

Mrs. Mulligan turned to pint down the road to the place
where she had dhropped the King, when, lo and behold,
up the boreen and through the field they saw, coming at a
thraymendous pace, Dark-eyed Susan and the King, riding
her like a dhragoon.

Mrs. Mulligan gave one screech and, lifting her petti-
coats, flew; the childher scurried off afther her like young
rabbits.

Tom, not being able to run bekase of his wooden leg,
stood his ground, but at the same time raymembering more
prayers an' raypentin' of more mane things he'd done than
ever before since he was born.

He was sure it was Ould Nick himself that was in it.

And now a new danger jumped suddenly before the
King. The pig headed for her favourite hole through the
hedge, and whin the King saw the size of the hole he let a
howl out of him, for he knew he'd be trun. He scrooched
close to the baste's back and dhrew up his legs. Sure
enough he was slithered off her back and left sitting on
the hard ground, half the clothes torn from his rile back.

That howl finished Tom entirely, so that whin his Majesty crawled through the hole afther the pig and came
over to him, the ballad-maker wouldn't have given

tuppence for his sowl's salvation. Howsumever, he put on the best and friendliest face he could undher the sarcumstances. Scraping with his wooden leg and pulling at a tuft of carroty hair on his fore-head, Tom said, mighty wheedling:

"The top o' the day to your Honour. Sure, how's Mrs. Balzebub and the childher. I hear it's a fine, bright family your Lordship has. Arrah, it isn't the likes of me, poor Tom Mulligan, the ballad-maker, that your riverence'd be wanting."

Hearing them words, the King looked mighty plazed. "If you're Tom Mulligan, the ballad- maker," he says, coming over smiling, "it's proud and happy I am to meet you! I'm no less than Brian Connors, the King of the Good People," he says, dhrawing himself up and trying to look grand. "It's many's the fine ballad of yours we sing in Sleive-na-mon."

"But little Patsy," stammered Tom; "sure your Majesty wouldn't take him from us; he's our twelfth and rounds out the dozen, you know."

"Have no fear," says the fairy; "Patsy'll be here safe and sound at nightfall. If you stand friend to me this day the divil a friend you'll ever need agin as long as you live!" With that the King up and tould him all the day's happenin's and misfortunes. Tom could hardly belave his eyes or his ears. He was so happy he begun in his mind making a ballad about himself and the King that minute.

"Ow!" says the King, bending his back and houlding his head, "whin I think of the ondacencies I wint true this day!"

"Your Majesty'll go through no more," says Tom. With that he went stumping away to call back the wife and childher.

In a few minutes the ruler of the night-time was sitting on Mulligan's table ating the last petatie and dhrinking the last sup of new milk that was in the house. The King dhrained the cup an' smacked his lips. "Now

sing us a ballad, Tom Mulligan, my lad," says he, leaning
back against the empty milk-crock and crossing his legs
like a tailor. Ann Mulligan nodded approvin' from where
she sat, proud and contented on the bed, the childher
smiled up from the mud floor. So Tom, who was a most
maylodious man, just as his wife was a most harmonious
woman, up and sang the ballad of Hugh Reynolds:

> "Me name is Hugh Reynolds, I came of dacint
>   parents;
> I was born in County Cavin, as you may
>   plainly see.
> Be lovin' of a maid named Catherine McCabe,
> My love has been bethrayed, she's a sore loss
>   to me."

There's most of the time thirty-two varses to that song,
and Tom sang them all without skippin' a word.

"Bate that, King Brian Connors," he says at last. "I
challenge you!"

Then King Brian trew back his head and, shutting his
eyes, sung another ballad of forty-seven varses, which was
Catherine McCabe's answer to Hugh Reynolds, and which
begins this away:

> "Come all ye purty fair maids wherever you
>   may be,
> And if you'll pay attention and listen unto me,
> I'll tell of a desayver that you may beware of
>   the same,
> He comes from the town of Drumscullen in
>   the County Cavan,
> an' Hugh Reynolds is his name."

One song brought out another finer than the first, until
the whole family, childher and all, jined in singing "Willie
Reilly and His Dear Colleen Bawn."

'Twould make your heart young agin to hear them. At the ind of aich varse all the Mulligans'd stop quick to let the King wobble his woice alone. Dark-eyed Susan was standing scratching herself inside the closed door, plazed but wondherin'; so, with sweet songs and ould tales, the hours flew like minutes till at last the ballad-maker pushed back the table and tuned his fiddle, while the whole family—at laste all of them ould enough to stand—smiling, faced one another for a dance.

The King chose Mrs. Ann Mulligan for a partner. The fiddle struck a note, the bare, nimble feet raised. "Rocky Roads to Dublin" was the tune.

"Deedle, deedle, dee; deedle, deedle, diddle um.
Deedle, deedle, dee, rocky roads to Dubalin"

The twinkling feet fell together. Smiles and laughter and jostling and jollity broke like a summer storm through the room. And singing and pattherin' and jiggering, rose and swirled to the mad music, till suddenly "knock, knock, knock!" the blows of a whip-handle fell upon the door and every leg stopped stiff.

"Murther in Irish," whispered little Mickey Mulligan, "'tis Father Scanlan himself that's in it!"

Ochone mavrone! what a change from merry-making and happiness to fright and scandalation was there! The Master of the Fairies, sure that Father Scanlan had the scent of him, tried to climb up on to the settle-bed, but was too wake from fear, so Mrs. Mulligan histed him and piled three childher on top of the King to hide him just as Father Scanlan pushed open the door.

The priest stood outside, houlding his horse with one hand and pintin' his whip with the other.

"What are you hiding on that bed, you vagabone?" he says.

"Whist!" says Tom Mulligan, hobblin' over and going outside, with the fiddle undher his arrum, "'tis little Patsy, the baby, and he ain't dressed dacint enough for your riverence to see," whuspered the villain.

"Tom Mulligan," says the priest, shaking his whip, "you're an idle, shiftless, thriftless man, and a cryin' shame and a disgrace to my flock; if you had two legs I'd bate you within an inch of your life!" he says, lookin' stern at the fiddler.

"Faith, and it's sorry I am now for my other leg," says Tom, "for it's well I know that whin your riverence scolds and berates a man you only give him half a shilling or so, but if you bate him as well, your riverence sometimes empties your pockets to him."

'Twas hard for the priest to keep an ill-natured face, so he smiled; but as he did, without knowing it, he let fly a shot that brought terror to the heart of the ballad-maker.

"God help me with you and the likes of you," says the priest, thrying to look savare; "you keep me from morning till night robbing Pether to pay Paul. Barney Casey, the honest man, gives me a crown for baptising his child, and tin minutes afther I must give that same money to a blaggard!"

Well, whin Mulligan heard that his own little Patsy had been baptised agin at the instigation of that owdacious imposthure, Barney Casey, the ballad-maker's neck swelled with rage. But worse was to come. Gulping a great lump down his throat he axed:

"What name did your riverence give the baby?"

There was a thremble in the poor man's woice.

"Bonyface," says the priest, his toe in the stirrup. "To-day is the feast of St. Bonyface, a gr-r-reat bishop. He was a German man," says Father Scanlan.

The groan Tom Mulligan let out of him was heart-rendering. "Bonyface! Oh, my poor little Patsy; bad scran to you, Barney Casey! My own child turned into a German man—oh, Bonyface!"

The priest was too busy mounting his horse to hear what the ballad-maker said, but just before starting the good man turned in his saddle.

"I came near forgetting my errant," he says. "There's a little ould man—dwarves they call the likes of thim—who has been lost from some thravelling show or carawan, or was stole by ould Peggy Collins this morning from some place—I don't rightly know which. Sind the childher looking for him and use him kind. I'm going up the road spreading the news. Ignorant people might misthrate him," says his riverence, moving off.

"You'll find no ignorant person up this road," called Tom, in a broken woice, "but Felix O'Shaughnessy, and he's not so bad, only he don't belave in ghosts," cried Mulligan.

Even as the ballad-maker turned to go in the door the sun, shooting one red, angry look at the world, dhropped below the western mountains. The King jumped from the bed.

"The charms have come back to me. I feel in my four bones the power, for 'tis sunset. I'm a greater man now than any king on his trone," says he. "Do you sind word to Barney and Judy Casey that if they don't bring little Patsy and my green velvet cloak and the silver-topped noggin and stand ferninst me on this floor within half an hour, I'll have the both of thim presners in Sleive-na-mon before midnight, to walk on all-fours the rest of their lives. As for you, my rayspected people," he says, "a pleasanter afthernoon I seldom spint, and be ready to get your reward."

With thim words he vanished. Their surprise at his disappearance was no sooner over than the Mulligans began hunting vessels in which to put the goold the fairy was going to give them.

Ann Mulligan was dragging in from outside an empty tub when shamefaced Judy Casey passed in, carrying little Patsy Mulligan. Behind her slunk Barney, her husband, houlding the green cloak and the silver-topped noggin.

"I had him for one day, Ann Mulligan," says Judy, handing little Patsy to his mother, "and though it breaks my poor, withered heart to give him up, he's yours by right, and here he is."

Whilst she was speaking those words the ruler of the fairies sprung over the threshold and laid a white bundle on the table. The household crowded up close around.

Without a word the fairy dhrew the cover from the white bundle, an' there, like a sweet, pink rose, lay sleepin' on its white pillow the purtiest baby you ever set your two livin' eyes on.

Judy gave a great gasp, for it was the identical child the fairies stole from her down in the County Mayo.

"You don't desarve much from me," says the King, "but because Ann Mulligan—fine woman—asked it, I'll do you a favour. You may take back the baby or I'll give you a hundhred pounds. Take your choice, Barney Casey."

Barney stood a long time with bowed head, looking at the child and thinking hard. You can surely see what a saryous question he had. One's own child is worth more than a hundred pounds, but other people's childhren are plenty and full of failings. Mulligan's family peered up into his face, and his wife Judy sarched him with hungry eyes. At last he said, very slow:

"My mind has changed," says he. "Though people always tould me that childher were a throuble, a worry and a care, yesterday I'd give the County Clare for that little one. After this day's work I know that sayin's thrue, so I'll take the hundhred pounds," he says.

"Divil a fear of you takin' the hundhred pounds!" snapped his wife, Judy, grabbing up the child. An' thin the two women, turning on him, fell to abusin' and ballyraggin' the Man without Childher, till sorra bit of courage was left in his heart.

"I promised you yer choice, and they'll lave you no choice," says the King, looking vexed. "Well, here's the hundhred pounds, and let Judy keep the child."

Whin the fairy turned to the ballad-maker the hearts of all the Mulligans stopped still.

"Now, my grand fellow, me one-legged jaynious," he says, "you're goin' to be disappinted. You think I'll give you riches, but I won't." At that Tom's jaw dhropped to his chist, and the littlest Mulligans began to cry.

"I'll not make you rich bekase you're a born ballad-maker, and a weaver of fine tales, and a jaynious—if you make a jaynious rich you take all the songs out of him and you spile him. A man's heart-sthrings must be often stretched almost to the breaking to get good music from him. I'll not spile you, Tom Mulligan.

"Besides," he says, "as you are a natural-born ballad-maker, you'd kill yourself the first year thryin' to spind all your money at wanst. But I'll do betther for you than to make you rich. Ann Mulligan, do you clear the table an' put my silver-topped noggin on the edge of it," says he.

When Ann Mulligan did as she was bid the King put the green cloak on his chowlders and, raising his hand, pointed to the silver-covered noggin. Everyone grew still and frightened.

"Noggin, noggin, where's your manners?" he says, very solemn.

At the last word the silver lid flew open, and out of the cup hopped two little men dhressed all in black, dhragging something afther them that began to grow and grow amazing. So quickly did they work, and so swiftly did this thing they brought twirl and change and turn into different articles that the people hadn't time to mark what form it was at first, only they saw grow before their astonished eyes taycups and dishes and great bowls, an' things like that.

In a minute the table was laid with a white cloth like the quality have, and chiny dishes and knives and forks.

"Noggin, noggin, where's your manners?" says the King again. The little men dhragged from the noggin other things that grew into a roast of mutton and biled turnips, and white bread an' butther, and petaties, and pots of tay.

"Noggin, noggin, where's your manners?" says the King, for the last time.

At that the little black men, afther puttin' a silver shillin' beside every plate at the table, jumped into the noggin an' pulled down its lid.

Whin the ating and drinking and jollity were at their hoight the King arose, drew tight his crown on his head, and pointing once more to the silver-covered noggin, said:

"This is my gift to you and your reward, Tom Mulligan, maker of ballads and journeyman worker in fine tales. 'Tis more than your wish was. Nayther you nor anyone who sits at your table, through all your life, will ever want a bite to ate or a sup to dhrink, nor yet a silver shilling to cheer him on his way. Good luck to all here and good-bye!" Even as they looked at the King he was gone, vanished like a light that's blown out—and they never saw him more.

But the news spread. Musicianers, poets, and story-tellers, and jayniouses flocked to the ballad-maker's cabin from all over Ireland. Any fine day in the year one might see them gather in a dozen knots before his door and into as many little crowds about the stable. In each crowd, from morning till night, there was a chune being played, a ballad sung, or a story being tould. Always one could find there blacksmiths, schoolmasters, and tinkers, and all trades, but the greater number be far, av coorse, were beggarmen.

Nor is that same to be wondhered at, bekase every jaynious, if he had his own way and could folly his own heart's desire'd start to-morrow at daybreak with the beggarman's staff and bag.

But wherever they came from, and whatever their station, Tom Mulligan stumped on his wooden leg from crowd to crowd, the jovial, happy master of them all.

THE BANSHEE'S COMB

Chapter I
The Diplomacy of Bridget

I

'Twas the mendin' of clothes that All Sowls' afthernoon in Elizabeth Ann Egan's kitchen that naturally brought up the subject of husbands an' the best ways to manage them. An' if there's one thing more than another that makes me take me hat off to the women, 'tis the owdacious way the most down-throdden of their sex will brag about her blaggard husband.

Not that ayther one or the other of the foive busy-tongued and busy-fingered neighbour women who bint above their sewing or knitting that afthernoon were down-throdden; be no manner of manes; far, far from it. They were so filled with matrimonial contintedness that they fairly thrampled down one another to be first in praising the wondherful men of their choice. Every woman proudly claimed to own an' conthrol the handsomest, loikeliest man that ever throd in brogues.

They talked so fast an' they talked so loud that 'twas a thryin' long while before meek-woiced little Margit Doyle could squeege her husband, Dan'l John, sideways into the argyment. An' even when she did get him to the fore, the other women had appropryated all the hayroic quali-fications for their own men, so that there was nothing left

for Dan'l but the common lavings; an' that dayprivation
nettled Margit an' vexed her sore. But she took her chanst
when it came, poor as it was, an' boulted in.

Jabbing the air as though her needle were a dagger,
she broke into the discoorse.

"I wouldn't thrade my Dan for the King of Rooshia or
the Imperor of Chiney," says she, peering dayfiant around
the room. No one sided with that raymark, an' no one
argyed agin it, an' this vexed her the more.

"The Kingdom of Chiney is where the most supharior
tay comes from," says Caycelia Crow. She was a large,
solemn woman, was Misthress Crow, an a gr-r-reat histhorian.

"No," says Margit, scorning the intherruption, "not if
the two men were rowled into one," says she.

"Why," says Caycelia Crow, an' her deep woice tolled
like a passing bell— "why," says she, "should any dacint
woman be wantin' to marry one of thim haythen Imperors?
Sure they're all ambiguious," she says, looking around
proud of the grand worrud.

Elizabeth Ann sthopped the spinning-wheel the betther
to listen, while the others turned bothered faces to the
histhorian.

"Ambiguious," says Misthress Crow, raisin' her woice
in the middle part of the worrud; "ambiguious," she says
again, "manes that accordin' to the laygal laws of some
furrin parts, a man may marry four or five wives if he has
a mind to."

At this Margit bristled up like a bantam-hin.

"Do you mane to say, Caycelia Crow," says she,
dhroppin' in her lap the weskit she was mendin', "do you
intind to substantiate that I'm wishin' to marry the Imperor
of Chiney, or," she says, her woice growin' high an' cutting
as an east wind, "do you wish to inferentiate that if my
Dan'l had the lave he'd be ambiguious? Will you plaze tell
these friends an' neighbours," she says, wavin' a hand, "which
of the two of us you was minded to insinuate against?"

The attackt was so sudden an' so unexpected that Misthress Crow was too bewildhered to dayfind herself. The poor woman only sat starin' stupid at Margit.

The others sunk back in their chairs spacheless with consternaytion till Mollie Scanlan, wishin' to pacificate the sitiwation, an' winkin' friendly at Caycelia, spoke up sootherin'.

"Thrue for ye, Margit Doyle," says she. "What kind of talk is that for ye to be talkin', Caycelia?" says she. "Sure if Dan'l John were to be med the Imperor of Chiney tomorrow he'd hesitate an' dayliberate a long time before bringin' in one of them ambiguious women to you an' the childher. I'd like to see him thry it. It'ud be a sore an' a sorrowful day for him, I'm thinkin'.'"

At thim worruds, Margit, in her mind's eye, saw Dan'l John standin' ferninst her with an ambiguious haythen woman on aich side of him, an' the picture riled the blood in her heart.

"Oh, ho!" says she, turning on poor, shrinkin' Mollie with a smile, an' that same smile had loaded guns an' pistols in it. "An' will you plaze be so kind an' condesinden', Misthress Scanlan," says she, "to explain what you ever saw or heerd tell of in my Dan'l John's actions, that'ud make you think he'd contimplate such schoundrel endayvours," says she, thrimblin'.

The only answer to the question was from the tay-kettle. It was singin' high an' impident on the hob.

Now, Bridget O'Gill, knowin' woman that she was, had wisely kept out of the discoorse. She sat apart, calmly knittin' one of Darby's winther stockings. As she listened, howsumever, she couldn't keep back a sly smile that lifted one corner of her mouth.

"Isn't it a poor an' a pittiful case," said Misthress Doyle, glaring savage from one to the other, "that a dacint man, the father of noine childher, eight of them livin', an' one gone for a sojer—isn't it a burnin' shame," she says, whumperin', "that such a daycint man must have his char-ack-ther thrajuiced before his own wife— Will you be so good as to tell me what you're laughing at, Bridget O'Gill, ma'am?" she blazed.

Bridget, flutthering guilty, thried to hide the misfortunate smile, but 'twas too late.

"Bekase, if it is my husband you're mocking at," says Margit, "let me tell you, fair an' plain, his ayquils don't live in the County of Tipperary, let alone this parish! 'Tis thrue," she says, tossin' her head, "he hasn't spint six months with the Good People—he knows nothin' of the fairies—but he has more sinse than those that have. At any rate, he isn't afeard of ghosts like a knowledgeable man that I could mintion."

That last thrust touched a sore spot in the heart of Bridget. Although Darby O'Gill would fight a dozen livin' men, if needful, 'twas well known he had an unraysonable fear of ghosts. So, Bridget said never a worrud, but her brown eyes began to sparkle, an' her red lips were dhrawn up to the size of a button.

Margit saw how hard she'd hit, an' she wint on thriumphant.

"My Dan'l John'ud sleep in a churchyard. He's done it," says she, crowin'.

Bridget could hould in no longer. "I'd be sore an' sorry," she says, "if a husband of mine were druv to do such a thing as that for the sake of a little pace and quiet," says she, turnin' her chowlder.

Tare an' 'ounds, but that was the sthroke! "The Lord bless us!" mutthered Mollie Scanlan. Margit's mind wint up in the air an' staid there whirlin', whilst she herself sat gasping an' panting for a rayply. 'Twas a thrilling, suspenseful minute.

The chiney shepherd and shepherdess on the mantel sthopped ogling their eyes an' looked shocked at aich other; at the same time Bob, the linnet, in his wooden cage at the door, quit his singin' an' cocked his head the betther to listen; the surprised tay-kettle gave a gasp an'

a gurgle, an' splutthered over the fire. In the turrible silence Elizabeth Egan got up to wet the tay. Settin' the
taypot in the fender she spoke, an' she spoke raysentful.

"Any sinsible man is afeard of ghosts," says she.

"Oh, indade," says Margit, ketching her breath. "Is that
so? Well, sinsible or onsinsible," says she, "this will be
Halloween, an' there's not a man in the parish who would
walk past the churchyard up to Cormac McCarthy's house,
where the Banshee keened last night, except my Dan'l!"
says she, thriumphant.

The hurt pride in Bridget rose at that an' forced from
her angry lips a foolish promise.

"Huh! we hear ducks talkin'," she says, coolly rowling
up Darby's stocking, an' sticking the needle in the ball of
yarn. "This afthernoon I was at Cormac McCarthy's," she
says, "an' there wasn't a bit of tay in the house for poor
Eileen, so I promised Cormac I'd send him up a handful.
Now, be the same token, I promise you my Darby will make
no bones of going on that errant this night."

"Ho! ho! ho!" laughed Margit. "If he has the courage to
do it bid him sthop in to me on his way back, an' I'll send
to you a fine settin' of eggs from my black Spanish hin."

What sharp worrud Misthress O'Gill would have flung
back in answer no one knows, bekase whin once purvoked
she has few ayquils for sarcastic langwidge, but just then
Elizabeth Ann put in Bridget's hand a steaming cup of
good, sthrong tay. Now, whusky, ale, an' porther are all
good enough in their places, yer honour—I've nothing to
intimidate aginst them—but for a comforting, soothering,
edayfing buverage give me a cup of foine black tay. So
this day the cups were filled only the second time, when
the subject of husbands was complately dhropped, an' the
conwersation wandhered to the misdajmeanours of Anthony Sullivan's goat.

All this time the women had been so busy with their
talkin' an' argyfyin' that the creeping darkness of a coming
storm had stolen unnoticed into the room, making the

fire glow brighter and redder on the hearth. A faint flare
of lightning, follyed be a low grumble of thunder, brought
the women to their feet.

"Marcy on us!" says Caycelia Crow, glad of an excuse
to be gone, "do you hear that? We'll all be dhrownded before we raich home," says she.

In a minute the wisitors, afther dhraining their cups,
were out in the road, aich hurryin' on her separate way,
an' tying her bonnet-sthrings as she wint.

'Twas a heavy an' a guilty heart that Bridget carried
home with her through the gathering storm. Although
Darby was a nuntimate friend of the fairies, yet, as Margit
Doyle said, he had such a black dhread of all other kinds
of ghosts that to get him out on this threatening Halloween night, to walk past the churchyard, as he must do on
his way to Cormac McCarthy's cottage, was a job ayquil
to liftin' the Shannon bridge. How she was to manage it
she couldn't for the life of her tell; but if the errant was
left undone she would be the laughin'-stock of every
woman in the parish.

But worst of all, an' what cut her heart the sorest, was
that she had turned an act of neighbourly kindness into a
wainglorious boast; an' that, she doubted not, was a mortal sin.

She had promised Cormac in the afthernoon that as
soon as she got home she would send Darby over with
some tay for poor little Eileen, an' now a big storm was
gathering, an' before she could have supper ready, thry
as hard as she could, black night might be upon them.

"To bring aise to the dying is the comfortingist privilege a
man or woman can have, an' I've thraded it for a miserable
settin' of eggs," she says. "Amn't I the unfortunit crachure,"
she thought, "to have let me pride rune me this away. What'll
I do at all at all?" she cried. "Bad luck to the thought that
took me out of me way to Elizabeth Egan's house!"

Then she med a wish that she might be able to get
home in time to send Darby on his errant before the night

came on. "If they laugh at me, that'll be my punishment, an' maybe it'll clane my sin," says she.

But the wish was in wain. For just as she crossed the stile to her own field the sun dhropped behind the hills as though he had been shot, an' the east wind swept up, carrying with it a sky full of black clouds an' rain.

II

That same All Sowls' night Darby O'Gill, the friend of the fairies, sat, as he had often sat before, amidst the dancin' shadows, ferninst his own crackling turf and wood fire, listening to the storm beat against his cottage windows. Little Mickey, his six-year-ould, cuddled asleep on his daddy's lap, whilst Bridget sat beside thim, the other childher cruedled around her. My, oh my, how the rain powered and hammered an' swirled!

Out in the highway the big dhrops smashed agin wayfarers' faces like blows from a fist, and once in a while, over the flooded moors and the far row of lonesome hills, the sullen lightning spurted red and angry, like the wicious flare of a wolcano.

You may well say 'twas perfect weather for Halloween—to-night whin the spirits of the dayparted dead visit once again their homes, and sit unseen, listening an' yearnin' about the ould hearthstones.

More than once that avenin' Darby'd shivered and shuddered at the wild shrieks and wails that swept over the chimney-tops; he bein' sartin sure that it wasn't the wind at all, but despairing woices that cried out to him from the could lips of the dead.

At last, afther one particular doleful cry that rose and fell and lingered around the roof, the knowledgeable man raised his head and fetched a deep breath, and said to his wife Bridget:

"Do you hear that cry, avourneen? The dear Lord be marciful to the souls of the dayparted!" sighed he.

Bridget turned a throubled face toward him. "Amen," she says, speakin' softly; "and may He presarve them who are dying this night. Poor Eileen McCarthy—an' she the purty, light-footed colleen only married the few months! Haven't we the raysons to be thankul and grateful. We can never pray enough, Darby," says she.

Now the family had just got off their knees from night prayers, that had lasted half an hour, so thim last worruds worried Darby greatly.

"That woman," he says to himself, mighty sour, "is this minute contimplaytin' an' insinuatin' that we haven't said prayers enough for Eileen, when as it is, me two poor knees have blisters on thim as big as hin's eggs from kneelin'. An' if I don't look out," he says to himself again, "she'll put the childher to bed and then she's down on her knees for another hour, and me wid her; I'd never advise anyone to marry such a pious woman. I'm fairly kilt with rayligion, so I am. I must disthract her mind an' prevent her intintions," he says to himself.

"Maybe, Bridget," he says, out loud, as he was readying his pipe, "it ain't so bad afther all for Eileen. If we keep hoping for the best, we'll chate the worst out of a few good hours at any rate," says the knowledgeable man.

But Bridget only rowled the apron about her folded arms and shook her head sorrowful at the fire. Darby squinted carefully down the stem of his pipe, blew in it, took a sly glance at his wife, and wint on:

"Don't you raymember, Bridget," he says, "whin ould Mrs. Rafferty lay sick of a bad informaytion of the stomick; well, the banshee sat for a full hour keening an' cryin' before their house—just as it did last night outside Cormac McCarthy's. An' you know the banshee cried but once at Rafferty's, but never rayturned the second time. The informaytion left Julia, and all the wide worruld knows, even the King of Spain might know if he'd send to ax, that Julia Rafferty, as strong as a horse, was diggin' petaties in her own field as late as yesterday."

"The banshee comes three nights before anyone dies, doesn't it, daddy?" says little Mickey, waking up, all excited.

"It does that," says Darby, smilin' proud at the child's knowledgeableness; "and it's come but once to Eileen McCarthy."

"An' while the banshee cries, she sits combing her hair with a comb of goold, don't she, daddy?"

Bridget sat onaisy, bitin' her lips. Always an' ever she had sthrove to keep from the childher tidings of fairies and of banshees an' ghosts an' other onnatural people. Twice she trun a warning look at Darby, but he, not noticin', wint on, strokin' the little lad's hair, an' sayin' to him:

"It does, indade, avick; an' as she came but once to Mrs. Rafferty's, so we have rayson to hope she'll come no more to Cormac McCarthy's."

"Hush that nonsinse!" says Bridget, lookin' daggers; "sure Jack Doolan says that 'twas no banshee at all that come to Rafferty's, but only himself who had taken a drop too much at the fair, an' on his way home sat down to rest himself by Rafferty's door. He says that he stharted singin' pious hymns to kape off the evil spirits, and everyone knows that the same Jack Doolan has as turrible a woice for singin' as any banshee that ever twishted a lip," she says.

The woman's conthrayriness vexed Darby so he pounded his knee with his fist as he answered her: "You'll not deny, maybe," he says, "that the Costa Bower sthopped one night at the Hall, and—"

"Whist!" cried Bridget; "lave off," she says; "sure that's no kind of talk to be talkin' this night before the childher," says she.

"But mammy, I _know_ what the Costa Bower is," cried little Mickey, sitting up straight in Darby's lap an' pinting his finger at his mother; "'tis I that knows well. The Costa Bower is a gr-r-reat black coach that comes in the night to carry down to Croagmah the dead people the banshee keened for."

The other childher by now were sitting boult upright, stiff as ramrods, and staring wild-eyed at Mickey.

"The coachman's head is cut off an' he houlds the reins this away," says the child, lettin' his hands fall limp an' open at his side. "Sometimes it's all wisable, an' then agin it's unwisable, but always whin it comes one can hear the turrible rumble of its wheels." Mickey's woice fell and, spreading out his hands, he spoke slow an' solemn. "One Halloween night in the woods down at the black pond, Danny Hogan heard it coming an' he jumped behind a stone. The threes couldn't sthop it, they wint right through it, an' as it passed Danny Hogan says he saw one white, dead face laned back agin the dark cushions, an' this is the night—All Sowls' night—whin it's sure to be out; now don't I know?" he says, thriumphant.

At that Bridget started to her feet. For a minute she stood spacheless with vexation at the wild, frighting notions that had got into the heads of her childher; then "Glory be!" she says, looking hard at Darby. You could have heard a pin dhrop in the room. Ould Malachi, the big yellow cat, who until this time lay coiled asleep on a stool, was the best judge of Bridget's charack-ter in that house. So, no sooner did he hear the worruds an' see Bridget start up, than he was on his own four feet, his back arched, his tail straight up, an' his two goolden eyes searchin' her face. One look was enough for him. The next instant he lept to the ground an' started for the far room. As he scampered through the door, he trew a swift look back at his comerades, the childher, an' that look said plain as any worruds could say:

"Run for it while you've time! Folly me; some one of us vagebones has done something murtherin'!"

Malachi was right; there would have been sayrious throuble for all hands, only that a softening thought was on Bridget that night which sobered her temper. She stopped a bit, the frown on her face clearing as she looked at the childher, an' she only said: "Come out of this! To

bed with yez! I'm raising a pack of owdacious young ro-
mancers, an' I didn't know it. Mickey sthop that whimpering an' make haste with your clothes. The Lord help us,
he's broke off another button. Look at that, now!" she says.

There was no help for thim. So, with longin' looks trun
back at their father, sittin' cosey before the fire, an' with
consolin' winks an' nods from him, the childher followed
their mother to the bedroom.

Thin, whilst Bridget was tucking the covers about them,
an' hushing their complainings, Darby sat with his el-
bows on his knees, doing in his head a sum in figures; an'
that sum was this:

"How much would it be worth this All Sowls' night for
a man to go out that door and walk past the churchyard
up to Cormac McCarthy, the stone-cutter's house?" One
time he made the answer as low as tin pounds two shillings and thruppence, but as he did so a purticular loud
blast went shrieking past outside, an' he raised the answer to one thousand five hundred an' tunty pounds ster-
ling. "And cheap at that," he said aloud.

While he was studyin' thim saygacious questions,
Bridget stole quietly behind and put a light hand on his
chowlder. For a minute, thin, nayther of thim said a
worrud.

Surprised at the silence, an' puzzled that little Mickey
had escaped a larruping, Malachi crept from the far room
an' stood still in the doorway judging his misthress. An'
expression was on her face the cat couldn't quite make
out. 'Twas an elevayted, pitying, good-hearted, daytermined look, such as a man wears when he goes into
the sty to kill one of his own pigs for Christmas.

Malachi, being a wise an' expayieranced baste, daycided
to take no chances, so he backed through the door again
an' hid undher the dhresser to listen.

"I was just thinking, Darby avourneen," says the
woman, half whuspering, "how we might this blessed night
earn great credit for our two sowls."

"Wait!" says the sly man, straightening himself, an' raising a hand. "The very thing you're going to spake was in my own mind. I was just dayliberatin' that I hadn't done justice to-night to poor Eileen. I haven't said me prayers farvint enough. I niver can whin we're praying together, or whin I'm kneeling down. Thin, like every way else, there's something quare about me. The foinest prayers I ever say is whin I'm be myself alone in the fields," says the conniving villyan. "So, do you, Bridget, go in an' kneel down by the childher for a half hour or so, an' I'll sit here doing my best. If you should happen to look out at me ye might aisily think," he says, "that I was only sittin' here comfortably smoking my pipe, but at the same time prayers'll be whirlin' inside of me like a wind-mill," says he.

"Oh, thin, ain't I glad an' happy to hear you say thim worruds," says his wife, puttin' one foine arrum about his neck; "you've taken a load off my heart that's been weighing heavy on it all night, for I thought maybe you'd be afeard."

"Afeard of what?" axed Darby, liftin' his eyebrows. Malachi throtted bouldly in an' jumped up on the stool.

"You know Father Cassidy says," whuspered Bridget, "that a loving deed of the hands done for the disthressed is itself a prayer worth a week of common prayers."

"I have nothin' agin that sayin'," says Darby, his head cocked, an' he growin' suspicious.

Bridget wiped her forehead with her apron. "Well, this afthernoon I was at McCarthy's house," she wint on, soothering his hair with one hand, "an', oh, but the poor child was disthressed! Her cheeks were flaming with the faver. An', Darby, the thirst, the awful thirst! I looked about for a pinch of tay—there's nothing so coolin' for one in the faver as a cup of wake tay—an' the sorra scrap of it was in the house, so I tould Cormac that to-night, as soon as the childher were in bed, I'd send you over with a pinch."

Every one of Darby's four bones stiffened an' a mortial chill sthruck into his heart.

"Listen, darlint," she says, "the storm's dying down, so while you're putting on your greatcoat I'll wrap up the bit of tay." He shook her hand from his chowldhers.

"Woman," he says, with bitther politeness, "I think you said that *we* had a great chanst to get credit for our *two* sowls. That's what I think you raymarked and stibulated," says he.

"Arrah, shouldn't a woman have great praise an' credit who'll send her husband out on such a night as this," his wife says. "The worse the conditions, the more credit she'll get. If a ghost were to jump at ye as you go past the church-yard, oughtn't I be the happy woman entirely?" says Bridget.

There was a kind of a tinkle in her woice, such as comes when Bridget is telling jokes, so Darby, with a sudden hope in his mind, turned quick to look at her. But there she stood grim, unfeeling, an' daytermined as a pinted gun.

"Oh, ho! is that the way it is?" he says. "Well, here's luck an' good fortune to the ghost or skellington that lays his hand on me this blessed night!" He stuck his two hands deep in his pockets and whirled one leg across the other—the most aggrawating thing a man can do. But Bridget was not the laste discouraged; she only made up her mind to come at him on his soft side, so she spoke up an' said:

"Suppose I was dying of the faver, Darby O'Gill, an' Cormac rayfused to bring over a pinch of tay to *me*. What, then, would ye think of the stone-cutter?"

Malachi, the cat, stopped licking his paws, an' trun a sharp, inquiring eye at his master.

"Bridget," says the knowledgeable man, giving his hand an argifying wave. "We have two separate ways of being good. Your way is to scurry round an' do good acts. My way is to keep from doing bad ones. An' who knows," he says, with a pious sigh, "which way is the betther one. It isn't for us to judge," says he, shakin' his head solemn at the fire.

Bridget walked out in front of him an' fowlded her arms tight.

"So you won't go," she says, sharp an' suddin'.

"The divil a foot!" says he, beginnin' to whustle.

You'd think, now, Bridget was bate, but she still hildt her trump card, an' until that was played an' lost the lad wasn't safe. "All right, me brave hayro," says she; "do you sit there be the fire; I'll go meself," she says. With that she bounced into the childher's room an' began to get ready her cloak an' hood.

For a minute Darby sat pokin' the fire, muttherin' to himself an' feeling very discommodious. Thin, just to show he wasn't the laste bit onaisy, the lad cleared his throat, and waggin' his head at the fire, began to sing:

> "Yarra! as I walked out one mor-r-nin' all in
>   the month of June
> The primrosies and daisies an' cowslips were
>   in bloom,
> I spied a purty fair maid a-sthrollin' on the lea,
> An' Rory Bory Alice, nor any other ould an-
>   cient haythan goddess was not half so fair
>   as she.
> Says I, 'Me purty fair maid, I'll take you for
>   me bride.
> An' if you'll pay no at-*tin*-tion—'"

Glancing up sudden, he saw Malachi's eye on him, and if ever the faytures of a cat spoke silent but plain langwidge Malachi's face talked that minute to its master, and this is what it said:

"Well, of all the cowardly, creaking bostheens I ever see in all me born days you are the worst, Darby O'Gill. You've not only guve impidence to your wife—an' she's worth four of you—but you've gone back on the friends you purtended to—"

Malachi's faytures got no further in their insultin' raymarks, for at that Darby swooped up a big sod of turf an' let it fly at the owdacious baste.

Now it is well known that be a spontaneous trow like that no one ever yet hit a sinsible cat, but always an' ever in that unlucky endayvour he strikes a damaginger blow where it's not intinded. So it was this time.

Bridget, wearing her red cloak an' hood, was just coming through the door, an' that misfortunate sod of turf caught her fair an' square, right below the chist, an' she staggered back agin the wall.

Darby's consthernaytion an' complycation an' turpitaytion were beyant imaginaytion.

Bridget laned there gasping. If she felt as bad as she looked, four Dublint surgunts with their saws an' knives couldn't have done her a ha-'porth of good. Howsumever, for all that, the sly woman had seen Malachi dodge an' go gallopin' away, but she purtendid to think 'twas at herself the turf was trun. Not that she scolded, or anything so common as that, but she went on like an early Christian marthyer who was just goin' to be inthrojuiced to the roaring loins.

Well, as you may aisy see, the poor man, her husband, hadn't a chanst in the worruld afther that. Of course, to rightify himself, he'd face all the ghosts in Croaghmah. So, in a minute, he was standing in his greatcoat with his hand on the latch. There was a packet of tay in his pocket, an' he was a subdued an' conquered man.

He looked so woful that Bridget raypented an' almost raylinted.

"Raymember," he says, mournful, "if I'm caught this night be the Costa Bower, or be the banshee, take good care of the childher, an' raymember what I say—I didn't mane, Bridget, to hit ye with that sod of turf."

"Oh, ain't ye the foolish darlin' to be afeared," smiled Bridget back at him, but she was sayrious, too. "Don't you know that when one goes on an errant of marcy a score of God's white angels with swoords in their hands march before an' beside an' afther him, keeping his path free from danger?" With that she pulled his face down to hers, an' kissed him as she used in the ould courtin' days.

There's nothing puts so much high courage an' clear, steadfast purpose in a man's heart, if it be properly given, as a kiss from the woman he loves. So, with the warmth of that kiss to cheer him, Darby set his face agin the storm.

Chapter II
The Banshee's Halloween

I

Halloween night, to all unhappy ghosts, is about the same as St. Patrick's Day is to you or to me—'tis a great holiday in every churchyard. An' no one knew this bether or felt it keener than did Darby O'Gill, that same Hallow-een night, as he stood on his own doorstep with the paper of black tay for Eileen McCarthy safely stowed away in the crown of his top-hat.

No one in that barony was quicker than he at an act of neighbourly kindness, but now, as he huddled himself together in the shelter of his own eaves, and thought of the dangers before, an' of the cheerful fire an' comfort-able bed he was leaving behint, black raybellion rushed shouting across his heart.

"Oh, my, oh, my, what a perishin' night to turn a man out into!" he says. "It'd be half a comfort to know I was goin' to be kilt before I got back, just as a warnin' to Bridget," says he.

The misthrayted lad turned a sour eye on the chumultuous weather, an' groaned deep as he pulled closer about his chowldhers the cape of his greatcoat an' plunged into the daysarted an' flooded roadway.

Howsumever, 'twas not the pelting rain, nor the lash-ing wind, nor yet the pitchy darkness that bothered the heart out of him as he wint splashin' an' stumbling along the road. A thought of something more raylentless than the storm, more mystarious than the night's blackness put pounds of lead into the lad's unwilling brogues; for somewhere in the shrouding darkness that covered McCarthy's house the banshee was waiting this minute, purhaps, ready to jump out at him as soon as he came near her.

And, oh, if the banshee nabbed him there, what in the worruld would the poor lad do to save himself?

At the raylisation of this sitiwation, the goose-flesh crept up his back an' settled on his neck an' chowldhers. He began to cast about in his mind for a bit of cheer or a scrap of comfort, as a man in such sarcumstances will do. So, grumblin' an' sore-hearted, he turned over Bridget's parting words. "If one goes on an errant of marcy," Bridget had said, "a score of God's white angels with swoords in their hands march before an' beside an' afther him, keeping his path free from danger."

He felt anxious in his hat for the bit of charitable tay he was bringin', and was glad to find it there safe an' dhry enough, though the rest of him was drenched through an' through.

"Isn't this an act of charity I'm doin', to be bringin' a cooling drink to a dyin' woman?" he axed himself aloud. "To be sure it is. Well, then, what rayson have I to be af eared?" says he, pokin' his two hands into his pockets. Arrah, it's aisy enough to bolsther up one's heart with wise sayin' an' hayroic praycepts when sitting comodious by one's own fire; but talkin' wise words to one's self is mighty poor comfort when you're on the lonely high-road of a Halloween night, with a churchyard waitin' for ye on the top of the hill not two hundred yards away. If there was only one star to break through the thick sky an' shine for him, if there was but one friendly cow to low or a distant cock to break the teeming silence, 'twould put some heart into the man. But not a sound was there—only the swish and wailing of the wind through the inwisible hedges.

"What's the matther with the whole worruld? Where is it wanished to?" says Darby. "If a ghost were to jump at

me from the churchyard wall, where would I look for help?
To run is no use," he says, "an' to face it is—"

Just then the current of his misdoubtings ran whack
up against a sayin' of ould Peggy O'Callaghan. Mrs.
O'Callaghan's repitation for truth and voracity, whin it
come to fairy tales or ghost stories, be it known, was ayquil
if not shuparior to the best in Tipperary. Now, Peggy had
towld Ned Mullin, an' Ned Mullin had towld Bill Donahue,
the tinker, an' the tinker had adwised Darby that no one
need ever be afeared of ghosts if he only had the courage
to face them.

Peggy said, "The poor crachures ain't roamin' about
shakin' chains an' moanin' an' groanin', just for the sport
of scarin' people, nor yet out of maneness. 'Tis always a
throuble that's on their minds—a message they want sint,
a saycret they're endayvouring to unload. So instead of
flyin' from the onhappy things, as most people generally
do," she said, "one should walk up bowld to the apparray-
tion, be it gentle or common, male or faymale, an' say,
'What throubles ye, sir?' or 'What's amiss with ye, ma'am?'
An' take my worrud for it," says she, "ye'll find yourself a
boneyfactor to them when you laste expect it," she says.

'Twas a quare idee, but not so onraysonable afther all
whin one comes to think of it; an' the knowledgeable man
fell to dayliberatin' whether he'd have the hardness to folly
it out if the chanst came. Sometimes he thought he would,
then agin he was sure he wouldn't. For Darby O'Gill was
one who bint quick undher trouble like a young three before a hurrycane, but he only bint—the throuble never
broke him. So, at times his courage wint down to a spark
like the light of a candle in a gust of wind, but before you
could turn on your heel 'twas blazing up sthrong and
fiercer than before.

Whilst thus contimplatin' an' meditaytin', his foot
sthruck the bridge in the hollow just below the berrin'-
ground, an' there as the boy paused a minute, churning
up bravery enough to carry him up the hill an' past the

mystarious gravestones, there came a short quiver of lightning, an' in its sudden flare he was sure he saw not tin
yards away, an' comin' down the hill toward him, a dim
shape that took the breath out of his body.

"Oh, be the powers!" he gasped, his courage emptying
out like wather from a spilt pail.

It moved, a slow, grey, formless thing without a head,
an' so far as he was able to judge it might be about the
size of an ulephant. The parsecuted lad swung himself
sideways in the road, one arrum over his eyes an' the other
stretched out at full length, as if to ward off the turrible
wisitor.

The first thing that began to take any shape in his
bewildhered brain was Peggy O'Callaghan's adwice. He
thried to folly it out, but a chatterin' of teeth was the only
sound he made. An' all this time a thraymendous splashin',
like the floppin' of whales, was coming nearer an' nearer.

The splashin' stopped not three feet away, an' the ha'nted
man felt in the spine of his back an' in the calves of his
legs that a powerful, unholwy monsther towered over him.

Why he didn't swoonge in his tracks is the wondher.
He says he would have dhropped at last if it weren't for
the distant bark of his own good dog, Sayser, that put a
throb of courage intil his bones. At that friendly sound he
opened his two dhry lips an' stutthered this sayin':

"Whoever you are, an' whatever shape ye come in, take
heed that I'm not afeared," he says. "I command ye to tell
me your throubles an' I'll be your boneyfactor. Then go
back dacint an' rayspectable where you're buried. Spake
an' I'll listen," says he.

He waited for a reply, an' getting none, a hot splinther
of shame at bein' so badly frightened turned his sowl into
wexation. "Spake up," he says, "but come no furder, for if
you do, be the hokey I'll take one thry at ye, ghost or no
ghost!" he says. Once more he waited, an' as he was lowering the arrum from his eyes for a peek, the ghost spoke
up, an' its answer came in two pitiful, disthressed roars.

A damp breath puffed acrost his face, an' openin' his eyes, what should the lad see but the two dhroopin' ears of Solomon, Mrs. Kilcannon's grey donkey. Foive different kinds of disgust biled up into Darby's throat an' almost sthrangled him. "Ye murdherin', big-headed imposture!" he gasped.

Half a minute afther a brown hoot-owl, which was shelthered in a nearby black-thorn three, called out to his brother's fambly which inhabited the belfry of the chapel above on the hill that some black-minded spalpeen had hoult of Solomon Kilcannon be the two ears an' was kickin' the ribs out of him, an' that the langwidge the man was usin' to the poor baste was worse than scan'lous.

Although Darby couldn't undherstand what the owl was sayin', he was startled be the blood-curdlin' hoot, an' that same hoot saved Solomon from any further exthrayornery throuncin', bekase as the angry man sthopped to hear-ken there flashed on him the rayilisation that he was bating an' crool maulthraytin' a blessing in dishguise. For this same Solomon had the repitation of being the knowingest, sensiblist thing which walked on four legs in that parish. He was a fayvourite with young an' old, especially with childher, an' Mrs. Kilcannon said she could talk to him as if he were a human, an' she was sure he understhood. In the face of thim facts the knowledgeable man changed his chune, an' puttin' his arrum friendly around the dis-thressed animal's neck, he said:

"Aren't ye ashamed of yerself, Solomon, to be payradin' an' mayandherin' around the churchyard Halloween night, dishguisin' yerself this away as an outlandish ghost, an' you havin' the foine repitation for daciency an' good man-ners?" he says, excusin' himself. "I'm ashamed of you, so I am, Solomon," says he, hauling the baste about in the road, an' turning him till his head faced once more the hillside. "Come back with me now to Cormac McCarthy's, avourneen. We've aich been in worse company, I'm thinkin'; at laste you have, Solomon," says he.

At that, kind an' friendly enough, the forgivin' baste turned with him, an' the two keeping aich other slitherin' company, went stumblin' an' scramblin' up the hill toward the chapel. On the way Darby kept up a one-sided conwersation about all manner of things, just so that the ring of a human woice, even if 'twas only his own, would take a bit of the crool lonesomeness out of the dark hedges.

"Did you notice McDonald's sthrame as you came along the night, Solomon? It must be a roarin' torrent be this, with the pourin' rains, an' we'll have to cross it," says he. "We could go over McDonald's stone bridge that stands ferninst McCarthy's house, with only Nolan's meadow betwixt the two, but," says Darby, laying a hand, confaydential on the ass's wet back, "'tis only a fortnit since long Faylix, the blind beggarman, fell from the same bridge and broke his neck, an' what more natural," he axed, "than that the ghost of Faylix would be celebraytin' its first Halloween, *as* a ghost, at the spot where he was kilt?"

You may believe me or believe me not, but at thim worruds Solomon sthopped dead still in his thracks an' rayfused to go another step till Darby coaxed him on be sayin':

"Oh, thin, we won't cross it if you're afeared, little man," says he, "but we'll take the path through the fields on this side of it, and we'll cross the sthrame by McCarthy's own wooden foot-bridge. 'Tis within tunty feet of the house. Oh, ye needn't be afeared," he says agin; "I've seen the cows cross it, so it'll surely hould the both of us."

A sudden raymembrance whipped into his mind of how tall the stile was, ladin' into Nolan's meadow, an' the boy was puzzling deep in his mind to know how was Solomon to climb acrost that stile, whin all at once the gloomy western gate of the graveyard rose quick be their side.

The two shied to the opposite hedge, an' no wondher they did.

Fufty ghosts, all in their shrouds, sat cheek be jowl along the churchyard wall, never caring a ha'-porth for the wind or the rain.

There was little Ted Rogers, the humpback, who was dhrownded in Mullin's well four years come Michaelmas; there was black Mulligan, the gamekeeper, who shot Ryan, the poacher, sittin' with a gun on his lap, an' he glowerin'; beside the gamekeeper sat the poacher, with a jagged black hole in his forehead; there was Thady Finnegan, the scholar, who was disappointed in love an' died of a daycline; furder on sat Mrs. Houlihan, who dayparted this life from ating of pizen musherooms; next to *her* sat—oh, a hundhred others!

Not that Darby *saw* thim, do ye mind. He had too good sinse to look that way at all. He walked with his head turned out to the open fields, an' his eyes squeeged shut. But something in his mind toult him they were there, an' he felt in the marrow of his bones that if he gave them the encouragement of one glance two or three'd slip off the wall an' come moanin' over to tell him their throubles.

What Solomon saw an' what Solomon heard, as the two wint shrinkin' along'll never be known to living man, but once he gave a jump, an' twice Darby felt him thrimblin', an' whin they raiched at last the chapel wall the baste broke into a swift throt. Purty soon he galloped, an' Darby wint gallopin' with him, till two yellow blurs of light across in a field to the left marked the windys of the stone-cutter's cottage.

'Twas a few steps only, thin, to the stile over into Nolan's meadow, an' there the two stopped, lookin' helpless at aich other. Solomon had to be lifted, and there was the throuble. Three times Darby thried be main strength to hist his compagnen up the steps, but in vain, an' Solomon was clane dishgusted.

Only for the tendher corn on our hayro's left little toe, I think maybe that at length an' at last the pair would have got safe over. The kind-hearted lad had the donkey's two little hoofs planted on the top step, an' whilst he himself was liftin' the rest of the baste in his arrums, Solomon got onaisy that he was goin' to be trun, an' so began to

twisht an' squirm; of course, as he did, Darby slipped an'
wint thump on his back agin the stile, with Solomon sittin'
comfortable on top of the lad's chist. But that wasn't the
worst of it, for as the baste scrambled up he planted one
hard little hoof on Darby's left foot, an' the knowledgeable man let a yowl out of him that must have frightened
all the ghosts within miles.

Seein' he'd done wrong, Solomon boulted for the middle
of the road an' stood there wiry an' attentive, listening to
the names flung at him from where his late comerade sat
on the lowest step of the stile nursin' the hurted foot.

'Twas an excited owl in the belfry that this time spoke
up an' shouted to his brother down in the black-thorn:

"Come up, come up quick!" it says. "Darby O'Gill is just
afther calling Solomon Kilcannon a malayfactor."

Darby rose at last, an' as he climbed over the stile he
turned to shake his fist toward the middle of the road.

"Bad luck to ye for a thick-headed, on-grateful informer!" he says; "you go your way an' I'll go mine—we're
sundhers," says he.

So sayin', the crippled man wint limpin' an' grumplin'
down the boreen, through the meadow, whilst his desarted
friend sint rayproachful brays afther him that would go
to your heart.

The throbbin' of our hayro's toe banished all pity for
the baste, an' even all thoughts of the banshee, till a long,
gurgling, swooping sound in front toult him that his fears
about the rise in McDonald's sthrame were undher rather
than over the actwil conditions.

Fearin' that the wooden foot-bridge might be swept
away, as it had been the year purvious, he hurried on.

Most times this sthrame was only a quiet little brook
that ran betwixt purty green banks, with hardly enough
wather in it to turn the broken wheel in Chartres' runed
mill; but to-night it swept along an angry, snarlin', growlin'
river that overlept its banks an' dhragged wildly at the
swaying willows.

Be a narrow throw of light from McCarthy's side windy our thraveller could see the maddened wather sthrivin' an' tearing to pull with it the props of the little foot-bridge; an' the boards shook an' the centre swayed undher his feet as he passed over. "Bedad, I'll not cross this way goin' home, at any rate," he says, looking back at it.

The worruds were no sooner out of his mouth than there was a crack, an' the middle of the foot-bridge lifted in the air, twishted round for a second, an then hurled itself into the sthrame, laving the two inds still standing in their place on the banks.

"Tunder an' turf!" he cried, "I mustn't forget to tell the people within of this, for if ever there was a thrap set by evil spirits to drownd a poor, unwary mortial, there it stands. Oh, ain't the ghosts turrible wicious on Halloween!"

He stood dhrippin' a minute on the threshold, listening; thin, without knockin', lifted the latch an' stepped softly into the house.

II

Two candles burned above the blue and white chiney dishes on the table, a bright fire blazed on the hearth, an' over in the corner where the low bed was set the stone-cutter was on his knees beside it.

Eileen lay on her side, her shining hair sthrealed out on the pillow. Her purty, flushed face was turned to Cormac, who knelt with his forehead hid on the bedcovers. The colleen's two little hands were clasped about the great fist of her husband, an' she was talking low, but so airnest that her whole life was in every worrud.

"God save all here!" said Darby, takin' off his hat, but there was no answer. So deep were Cormac an' Eileen in some conwersation they were having together that they didn't hear his coming. The knowledgeable man didn't know what to do. He raylised that a husband and wife about to part for ever were lookin' into aich other's hearts, for maybe the last time. So he just sthood shifting from one foot to the other, watching thim, unable to daypart, an' not wishin' to obtrude.

"Oh, it isn't death at all that I fear," Eileen was saying. "No, no, Cormac asthore, 'tis not that I'm misdoubtful of; but, ochone mavrone, 'tis you I fear!"

The kneelin' man gave one swift upward glance, and dhrew his face nearer to the sick wife. She wint on, thin, spakin' tindher an' half smiling an' sthrokin' his hand:

"I know, darlint, I know well, so you needn't tell me, that if I were to live with you a thousand years you'd never sthray in mind or thought to any other woman, but it's when I'm gone—when the lonesome avenings folly aich other through days an' months, an' maybe years, an' you sitting here at this fireside without one to speak to, an' you so handsome an' gran', an' with the penny or two we've put away—"

"Oh, asthore machree, why can't ye banish thim black thoughts!" says the stone-cutter. "Maybe," he says, "the banshee will not come again. Ain't all the counthry-side prayin' for ye this night, an' didn't Father Cassidy himself bid you to hope? The saints in Heaven couldn't be so crool!" says he.

But the colleen wint on as though she hadn't heard him, or as if he hadn't intherrupted her:

"An' listen," says she; "they'll come urging ye, the neighbours, an' raysonin' with you. You're own flesh an' blood'll come, an', no doubt, me own with them, an' they all sthriving to push me out of your heart, an' to put another woman there in my place. I'll know it all, but I won't be able to call to you, Cormac machree, for I'll be lying silent undher the grass, or undher the snow up behind the church."

While she was sayin' thim last worruds, although Darby's heart was meltin' for Eileen, his mind began running over the colleens of that townland to pick out the one

who'd be most likely to marry Cormac in the ind. You know
how far-seeing an' quick-minded was the knowledgeable
man. He settled sudden on the Hanlon girl, an' daycided
at once that she'd have Cormac before the year was out.
The ondaycency of such a thing made him furious at her.

He says to himself, half crying, "Why, then, bad cess
to you for a shameless, red-haired, forward baggage,
Bridget Hanlon, to be runnin' afther the man, an' throwing yourself in his way, an' Eileen not yet cowld in her
grave!" he says.

While he was saying them things to himself, McCarthy
had been whuspering fierce to his wife, but what it was
the stone-cutter said the friend of the fairies couldn't hear.
Eileen herself spoke clean enough in answer, for the faver
gave her onnatural strength.

"Don't think," she says, "that it's the first time this
thought has come to me. Two months ago, whin I was
sthrong an' well an' sittin' happy as a meadow-lark at your
side, the same black shadow dhrifted over me heart. The
worst of it an' the hardest to bear of all is that they'll be
in the right, for what good can I do for you when I'm undher
the clay," says she.

"It's different with a woman. If you were taken an' I
left I'd wear your face in my heart through all me life, an'
ax for no sweeter company."

"Eileen," says Cormac, liftin' his hand, an' his woice
was hoarse as the roar of the say, "I swear to you on me
bendid knees—"

With her hand on his lips, she sthopped him. "There'll
come on ye by daygrees a great cravin' for sympathy, a
hunger an' a longing for affection, an' you'll have only the
shadow of my poor, wanished face to comfort you, an' a
recollection of a woice that is gone for ever. A new, warm
face'll keep pushin' itself betwixt us—"

"Bad luck to that red-headed hussy!" mutthered Darby,
looking around disthressed. "I'll warn father Cassidy of
her an' of her intintions the day afther the funeral."

There was silence for a minute; Cormac, the poor lad, was sobbing like a child. By-and-by Eileen wint on again, but her woice was failing an' Darby could see that her cheeks were wet.

"The day'll come when you'll give over," she says. "Ah, I see how it'll all ind. Afther that you'll visit the church-yard be stealth, so as not to make the other woman sore-hearted."

"My, oh, my, isn't she the far-seein' woman?" thought Darby.

"Little childher'll come," she says, "an' their soft, warm arrums will hould you away. By-and-by you'll not go where I'm laid at all, an' all thoughts of these few happy months we've spent together—Oh! Mother in Heaven, how happy they were—"

The girl started to her elbow, for, sharp an' sudden, a wild, wailing cry just outside the windy startled the shud-dering darkness. 'Twas a long cry of terror and of grief, not shrill, but piercing as a knife-thrust. Every hair on Darby's head stood up an' pricked him like a needle. 'Twas the banshee!

"Whist, listen!" says Eileen. "Oh, Cormac asthore, it's come for me again!" With that, stiff with terror, she buried herself undher the pillows.

A second cry follyed the first, only this time it was longer, and rose an' swelled into a kind of a song that broke at last into the heart-breakingest moan that ever fell on mortial ears. "Ochone!" it sobbed.

The knowledgeable man, his blood turned to ice, his legs thremblin' like a hare's, stood looking in spite of him-self at the black windy-panes, expecting some frightful wision.

Afther that second cry the woice balanced itself up an' down into the awful death keen. One word made the whole song, and that was the turruble worrud, "Forever!"

"Forever an' forever, oh, forever!" swung the wild keen, until all the deep meaning of the worrud burned itself into

Darby's sowl, thin the heart-breakin' sob, "Ochone!" inded
always the varse.

Darby was just wondherin' whether he himself wouldn't
go mad with fright, whin he gave a sudden jump at a hard,
sthrained woice which spoke up at his very elbow.

"Darby O'Gill," it said, and it was the stone-cutter who
spoke, "do you hear the death keen? It came last night;
it'll come to-morrow night at this same hour, and thin—
oh, my God!"

Darby tried to answer, but he could only stare at the
white, set face an' the sunken eyes of the man before him.

There was, too, a kind of fierce quiet in the way
McCarthy spoke that made Darby shiver.

The stone-cutter wint on talkin' the same as though
he was goin' to dhrive a bargain. "They say you're a knowledgeable man, Darby O'Gill," he says, "an' that on a time
you spint six months with the fairies. Now I make you
this fair, square offer," he says, laying a forefinger in the
palm of the other hand. "I have fifty-three pounds that
Father Cassidy's keeping for me. Fifty-three pounds," he
says agin. "An' I have this good bit of a farm that me father
was born on, an' his father was born on, too, and the grand-
father of him. An' I have the grass of seven cows. You know
that. Well, I'll give it all to you, all, every stiver of it, if you'll
only go outside an' dhrive away that cursed singer." He trew
his head to one side an' looked anxious up at Darby.

The knowledgeable man racked his brains for something to speak, but all he could say was, "I've brought you
a bit of tay from the wife, Cormac." McCarthy took the tay
with unfeeling hands, an' wint on talking in the same dull
way. Only this time there came a hard lump in his throat
now and then that he stopped to swally.

"The three cows I have go, of course, with the farm,"
says he. "So does the pony an' the five pigs. I have a good
plough an' a foine harrow; but you must lave my stone-
cutting tools, so little Eileen an' I can earn our way wherever
we go, an' it's little the crachure ates the best of times."

The man's eyes were dhry an' blazin'; no doubt his mind was cracked with grief. There was a lump in Darby's throat, too, but for all that he spoke up scolding-like.

"Arrah, talk rayson, man," he says, putting two hands on Cormac's chowlders; "if I had the wit or the art to banish the banshee, wouldn't I be happy to do it an' not a fardin' to pay?"

"Well, then," says Cormac, scowling, an' pushin' Darby to one side, "I'll face her myself—I'll face her an' choke that song in her throat if Sattin himself stood at her side."

With those words, an' before Darby could sthop him, the stone-cutter flung open the door an' plunged out into the night. As he did so the song outside sthopped. Suddenly a quick splashing of feet, hoarse cries, and shouts gave tidings of a chase. The half-crazed gossoon had stharted the banshee—of that there could be no manner of doubt. A raymembrance of the awful things that she might do to his friend paythrefied the heart of Darby.

Even afther these cries died away he stood listening a full minute, the sowls of his two brogues glued to the floor. The only sounds he heard now were the deep ticking of a clock and a cricket that chirped slow an' solemn on the hearth, an' from somewhere outside came the sorrowful cry of a whipperwill. All at once a thought of the broken bridge an' of the black, treacherous waters caught him like the blow of a whip, an' for a second drove from his mind even the fear of the banshee.

In that one second, an' before he rayalised it, the lad was out undher the dhripping trees, and running for his life toward the broken foot-bridge. The night was whirling an' beating above him like the flapping of thraymendous wings, but as he ran Darby thought he heard above the rush of the water and through, the swish of the wind Cormac's woice calling him.

The friend of the fairies stopped at the edge of the foot-bridge to listen. Although the storm had almost passed, a spiteful flare of lightning lept up now an' agin out of the

western hills, an' afther it came the dull rumble of distant thunder; the water splashed spiteful against the bank,
and Darby saw that seven good feet of the bridge had been
torn out of its centre, laving uncovered that much of the
black, deep flood.

He stood sthraining his eyes an' ears in wondheration,
for now the woice of Cormac sounded from the other side
of the sthrame, and seemed to be floating toward him
through the field over the path Darby himself had just
thravelled. At first he was mightily bewildhered at what
might bring Cormac on the other side of the brook, till all
at once the murdhering scheme of the banshee burst in
his mind like a gun-powdher explosion.

Her plan was as plain as day—she meant to dhrown
the stone-cutter. She had led the poor, daysthracted man
straight from his own door down to and over the new stone
bridge, an' was now dayludherin' him on the other side of
the sthrame, back agin up the path that led to the broken
foot-bridge. In the glare of a sudden blinding flash from
the middle of the sky Darby saw a sight he'll never forget
till the day he dies. Cormac, the stone-cutter, was running toward the death-trap, his bare head trun back, an'
his two arrums stretched out in front of him. A little above
an' just out of raich of them, plain an' clear as Darby ever
saw his wife Bridget, was the misty white figure of a
woman. Her long, waving hair sthrealed back from her
face, an' her face was the face of the dead.

At the sight of her Darby thried to call out a warning,
but the words fell back into his throat. Thin again came
the stifling darkness. He thried to run away, but his knees
failed him, so he turned around to face the danger.

As he did so he could hear the splash of the man's feet
in the soft mud. In less than a minute Cormac would be
sthruggling in the wather. At the thought Darby, bracing
himself body and sowl, let a warning howl out of him.

"Hould where you are!" he shouted; "she wants to
drownd ye—the bridge is broke in the middle!" but he could

tell, from the rushing footsteps an' from the hoarse swelling curses which came nearer an' nearer every second, that the dayludhered man, crazed with grief, was deaf an' blind to everything but the figure that floated before his eyes.

At that hopeless instant Bridget's parting words popped into Darby's head.

"When one goes on an errant of marcy a score of God's white angels, with swoords in their hands, march before an' beside an' afther him, keeping his path free from danger."

How it all come to pass he could never rightly tell, for he was like a man in a dhrame,but he recollects well standing on the broken ind of the bridge, Bridget's words ringing in his ears, the glistening black gulf benathe his feet, an' he swinging his arrums for a jump. Just one thought of herself and the childher, as he gathered himself for a spring, an' then he cleared the gap like a bird.

As his two feet touched the other side of the gap a turrific screech—not a screech, ayther, but an angry, frightened shriek—almost split his ears. He felt a rush of cowld, dead air agin his face, and caught a whiff of newly turned clay in his nosthrils; something white stopped quick before him, an' then, with a second shriek, it shot high in the darkness an' disappeared. Darby had frightened the wits out of the banshee.

The instant afther the two men were clinched an' rowling over an' over aich other down the muddy bank, their legs splashing as far as the knees in the dangerous wather, an' McCarthy raining wake blows on the knowledgeable man's head an' breast.

Darby felt himself goin' into the river. Bits of the bank caved undher him, splashing into the current, an' the lad's heart began clunking up an' down like a churn-dash.

"Lave off, lave off!" he cried, as soon as he could ketch his breath. "Do you take me for the banshee?" says he, giving a dusperate lurch an' rowling himself on top of the other.

"Who are you, then? If you're not a ghost you're the divil, at any rate," gasped the stone-cutter.

"Bad luck to ye!" cried Darby, clasping both arrums of the haunted man. "I'm no ghost, let lone the divil—I'm only your friend, Darby O'Gill."

Lying there, breathing hard, they stared into the faces of aich other a little space till the poor stonecutter began to cry. "Oh, is that you, Darby O'Gill? Where is the banshee? Oh, haven't I the bad fortune," he says, sthriving to raise himself.

"Rise up," says Darby, lifting the man to his feet an' steadying him there. The stone-cutter stared about like one stunned be a blow.

"I don't know where the banshee flew, but do you go back to Eileen as soon as you can," says the friend of the fairies. "Not that way, man alive," he says, as Cormac started to climb the foot-bridge, "it's broke in the middle; go down an' cross the stone bridge. I'll be afther you in a minute," he says.

Without a word, meek now and biddable as a child, Cormac turned, an' Darby saw him hurry away into the blackness.

The raysons Darby raymained behind were two: first an' foremost, he was a bit vexed at the way his clothes were muddied an' dhraggled, an' himself had been pounded an' hammered; an' second, he wanted to think. He had a quare cowld feeling in his mind that something was wrong—a kind of a foreboding, as one might say.

As he stood thinking a rayalisation of the caylamity sthruck him all at once like a rap on the jaw—he had lost his fine brier pipe. The lad groaned as he began the anxious sarch. He slapped furiously at his chist an' side pockets, he dived into his throwsers and greatcoat, and at last, sprawlin' on his hands an' feet like a monkey, he groped savagely through the wet, sticky clay.

"This comes," says the poor lad, grumblin' an' gropin', "of pokin' your nose into other people's business. Hallo,

what's this?" says he, straightening himself. "'Tis a comb.
Be the powers of pewther, 'tis the banshee's comb."

An' so indade it was. He had picked up a goold comb
the length of your hand an' almost the width of your two
fingers. About an inch of one ind was broken off, an'
dhropped into Darby's palm. Without thinkin', he put the
broken bit into his weskit pocket, an' raised the biggest
half close to his eyes, the betther to view it.

"May I never see sorrow," he says, "if the banshee mustn't
have dhropped her comb. Look at that, now. Folks do be
sayin' that 'tis this gives her the foine singing voice, bekase
the comb is enchanted," he says. "If that sayin' be thrue, it's
the faymous lad I am from this night. I'll thravel from fair to
fair, an' maybe at the ind they'll send me to parliament."

With these worruds he lifted his caubeen an' stuck the
comb in the top tuft of his hair.

Begor, he'd no sooner guv it a pull than a sour, singing feelin' begun at the bottom of his stomick, an' it rose
higher an' higher. When it raiched his chist he was just
going to let a bawl out of himself only that he caught sight
of a thing ferninst him that froze the marrow in his bones.

He gasped short an' jerked the comb out of his hair,
for there, not tin feet away, stood a dark, shadowy woman,
tall, thin, an' motionless, laning on a crutch.

During a breath or two the parsecuted hayro lost his
head completely, for he never doubted that the banshee
had changed her shuit of clothes to chase back afther him.

The first clear aymotion that rayturned to him was to
fling the comb on the ground an' make a boult of it. On
second thought he knew that 'twould be aisier to bate the
wind in a race than to run away from the banshee.

"Well, there's a good Tipperary man done for this time,"
groaned the knowledgeable man, "unless in some way I
can beguile her." He was fishing in his mind for its civilist
worrud when the woman spoke up, an' Darby's heart
jumped with gladness as he raycognised the cracked voice
of Sheelah Maguire, the spy for the fairies.

"The top of the avenin' to you, Darby O'Gill," says Sheelah, peering at him from undher her hood, the two eyes of her glowing like tallow candles; "amn't I kilt with a-stonishment to see you here alone this time of the night," says the ould witch.

Now, the clever man knew as well as though he had been tould, when Sheelah said thim worruds, that the banshee had sent her to look for the comb, an' his heart grew bould; but he answered her polite enough, "Why, thin, luck to ye, Misthress Maguire, ma'am," he says, bowing grand, "sure, if you're kilt with a-stonishment, amn't I sphlit with inkerdoolity to find yourself mayandherin' in this lonesome place on Halloween night."

Sheelah hobbled a step or two nearer, an' whuspered confaydential.

"I was wandherin' hereabouts only this morning," she says, "an' I lost from me hair a goold comb—one that I've had this forty years. Did ye see such a thing as that, agra?" An' her two eyes blazed.

"Faix, I dunno," says Darby, putting his two arrums behind him. "Was it about the length of ye're hand an' the width of ye're two fingers?" he axed.

"It was," says she, thrusting out a withered paw.

"Thin I didn't find it," says the tantalising man. "But maybe I did find something summillar, only 'twasn't yours at all, but the banshee's," he says, chuckling.

Whether the hag was intentioned to welt Darby with her staff, or whether she was only liftin' it for to make a sign of enchantment in the air, will never be known, but whatsomever she meant the hayro doubled his fists an' squared off; at that she lowered the stick, an' broke into a shrill, cackling laugh.

"Ho, ho!" she laughed, houldin' her sides, "but aren't ye the bould, distinguishable man. Becourse 'tis the banshee's comb; how well ye knew it! Be the same token I'm sint to bring it away; so make haste to give it up, for she's hiding an' waiting for me down at Chartres' mill.

Aren't you the courageous blaggard, to grabble at her, an' thry to ketch her. Sure, such a thing never happened before, since the worruld began," says Sheelah.

The idee that the banshee was hiding an' afeared to face him was great news to the hayro. But he only tossed his head an' smiled shuparior as he made answer.

"'Tis yourself that knows well, Sheelah Maguire, ma'am," answers back the proud man, slow an' dayliberate, "that whin one does a favour for an unearthly spirit he may daymand for pay the favours of three such wishes as the spirit has power to give. The worruld knows that. Now I'll take three good wishes, such as the banshee can bestow, or else I'll carry the goolden comb straight to Father Cassidy. The banshee hasn't goold nor wor'ly goods, as the sayin' is, but she has what suits me betther."

This cleverness angered the fairy-woman so she set in to abuse and to frighten Darby. She ballyragged, she browbate, she trajooced, she threatened, but 'twas no use. The bould man hildt firm, till at last she promised him the favours of the three wishes.

"First an' foremost," says he, "I'll want her never to put her spell on me or any of my kith an' kin."

"That wish she gives you, that wish she grants you, though it'll go sore agin the grain," snarled Sheelah.

"Then," says Darby, "my second wish is that the black spell be taken from Eileen McCarthy."

Sheelah flusthered about like an angry hin. "Wouldn't something else do as well?" she says.

"I'm not here to argify," says Darby, swingin' back an' forrud on his toes.

"Bad scran to you," says Sheelah. "I'll have to go an' ask the banshee herself about that. Don't stir from that spot till I come back."

You may believe it or not, but with that sayin' she bent the head of her crutch well forward, an' before Darby's very face she trew—savin' your presence—one leg over the stick as though it had been a horse, an' while one might say Jack Robinson the crutch riz into the air an' lifted her, an' she went sailing out of sight.

Darby was still gaping an' gawpin' at the darkness where she disappeared whin—whisk! she was back agin an' dismountin' at his side.

"The luck is with you," says she, spiteful. "That wish I give, that wish I grant you. You'll find seven crossed rushes undher McCarthy's door-step; uncross them, put them in fire or in wather, an' the spell is lifted. Be quick with the third wish—out with it!"

"I'm in a more particular hurry about that than you are," says Darby. "You must find me my brier pipe," says he.

"You omadhaun," sneered the fairy-woman, "'tis sthuck in the band of your hat, where you put it when you left your own house the night. No, no, not in front," she says, as Darby put up his hand to feel. "It's stuck in the back. Your caubeen's twishted," she says.

Whilst Darby was standing with the comb in one hand an' the pipe in the other, smiling daylighted, the comb was snatched from his fingers and he got a welt in the side of the head from the crutch. Looking up, he saw Sheelah tunty feet in the air, headed for Chartres' mill, an' she cacklin' an' screechin' with laughter. Rubbing his sore head an' mutthering unpious words to himself, Darby started for the new bridge.

In less than no time afther, he had found the seven crossed rushes undher McCarthy's door-step, an' had flung them into the stream. Thin, without knocking, he pushed open McCarthy's door an' tiptoed quietly in.

Cormac was kneelin' beside the bed with his face buried in the pillows, as he was when Darby first saw him that night. But Eileen was sleeping as sound as a child, with a sweet smile on her lips. Heavy pursperation beaded her forehead, showing that the faver was broke.

Without disturbing aither of them our hayro picked up the package of tay from the floor, put it on the dhresser,

an' with a glad heart sthole out of the house an' closed
the door softly behind him.

Turning toward Chartres' mill he lifted his hat an'
bowed low. "Thank you kindly, Misthress Banshee," he
says. "'Tis well for us all I found your comb this night.
Public or private, I'll always say this for you—you're a
woman of your worrud," he says.

Chapter III
The Ghosts at Chartres' Mill

For a little while afther Darby O'Gill sint the banshee
back her comb, there was the duckens to pay in that
townland. Aich night came stormier than the other. An'
the rain—never, since Noey the Phoenaycian histed sail
for Arrayat was there promised such a daynudherin' flood.
(In one way or another we're all, even the Germin min an'
the Fardowns, dayscendints of the Phoenaycians.)

Even at that the foul weather was the laste of the
throuble—the counthry-side was ha'nted. Every ghost
must have left Croaghmah as soon as twilight to wander
abroad in the lonesome places. The farmyards and even
the village itself was not safe.

One morning, just before cock-crow, big Joey Hooligan, the smith, woke up sudden, with a turrible feeling
that some gashly person was lookin' in at him through
the windy. Startin' up flurried in bed, what did he see but
two eyes that were like burnin' coals of fire, an' they peerin'
study into the room. One glance was enough. Givin' a
thraymendous gasp, Joey dhropped back quakin' into the
bed, an' covered his head with the bed-clothes. How long
afther that the two heegous eyes kept starin' at the bed
Joey can't rightly tell, for he never uncovered his head
nor stirred hand nor foot agin till his wife Nancy had
lighted the fire an' biled the stirabout.

Indade, it was a good month afther that before Joey found courage enough to get up first in the morning so as to light the fire. An' on that same mimorable mornin' he an' Nancy lay in bed argyfin' about it till nearly noon—the poor man was that frightened.

The avenin' afther Hooligan was wisited Mrs. Norah Clancy was in the stable milking her cow—Cornaylia be name—whin sudden she spied a tall, sthrange man in a topcoat standin' near the stable door an' he with his back turned toward her. At first she thought it a shadow, but it a-ppeared a thrifle thicker than a shadow, so, a little afeared, she called out: "God save you kindly, sir!"

At that the shadow turned a dim, grey face toward her, so full of rayproachful woe that Mrs. Clancy let a screech out of her an' tumbled over with the pail of milk betwixt her knees. She lay on her back in the spilt milk unconscionable for full fufteen minutes.

The next night a very rayliable tinker, named Bothered Bill Donahue, while wandherin' near Chartres' ruined mill, came quite accidental upon tunty skillingtons, an' they colloguing an' confabbing together on the flat roof of the mill-shed.

But worst of all, an' something that sthruck deeper terror into every heart, was the news that six different persons at six different places had met with the turrible phantom coach, the Costa Bower.

Peggy Collins, a wandherin' beggar woman from the west counthry, had a wild chase for it; an' if she'd been a second later raichin' the chapel steps an' laying her hand on the church-door it would have had her sure.

Things got on so that afther dark people only wentured out in couples or in crowds, an' in pint of piety that parish was growin' into an example an' patthron for the naytion.

But of all the persons whom thim con-ditions complicayted you may be sure that the worst harried an' implicayted was the knowledgeable man, Darby O'Gill.

There was a weight on his mind, but he couldn't tell why, an' a dhread in his heart that had no raysonable foundaytion. He moped an' he moothered. Some of the time he felt like singin' doleful ballads an' death keens, an' the rest of the time he could hardly keep from cryin'. His appetite left him, but what confuged him worse than all the rest was the fondness that had come over him for hard worruk—cuttin' turf an' diggin' petaties, an' things like that.

To make matters more onsociable, his friend, Brian Connors, the King of the Fairies, hadn't showed a nose inside Darby's door for more than a fortnit; so the knowledgeable man had no one to adwise with.

In thim dismal sarcumstances Darby, growin' dusperate, harnessed the pony Clayopathra one morning and dhrove up to Clonmel to see the Masther Doctor—the raynowned McNamara. Be this you may know how bad he felt, for no one, till he was almost at the pint of dissolation, ever wint to that crass, browbatin' ould codger.

So, loath enough was our own hayro to face him, an' hard-hearted enough was the welcome the crabbed little docthor hilt out to Darby whin they met.

"What did you ate for breakwus?" the physician says, peerin' savage from undher his great eyebrows at Darby's tongue.

"Only a bowl of stirabout, an' a couple of petaties, an' a bit of bacon, an' a few eggs." He was countin' on his fingers, "an'—an' somethin' or other I forgot. Do you think I'll go into a daycline, Doctor, agra?"

"Hump! ugh! ugh!" was all the comfort the sick man got from the blinkin' ould blaggard. But turnin' imaget to his medicine-table the surgent began studyin' the medicines. There was so much of it ferninst him he might have give a gallon an' never missed it. There was one foine big red bottle in particular Darby had his eye on, an' thought his dose 'ud surely come out of that. But NcNamara turns to a box the size of your hat, an' it filled to the top with little white, flat pills. Well, the stingy ould rascal counts out three and, handing them to Darby, says: "Take one before breakwus, another before dinner, an' the last one before supper, an' give me four silver shillings, an' that'll cure ye," he says.

You may be sure that Darby biled up inside with madness at the onraysonableness of the price of the pills, but, houlding himself in, he says, very cool an' quite: "Will you write me out a rayceipt for the money, Doctor McNamara, if you plaze?" he says. An', whilst the ould chayter was turned to the writing, be the hokey if our hayro didn't half fill his pockets with pills from the box. By manes of them, as he dhrove along home, he was able to do a power of good to the neighbour people he met with on the road.

Whin you once get in the habit of it there's no pleasure in life which ayquils givin' other people medicine.

Darby ginerously med ould Peggy O'Callaghan take six of the little round things. He gave a swally to half-witted Red Durgan, an' a good mouthful to poor sick Eileen McCarthy (only she had to gulp them whole, poor thing, an' couldn't ate them as the others did but maybe 'twas just as good). An' he gave a fistful aich to Judy Rafferty an' Dennis Hogan; an' he stood handsome thrate to a sthranger, who, the minute he got the taste well intil his mouth, wanted to fight Darby. Howsumever, the two only called aich other hard names for a while, then Darby joggled along, doin' good an' growin' lighter-hearted an' merrier-minded at every sthop he med. 'Twas this way with him till, just in front of Mrs. Kilcannon's, who should he see, scratching himself agin the wall, but Solomon, an' the baste lookin' bitther daynunciation out of the corner of his eye. Darby turned his head, ashamed to look the misthrayted donkey in the face. An' worse still nor that, just beyant Solomon, laning agin the same wall, was Bothered Bill Donahue, the deef tinker. That last sight dashed Darby entirely, for he knew as well as if he had been tould that the tinker was layin' in wait to ride home with him for a night's lodging.

It wasn't that Darby objected on his own account to takin' him home, for a tinker or a beggar-man, mind you, has a right, the worruld over, to claim a night's lodgin' an' a bit to ate wherever he goes; an' well, these honest people pay for it in the gossip an' news they furnish at the fireside an' in the good rayport of your family they'll spread through the counthry afterwards.

Darby liked well to have them come, but through some unknown wakeness in her char-ack-ther Bridget hated the sight of them. Worst of all, she hated Bothered Bill. She even went so far as to say that Bill was not half so bothered as he purtendid—that he could hear well enough what was a-greeable for him to hear, an' that he was deef only to what he didn't like to listen to.

Well, anyhow there was the tinker in the road waitin' for the cart to come up, an' for a while what to do Darby didn't well know.

He couldn't rayfuse one who axed food to ate or shelther for a wandherer's four bones during the night (that would be a sin, besides it would bring bad luck upon the house), an' still he had a mortial dislike to go agin Bridget in this purtick'ler—she'd surely blame him for bringin' Bothered Bill home.

But at length an' at last he daycided, with a sigh, to put the whole case before Bill an' then let him come or stay.

Whilst he was meditaytin' on some way of conveyin' the news that'd be complaymintary to the tinker, an' that'd elevayte instid of smashing that thraveller's sinsitiveness, Bill came up to the cart.

"The top iv the day to you, dacint man," he says. "'Tis gettin' toward dark an' I'll go home with ye for the night, I'm thinkin'," says he. The tinker, like most people who are hard of hearin', roared as though the listener was bothered.

Darby laid down the lines an' hilt out a handful of the little medicines.

"There's nothin' the matther with me, so why should I ate thim?" cried Bill.

"They're the best thing in the worruld for that," says Darby, forcing them into Bill's mouth. "You don't know whin you'll nade thim," he says, shoutin'. "It's betther meet sickness half-way," says he, "than to wait till it finds you."

And thin, whilst Bill, with an open hand aginst his ear, was chawin' the pills an' lookin' up plaintiff into Darby's face, the knowledgeable man wint on in a blandishin' way to pint out the sitiwation.

"You see, 'tis this away, Wullum," he says. "It's only too daylighted I'd be to take you home with me. Indade, Bridget herself has wondherful admiraytion for you in an ord'nary way," says he. "She believes you're a raymarkable man intirely," he says, dayplomatic, "only she thinks you're not clane," says he.

The tinker must have misundherstood altogether, for he bawled, in rayply, "Wisha good luck to her," he says, "an' ain't I glad to have so foine opinion from so foine a woman," says he. "But sure, all the women notice how tidy I am, an' that's why they like to have me in the house. But we best be movin'," says he, coolly dhropping his bags of tools intil the cart, "for the night's at hand, an' a black an' stormy one it'll be," says Bill.

He put a foot onto the wheel of the cart. As he did so Darby, growin' very red in the face, pressed a shilling into the tinker's hand. "Go into Mrs. Kilcannon's for the night, Wullum," he says, "an' come 'to us for your breakwus, an' your dinner an' maybe your supper, me good fellow," says he.

But the deef man only pocketed the shillin' an' clambered up onto the sate beside Darby. "Faith, the shillin's welcome," he says; "but I'd go to such a commodious house as yours any time, Darby O'Gill, without a fardin's pay," says he, pattin' Darby kindly on the back. But Darby's jaw was hangin' for the loss of the shillin' right on top of the unwelcome wisitor.

"We'd betther hurry on," says the tinker, lighting his pipe; "for afther sundown who knows what'll catch up with us on the road," says he.

Sure, there was nothing for it but to make the best of a bad bargain, an' the two went on together, Darby gloomy an' vexed an' the deef man solemn but comfortable till they were almost at McHale's bridge. Then the tinker spoke up.

"Did ye hear the black threats Sheelah Maguire is makin' agin you?" he says.

"No," says Darby; "what in the worruld ails her?" says he.

"Bless the one of me knows," says the tinker, "nor anybody else for that matther. Only that last Halloween night Sheelah Maguire was bate black an' blue from head to foot, an' she lays the raysponsibility on you, Darby," he says.

The knowledgeable man had his mouth open for a question whin who should go runnin' acrost the road in front of them but Neddy McHale himself, an' his arrum full of sticks. "Go back! go back!" cries Neddy, wavin' an arrum wild. "The bridge's butther-worruks are washed out be the flood an' McDonald's bridge is down, too, so yez must go around be the mill," says Neddy.

Now here was bitther news for ye! 'Twas two miles out of the way to go be Chartres' mill, an' do the best possible they'd be passing that ha'nted place in the pitch dark.

"Faith, an' I've had worse luck than in pickin' you up this night, Bothered Bill Donahue," says Darby, "for it's loath I'd be to go alone—"

He turned to speak just in time, for the tinker had gathered up his bag an' had put his right foot on the cart-wheel, purparin' for a jump. Darby clutched the lad be the back of his neck an' joulted him back hard into the sate.

"Sit still, Wullum, till we raich me own house, avourneen," he says, sarcastic, "for if ye thry that move agin I'll not lave a whole bone in your body. I'll never let it be said," he says, lofty, "that I turned one who axed me for a night's lodgin' from me door," he says. An' as he spoke he wheeled the cart quick around in the road.

"Lave me down, Misther O'Gill! I think I'll stop the night with Neddy McHale," says Wullum, shiverin'. "Bridget don't think I'm clane," says he, as the pony started off.

"Who tould ye that, I'd like to know?" shouted Darby, growin' fierce; "who dared say that of ye? You're bothered, Wullum, you know, an' so you misthrupit langwidge," he says.

But Bill only cowered down sulky, an' the pony galloped down the side lane intil the woods, strivin' to bate the rain an' the darkness. But the elements were too swiftfooted, an' the rain came down an' all the shadows met together, an' the dusk whirled quick intil blackness before they raiched the gloomy hill.

Ever and always Chartres' mill was a misfortunit place. It broke the heart of an' runed and kilt the man who built it; an' itself was a rune these last tunty years.

Many was the wild tale known throughout the counthry-side of the things that had been seen an' heard at that same mill, but the tale that kept Darby an' the tinker unwelcome company as the pony throtted along was what had happened there a couple of years before. One night, as Paddy Carroll was dhrivin' past the gloomy ould place, his best ear cocked an' his weather eye open for ghosts, there came sudden from the mill three agonised shrieks for help.

Thinkin' 'twas the spirits that were in it Paddy whipped up his pony an' hurried on his way. But the next morning, misdoubtin' whether 'twasn't a human woice, afther all, he had heard, Paddy gathered up a dozen of the neighbours an' went back to inwestigate. What did they find in one of the upper rooms but a peddler, lying flat on the floor, his pack ramsacked an' he dead as a door-nail. 'Twas *his* cries Paddy had heard as the poor thraveller was bein' murdhered.

Since that time a dozen people passing the mill at night had heard the cries of the same peddler, an' had seen the place blazin' with lights. So, that now no one who could help it ever alone passed the mill afther dark.

At the hill this side of that place the pony slowed down to a walk; nayther coaxin' nor batin' 'd injooce the baste to mend his steps. The horse'd stop a little an' wait, an' thin it'd go on thrimblin'.

They could all see the dim outlines of the empty mill glowerin' up at them, an' the nearer they came the more it glowered, an' the faster their two hearts bate. Half-way down the hill an ould sign-post pinted the way with its broken arm; just beyant that the bridge, an' afther that the long, level road an'—salwaytion.

But at the sign-post Clayopathra sthopped dead still, starin' into some bushes just beyant. She was shakin' an' snortin' and her limbs thrimblin'.

At the same time, to tell the truth, she was no worse off than the two Christians sittin' in the cart behint her, only they were not so daymonsthray-ta-tive about it. Small blame to the lads at that, for they were both sure an' sartin that lurking in the black shadows was a thing waiting to freeze their hearts with terror, an' maybe to put a mark on thim that they'd carry to their graves.

Afther coaxing Clayopathra an' raysonin' with her in wain, Darby, his knees knocking, turned to the tinker, an' in the excitement of the events forgettin' that Bill was deef, whuspered, as cool an' as aisy-like as he could:

"Would ye mind doin' me the favour of steppin' out, avick, an' seein' what's in that road ahead of us, Wullum?"

But Bothered Bill answered back at once, just as cool an' aisy:

"I would mind, Darby," he says; "an' I wouldn't get down, asthore, to save you an' your family an' all their laneyal daysindents from the gallus-rope," says he.

"I thought you was deef," says Darby, growin' disray-spectful.

"This is no time for explaynations," says Wullum. "An'
I thought meself," he wint on, turning his chowlder on
Darby, "that I was in company with a brave man; but I'm
sorry to find that I'm riding with no betther than an' outrageous coward," says he, bitther.

Whilst Wullum was sayin' them wexatious worruds
Darby stood laning out of the cart with a hand on
Clayopathra's back an' a foot on the shaft, goggling his
eyes an' sthrivin' to pierce the darkness at the pony's head.
Without turnin' round he med answer:

"Is that the way it is with you, Wullum?" he says, still
sarcastic. "Faix, thin ye'll have that complaint no longer,
for if yez don't climb down this minute I'll trow you bag
an' baggage in the ditch," he says; "so get out immaget,
darlint, or I'll trow you out," says he.

The worruds weren't well out of his mouth whin the
owdacious tinker whipped out his scissors an' sint the
sharp pint half an inch into Clayopathra's flank.
Clayopathra jumped, an' Darby, legs an' arrums flying,
took a back sommerset that he never ayquiled in his sup-
plest days, for it landed him flat agin the hedge; an' the
leap Clayopathra gave, if she could only keep it up'd fit
her for the Curragh races. An' keep it up for a surprisin'
while she did, at any rate, for as the knowledgeable man
scrambled to his feet he could hear her furious gallop a
hundhred yards down the road.

"Stop her, Wullum avourneen, I was only joking! Come
back, ye shameless rogue of the univarse, or I'll have ye
thransported!" he shouted, rushing a few steps afther
them. But the lash of the whip on Clayopathra's sides
was the only answer Wullum sint back to him.

To purshue was useless, so the daysarted man slacked
down to a throt. I'd hate bad to have befall me any one of
the hundhred things Darby wished aloud then an' there
for Wullum. Well, at all events, there was Darby, his head
bint, plodding along through the storm, an' a fiercer storm
than the wind or rain ever med kept ragin' in his heart.

Only that through the storm in his mind there flared now an' thin quivers of fear an' turpitation that sometimes hastened his steps an' thin again falthered thim. Howsumever, taking it all in all, he was making good progress, an' had got to the bunch of willows at the near side of the mill whin one particular raymembrance of Sheelah Maguire and of the banshee's comb halted the lad in the middle of the road an' sint him fumblin' with narvous hands in his weskit pocket.

There, sure enough, was the piece of the banshee's comb. The broken bit had lain forgotten in the lad's pocket since Halloween; an' now, as he felt it there next his thumping heart an' buried undher pipefuls of tobaccy, the rayalisation almost floored him with consthernaytion. All rushed over his sowl like a flood.

Who else could it be but the banshee that guv Sheelah Maguire that turrible batin' mintioned by the tinker? An' what was that bating for, unless the banshee a-ccused Sheelah of stealing the ind of the comb? An', mother of Moses! 'Twas sarchin' for that same bit of comb it was that brought the ghosts up from Croaghmah an' med the whole townland ha'nted.

Was ever such a dangerous purdicament! Here he was, with ghosts in the threes above him an' in the hedges, an' maybe lookin' over his chowlder, an' all of them sarchin' for the bit of enchanted comb that was in his own pocket. If they should find out where it lay what awful things they would do to him. Sure, they might call up the Costa Bower an' fling him into it, an' that 'ud be the last ever heard of Darby O'Gill in the land of the livin'.

With thim wild thoughts jumpin' up an' down in his mind he stood in the dark an' in the rain, gawmin' vacant over toward the shadowy ruin. An' he bein' much agitayted, the lad, without thinkin', did the foolishest thing a man in his sitiwaytion could well a-complish he took out of his pocket the enchanted sliver of goold an' hildt it to his two eyes for a look.

The consequences came suddin', for as he stuck it back into the tobaccy there burst from the darkness of the willows the hallowest, most blood-curdlin' laugh that ever fell on mortial ears. "Ho! ho! ho!" it laughed. The knowledgeable man's hair lifted the hat from his head.

An' as if the laugh wasn't enough to scatther the wits of anyone, at the same instant it sounded, an' quick as a flash, every windy in the ould mill blazed with a fierce blue light. Every batthered crack an' crevice seemed bursting with the glare for maybe the space of ten seconds, an' then, oh, Millia Murther! there broke from the upper floor three of the bitterest shrieks of pain an' terror ever heard in this worruld; an', with the last cry, the mill quinched itself into darkness agin an' stood lonely an' gloomy an' silent as before. The rain patthered down on the road an' the wind swished mournful in the threes, but there was no other sound.

The knowledgeable man turned to creep away very soft an' quiet; but as he did a monsthrous black thing that looked like a dog without a head crawled slowly out from the willows where the turrible laugh had come from, an' it crept into the gloom of the opposite hedge an' there it stood, waitin' for Darby to dhraw near.

But the knowledgeable man gave a leap backwards, an' as he did from the darkness just behindt him swelled a deep sigh that was almost a groan. From the hedge to his right came another sigh, only deeper than the first, and from the blackness on his left rose another moan, an' then a groaning, moaning chorus rose all round him, an' lost itself in the wailing of the wind. He was surrounded— the ghosts had captured Darby.

The lad never rayalised before that minute what a precious thing is daylight. If there would only come a flash of lightening to show him the faces of the surrounding spirrits, horrible though they might be, he'd bid it welcome. But though the rain drizzled an' the tunder rumpled, not a flare lit up the sky.

One swift, dusperate hope at the last minute saved the boy from sheer dispair; an' that same hope was that maybe some of the Good People might be flyin' about an' would hear him. Liftin' up his face to the sky an' crying out to the passin' wind, he says:

"Boys," he says, agonised, "lads," says he, "if there be any of yez to listen," he cried, "I'll take it as a great favour an' I'll thank ye kindly to tell King Brian Connors that his friend an' comerade, Darby O'Gill, is in deep throuble and wants to see him imaget," says he.

"Ho! ho! ho!" laughed the turrible thing in the hedge.

In spite of the laugh he was almost sure that off in the distance a cry answered him.

To make sure he called again, but this time, though he sthrained his ears till their drums ached, he caught no rayply.

And now, out of the murkiness in the road ahead of him, something began to grow slowly into a tall, slender, white figure. Motionless it stood, tightly wrapped in a winding sheet. In its presence a new an' awful fear pressed down the heart of Darby. He felt, too, that another shade had taken its place behindt him, an' he didn't want to look, an' sthrove against lookin', but something forced the lad to turn his head. There, sure enough, not foive feet away, stood still an' silent the tall, dark figure of a man in a topcoat.

Thin came from every direction low, hissing whuspers that the lad couldn't undherstand. Somethin' turrible would happen in a minute—he knew that well.

There's just so much fear in every man, just exactly as there is a certain amount of courage, an' whin the fear is all spilt a man aither fights or dies. So Darby had always said.

He raymembered there was a gap in the hedge nearly opposite the clump of willows, so he med up his mind that, come what might, he'd make a gran' charge for it, an' so into the upland meadow beyant. He waited an instant to get some strength back intil his knees, an' then he gave a spring. But that one spring was all he med—in that direction, at laste.

For, as he neared the ditch, a dozen white, ghostly hands raiched out eager for him. With a gasp he whirled in his thracks an' rushed mad to the willows opposite, but there a hundhred gashly fingers were stretched out to meet the poor lad; an' as he staggered back into the middle of the road agin, the hayro couldn't, to save his sowl, keep back a long cry of terror and disthress.

Imaget, from undher the willows and from the ditch near the hedge an' in the air above his head, from countless dead lips aychoed that triumphing, onairthly laugh, Ho! ho! ho!

'Twas then Darby just nearly guve up for lost. He felt his eyes growing dim an' his limbs numb. There was no air comin' into his lungs, for whin he thried to breathe he only gaped, so that he knew the black spell was on him, an' that all that was left for him to do was to sink down in the road an' thin to die.

But at that minute there floated from a great way off the faint cry of a woice the dispairing man knew well.

"Keep up your heart, Darby O'Gill," cried Brian Connors; "we're coming to resky you," an' from over the fields a wild cheer follyed thim worruds.

"Faugh-a-balla—clear the way!" sprang the shrill war-cry of a thousand of the Good People.

At the first sound of the King's worruds there rose about Darby the mighty flurrying an' rushing of wings in the darkness, as if thraymendous birds were rising sudden an' flying away, an' the air emptied itself of a smothering heaviness. So fast came the King's fairy army that the great cheer was still aychoing among the threes when the goold crown of Brian Connors sparkled up from beside the knowledgeable man's knees. At that the parsecuted man, sobbin' with joy, knelt down in the muddy road to shake hands with his friend, the masther of the Good People.

Brian Connors was not alone, for there crowded about Darby, sympathisin' with him, little Phelim Beg, an' Nial the fiddler, an' Shaun Rhue the smith, an' Phadrig Oge. Also every instant, flitthering out of the sky into the road, came be the score green-cloaked and red-hooded men, follying the King an' ready for throuble.

"If ever a man needed a dhrop of good whusky, you're the hayro, an' this is the time an' place for it," says the King, handin' up a silver-topped noggin. "Dhrink it all," he says, "an' then we'll escorch ye home. Come on," says he.

The masther of the night-time turned an' shouted to his subjects. "Boys," he cried, "we'll go wisible, the betther for company sake. An' do you make the 'luminaytion so Darby can see yez with him!"

At that the lovely rosy light which, as you may raymember, our hayro first saw in the fairy's home at Sleive-na-mon, lighted up the roadway, an' undher the leafy arches, bobbin' along like a ridgement of sojers, all in their green cloaks an' red caps, marched at laste a thousand of the Little People, with Phadrig Oge at their head actin' as gineral.

As they passed the mill foive dayfiant pipers med the batthered ould windys rattle with "Garry Owen."

Chapter IV
The Costa Bower

I

So the green-dhressed little army, all in the sweet, rosy light they made, wint marchin', to the merry music of the pipes, over the tree-bowered roadway, past the ha'nted brakes up the shivering hills, an' down into the waiting dales, making the grim night maylodious.

For a long space not a worrud, good, bad, or indifferent, said Darby.

But a sparrow woke her dhrowsy childher to look at the beautiful purcession, an' a robin called excited to her sleepy neighbours, the linnets an' the rabbits an' the hares, an' hundhreds like them crowded daylighted through the bushes, an' stood peerin' through the glistening leaves as their well-known champyions wint by. A dozen wentursome young owls flew from bough to bough, follying along, crackin' good-natured but friendly jokes at their friends, the fairies. Thin other birds came flying from miles around, twitthering jubilaytion.

But the stern-jawed, frowny-eyed Little People for once answered back never a worrud, but marched stiff an' silent, as sojers should. You'd swear 'twas the Enniskillins or 'twas the Eighteenth Hussars that 'twas in it.

"Isn't that Giniral Julius Sayser at the head?" says one brown owl, flapping an owdacious wing at Phadrig Oge.

"No!" cries his brother, another young villian. "'Tis only the Jook of Wellington. But look at the bothered face on Darby O'Gill! Musha, are the Good People goin' to hang Darby?"

And faix, thin, sure enough, there was mighty little elaytion on the faytures of our hayro. For, as he came marchin' along, silent an' moody, beside the King, what to do with the banshee's comb was botherin' the heart out of him. If he had only trun it to the ghosts whin he was there at the mill! But that turrible laugh had crunched all sense an' rayson out of him, so that he forgot to do that very wise thing. Ochone, now the ghosts knew he had it; so, to trow it away'd do no good, onless they'd find it afther. One thing was sartin—he must some way get it back to the banshee, or else be ha'nted all the rest of his days.

He was sore-hearted, too, at the King, an' a bit crasstimpered bekase the little man had stayed away so long frum wisitin' with him.

But at last the knowledgeable man found his tongue. "Be me faix, King," he complained, "'tis a cure for sore eyes to see ye. I might have been dead an' buried an' you none the wiser," says he, sulky.

"Sure, I've been out of the counthry a fortnit," says the King. "And I've only rayturned within the hour," he says. "I wint on a suddin call to purvent a turrible war betwixt the Frinch fairies and the German fairies. I've been for two weeks on an island in the River Ryan, betwixt France an' Germany. The river is called afther an Irishman be the name of Ryan."

"At laste ye might have sint me wurrud," says Darby.

"I didn't think I'd be so long gone," says the fairy; "but the disputaytion was thraymendous," he says.

The little man dhrew himself up dignayfied an' scowled solemn up at Darby. "They left it for me to daycide," he says, "an' this was the contintion:

"Fufty years ago a swan belongin' to the Frinch fairies laid a settin' of eggs on that same island, an' thin comes along a German swan, an' what does the impident craythure do but set herself down on the eggs laid be the Frinch swan an' hatched thim. Afther the hatchin' the German min claimed the young ones, but the Frinchmen pray-imp-thurribly daymanded thim back, d'ye mind. An' the German min dayfied thim, d'ye see. So, of course, the trouble started. For fufty years it has been growin', an' before fightin', as a last raysort, they sint for me.

"Well, I saw at once that at the bottom of all was the ould, ould question, which has been disthurbin' the worruld an' dhrivin' people crazy for three thousand years."

"I know," says Darby, scornful, "'twas whither the hin that laid the egg or the hin that hatched the egg is the mother of the young chicken."

"An' nothin' else but that!" cried the King, surprised. "Now, what d'ye think I daycided?" he says.

Now, yer honour, I'll always blame Darby for not listening to the King's daycision, bekase 'tis a matther I've studied meself considherable, an' never could rightly conclude; but Darby at the time was so bothered that he only said, in rayply to the King: "Sure, it's little I know, an' sorra little I care," he says, sulky. "I've something more important than hin's eggs throubling me mind, an' maybe ye can help me," he says, anxious.

"Arrah, out with it, man," says the King. "We'll find a way, avourneen," he says, cheerful.

With that Darby up an' toult everything that had happened Halloween night an' since, an', indeed, be sayin': "Now, here's that broken piece of comb in me pocket, an' what to do with it I don't know. Will ye take it to the banshee, King?" he says.

The King turned grave as a goat. "I wouldn't touch that thing in yer pocket, good friends as we are, to save yer life—not for a hundhred pounds. It might give them power over me. Yours is the only mortial hand that ever touched the banshee's comb, an' yours is the hand that should raystore it."

"Oh, my, look at that, now," says Darby, in despair, nodding his head very solemn.

"Besides," says the King, without noticin' him, "there's only one ghost in Croaghmah I 'ssociate with—an' that's Shaun. They are mostly oncultavayted, an' I almost said raydundant. Although I'd hate to call anyone raydundant onless I had to," says the just-minded ould man.

"I'll trow it here in the road an' let some of them find it," says Darby, dusperate. "I'll take the chanst," says he.

The King was shocked, an', trowing up a warnin' hand, he says:

"Be no manner of manes," the fairy says, "you forget that thim ghosts were once min an' women like yerself, so whin goold's consarned they're not to be thrusted. If one should find the comb he mightn't give it to the banshee at all—he might turn 'bezzler an' 'buzzle it. No, no, you must give it to herself pursnal, or else you an' Bridget an' the childher'll be ha'nted all yer days. An' there's no time to lose, ayther," says he.

"But Bridget an' the childher's waitin' for me this minute," wailed Darby. "An' the pony, what's become of her? An' me supper?" he cried.

A little lad who was marchin' just ahead turned an' spoke up.

"The pony's tied in the stable, an' Bothered Bill has gone sneakin' off to McCloskey's," the little man says. "I saw thim as I flew past."

"Phadrig!" shouted the King. "Donnell! Conn! Nial! Phelim!" he called.

With that the little min named rose from the ranks, their cloaks spread, an' come flyin' back like big green buttherflies, an' they sthopped huvering in the air above Darby an' the King.

"What's wanted?" axed Phelim.

"Does any of yez know where the banshee's due at this hour?" the King rayplied.

"She's due in County Roscommon at Castle O'Flinn, if I don't misraymimber," spoke up the little fiddler. "But I'm thinking that since Halloween she ain't worrukin' much, an' purhaps she won't lave Croaghmah."

"Well, has any one of yez seen Shaun the night, I dunno?" axed the master.

"Sorra one of *me* knows," says Phadrig. "Nor I," "Nor I," "Nor I," cried one afther the other.

"Well, find where the banshee's stayin'," says King Brian. "An' some of yez, exceptin' Phadrig, go look for Shaun, an' tell him I want to see him purtic'lar," says the King.

The foive huvering little lads wanished like a candle that's blown out.

"As for you, Phadrig," wint on the masther fairy, "tell the ridgiment they're to guard this townland the night, an' keep the ghosts out of it. Begin at once!" he commanded.

The worruds wern't well said till the whole ridgiment had blown itself out, an' agin the night closed in as black as yer hat. But as it did Darby caught a glimpse from afar of the goolden light of his own open door, an' he thought he could see on the thrashol the shadow of Bridget, with one of the childher clinging to her skirt, an' herself watchin' with a hand shading her eyes.

"Do you go home to yer supper, me poor man," says the King, "an' meantime I'll engage Shaun to guide us to the banshee. He's a great comerade of hers, an' he'll paycificate her if anyone can."

The idee of becomin' acquainted pursonal with the ghosts, an' in a friendly, pleasant way have dalings with them, was a new sinsation to Darby. "What'll I do now?" he axed.

"Go home to yer supper," says the King, "an' meet me by the withered three at Conroy's crass-roads on the sthroke of twelve. There'll be little danger to-night, I'm thinkin', but if ye should run against one of thim spalpeens trow the bit of comb at him; maybe he'll take it to the banshee an' maybe he won't. At any rate, 'tis the best yez can do."

"Don't keep me waitin' on the crass-roads, whatever else happens," warned Darby.

"I'll do me best endayvour," says the King. "But be sure to racognise me whin I come; make no mistake, for ye'll have to spake first," he says.

They were walking along all this time, an' now had come to Darby's own stile. The lad could see the heads of the childher bunched up agin the windy-pane. The King sthopped, an', laying a hand on Darby's arrum, spoke up umpressive:

"If I come to the crass-roads as a cow with a rope about me horns ye'll lade me," he says. "If I come as a horse with a saddle on me back, yez'll ride me," says he. "But if I come as a pig with a rope tied to me lift hind leg, ye'll dhrive me," says the King.

"Oh, my! Oh, my! Oh, tare an' ages!" says Darby.

"But," says the King, wavin' his hand aginst inthurruptions, "so that we'll know aich other we'll have a by-worrud bechuxt us. An' it'll be poethry," he says. "So that I'll know that 'tis you that's in it ye'll say 'Cabbage an' bacon'; an' so that ye'll know that 'tis me that's in it I'll answer, 'Will sthop the heart achin'.' Cabbage an' bacon will sthop the heart achin'," says the King, growin' unwisible. "That's good, satisfyin' poethry," he says. But the last worruds were sounded out of the empty air an' a little way above, for the masther of the night-time had wanished. At that Darby wint in to his supper.

I won't expaytiate to yer honour on how our hayro spint the avenin' at home, an' how, afther Bridget an' the childher were in bed, that a growin' daysire to meet an' talk sociable with a ghost fought with tunty black fears an' almost bate them. But whinever his mind hesitayted, as it always did at the thought of the Costa Bower, a finger poked into his weskit pocket where the broken bit of comb lay hid, turned the scale.

Howandever, at length an' at last, just before midnight our hayro, dhressed once more for the road, wint splashin' an' ploddin' up the lane toward Conroy's crass-roads.

II

A man is never so brave as whin sittin' ferninst his own comfortable fire, a hot supper asleep in his chist, a steamin' noggin of flaygrant punch in his fist, an' a well-thried pipe betwixt his teeth. At such times he rumynates on the ould ancient hayroes, an' he daycides they were no great shakes, afther all. They had the chanst to show themselves, an' that's the only difference betwixet himself an' themselves. But whin he's flung sudden out of thim pleasant surcumstances, as Darby was, to go chargin' around in the darkness, hunting unknown an' unwisible dangers, much of that courage oozes out of him.

An' so the sthrangest of all sthrange things was, that this night, whin 'twas his fortune to be taken up be the Costa Bower, that a dhread of that death-coach was present in his mind from the minute he shut the door on himself, an' it outweighed all other fears.

In spite of the insurance that King Brian had given, in spite of the knowledge that his friends, the Good People, were flyin' hither an' thither over that townland, there crept into his sowl an' fastened itself there the chanst that the headless dhriver might slip past thim all an' gobble him up.

In wain he tould himself that there were a million spots in Ireland where the death-carriage was more likely to be than in his own path. But in spite of all raysons, a dhreading, shiverin' feelin' was in his bones, so that as he splashed along he was flinging anxious looks behind or thremblin' at the black, wavering shadows in front.

Howsumever, there was some comfort to know that the weather was changin' for the betther. Strong winds had swept the worst of the storm out over the ocean, where it lingered slow, growlin' an' spputherin' lightening.

A few scatthered, frowning clouds, trowing ugly looks at the moon, sulked behind.

"Lord love your shining face," says Darby, looking up to where the full moon, big as the bottom of a tub, shone bright an' clear over his head. "An' it's I that hopes that the blaggard of a cloud I see creeping over at you from Sleive-na-mon won't raich you an' squinch your light before I meet up with Brian Connors."

The moon, in answer, brushed a cloud from her face, and shed a clearer, fuller light, that made the flooded fields an' dhropping threes quiver an' glisten.

On top of the little mound known as Conroy's Hill, an' which is just this side of where the roads crass, the friend of the fairies looked about over the lonesome counthry-side.

Here and there gleamed a distant farm-house, a still white speck in the moonlight. Only at Con Kelley's, which was a good mile down the road, was a friendly spark of light to be seen, an' that spark was so dim and so far that it only pressed down the loneliness heavier on Darby's heart.

"Wisha," says Darby, "how much I'd druther be there merry-makin' with the boys an' girls than standin' here lonesome and cowld, waiting for the divil knows what."

He sthrained his eyes for a sight of a horse, or a cow, or a pig, or anything that might turn out to be Brian Connors. The only thing that moved was the huge dark cloud that stretched up from Sleive-na-mon, and its heavy edge already touched the rim of the moon.

He started down the hill.

The withered three at the cross-roads where he was to meet the King waved its blackened arms and lifted them up in warning as he came toward it, an' it dhripped cowld tears upon his caubeen and down his neck when he stood quaking in its shadows.

"If the headless coachman were to ketch me here," he whumpered, "and fling me into his carriage, not a sowl on earth would ever know what became of me.

"I wish I wasn't so knowledgeable," he says, half cryin'. "I wish I was as ignorant about ghosts an' fairies as little Mrs. Bradigan, who laughs at them. The more you know the more you need know. Musha, there goes the moon."

And at them words the great blaggard cloud closed in on the moon and left the worruld as black as yer hat.

That wasn't the worst of it by no manner of manes, for at the same instant there came a rush of wind, an' with it a low, hollow rumble that froze the marrow in Darby's bones. He sthrained his eyes toward the sound, but it was so dark he couldn't see his hand before his face.

He thried to run, but his legs turned to blocks of wood and dayfied him.

All the time the rumble of the turrible coach dhrew nearer an' nearer, an' he felt himself helpless as a babe. He closed his eyes to shut out the horror of the headless dhriver an' of the poor, dead men laning back agin the sate.

At that last minute a swift hope that the King might be within hearing lent him a flash of strength, and he called out the by-word.

"Cabbage an' bacon!" he cried out, dispairing. "Cabbage an' bacon'll stop the heart achin'!" he roared, dismally, an' then he gave a great gasp, for there was a splash in the road ferninst the three, an' a thraymendous black coach, with four goint horses an' a coachman on the box, stood still as death before him.

The dhriver wore a brown greatcoat, the lines hung limp in his fingers, an' Darby's heart sthopped palpitaytin' at the sight of the two broad, headless chowlders.

The knowledgeable man sthrove to cry out agin, but he could only croak like a raven.

"Cabbage an' bacon'll stop the heart achin'," he says.

Something moved inside the coach. "Foolish man," a woice cried, "you've not only guv the by-word, but at the same time you've shouted out its answer!"

At the woice of the King—for 'twas the King who spoke—a great wakeness came over Darby, an' he laned limp agin the three.

"Suppose," the King went on, "that it was an inemy you'd met up with instead of a friend. Tare an' 'ounds! he'd have our saycret and maybe he'd put the comeither on ye. Shaun," he says, up to the dhriver, "this is the human bean we're to take with us down to Croaghmah to meet the banshee."

From a place down on the sate on the far side of the dhriver a deep, slow woice, that sounded as though it had fur on it, spoke up:

"I'm glad to substantiate any sarvice that will in any way conjuice to the amaylyro-ra-tion of any friend of the raynounded King Brian Connors, even though that friend be only a human bean. I was a humble human bean meself three or four hundhred years ago."

At that statement Darby out of politeness thried to look surprised.

"You must be a jook or an earl, or some other rich pillosopher, to have the most raynouned fairy in the worruld take such a shine to you," wint on the head.

"Haven't ye seen enough to make yerself like him?" cried the King, raising half his body through the open windy. "Didn't ye mark how ca'm an' bould he stood waitin' for ye, whin any other man in Ireland would be this time have wore his legs to the knees runnin' from ye? Where is the pillosopher except Darby O'Gill who would have guessed that 'twas meself that was in the coach, an' would have flung me the by-worrud so careless and handy?" cried the King, his face blazing with admyration.

The worruds put pride into the heart of our hayro, an' pride the worruld over is the twin sisther of courage. And then, too, whilst the King was talkin' that deep, obsthreperous cloud which had covered the sky slipped off the edge of the moon an' hurried to jine its fellows, who were waiting for it out over the ocean. And the moon, to make a-minds for its late obscuraytion, showered down sudden a flood of such cheerful, silver light that the drooping, separate leaves and the glistening blades of grass lept up clane an' laughin' to the eye. Some of that cheer wint into Darby's breast, an' with it crept back fresh his ould confidence in his champyion, the King.

But the headless dhriver was talking. "O'Gill," says the slow woice agin, "did I hear ye say O'Gill, Brian Connors? Surely not one of the O'Gills of Ballinthubber?"

Darby answered rayluctant an' haughty, for he had a feeling that the monsther was goin' to claim relaytionship, an' the idee put a bad taste in his mouth. "All me father's people came from Ballinthubber," he says.

"Come this or come that," says the deep woice, thremblin' with excitement, "I'll have one look at ye." No sooner said than done; for with that sayin' the coachman thwisted, an' picking up an extra'onary big head from the sate beside him, hilt it up in his two hands an' faced it to the road. 'Twas the face of a goint. The lad marked that its wiry red whuskers grew close undher its eyes, an' the flaming hair of the head curled an' rowled down to where the chowlders should have been. An' he saw, too, that the

166 of HERMINIE TEMPLETON KAVANAGH

nose was wide an' that the eyes were little. An uglier face you couldn't wish to observe.

But as he looked, the boy saw the great lips tighten an' grow wide; the eyelids half closed, an' the head gave a hoarse sob; the tears thrickled down its nose. The head was cry in'.

First Darby grew oncomfortable, then he felt insulted to be cried at that way be a total sthranger. An' as the tears rowled faster an' faster, an' the sobs came louder an' louder, an' the ugly eyes kep' leering at him affectionate, he grew hot with indignaytion.

Seeing which, the head spoke up, snivelling:

"Plaze don't get pugnaycious nor yet disputaytious," it begged, betwixt sobs. "'Tisn't yer face that hurts me an' makes me cry. I've seen worse—a great dale worse—many's the time. But 'tis the amazin' fam'ly raysimblance that's pathrifying me heart."

The dhriver lifted the tail of his coat an' wiped the head's two weepin' eyes. "'Twas in Ballinthubber I was born an' in Ballinthubber I was rared; an' it's there I came to me misfortune through love of a purty, fair maid named Margit Ellen O'Gill. There was a song about it," he says.

"I've heerd it many an' many the time," says the King, noddin', sympathisin', "though not for the last hundhred years or so." Darby glared, scornful, at the King.

"Vo! Vo! Vo!" wailed the head, "but you're like her. If it wasn't for yer bunchy red hair, an' for the big brown wen that was on her forehead, ye'd be as like as two pase."

"Arrah," says Darby, brustlin', "I'm ashamed to see a man of yer sinse an' station," he says, "an' high dictation—"

"Lave off!" broke in the King, pulling Darby be the sleeve. "Come inside! Whatever else you do, rayspect the sintimintalities—there all we have to live for, ghost or mortial," says he.

So, grumbling, Darby took a place within the coach beside his friend. He filled his poipe, an' was borrying a bit of fire from that of the King, whin looking up he saw

just back of the dhriver's seat, and opening into the carriage, a square hole of about the height an' the width of
yer two hands. An' set agin the hole, starin' affectionate
down at him, was the head, an' it smiling langwidging.

"Be this an' be that," Darby growled low to the King, "if
he don't take his face out of that windy, ghost or no ghost,
I'll take a poke at him!"

"Be no manner of manes," says the King, anxious.
"What'd we do without him? We'll be at Croaghmah in a
few minutes, then he needn't bother ye."

"Why don't ye dhrive on?" says Darby, lookin' up surly
at the head. "Why don't ye start?"

"We're goin' these last three minutes," smiled Shaun;
"we're comin' up to Kilmartin churchyard now."

"Have you passed Tom Grogan's public-house?" axed
the King, starting up, anxious.

"I have, but I can turn back agin," says the face, lighting up, intherested.

"They keep the best whusky there in this part of Ireland," says the King. "Would ye mind steppin' in an' bringing us out a sup, Darby agra?"

Misthress Tom Grogan was a tall, irritated woman, with
sharp corners all over her, an' a timper that was like an
east wind. She was standing at her own door, argyin' with
Garge McGibney an' Wullum Broderick, an' daling them
out harrud names, whilst her husband, Tom, a mild little
man, stood within laning on the bar, smoking saydately.
Garge an' Wullum were argying back at Misthress Grogan,
tellin' her what a foine-looking, rayspectable woman she
was, an' couldn't they have one dhrop more before going
home, whin they saw coming sliding along through the
air toward them, about four feet above the ground, a
daycint-dhressed man, sitting comfortable, his poipe in
his mouth an' one leg crossed over the other. The sthranger
stopped in the air not foive feet away, and in the moonlight they saw him plain knock the ashes from his poipe
an' stick it in the rim of his caubeen.

They ketched hould of aich other, gasping as he stepped
down out of the air to the ground, an' wishin' them the top of
the avening, he brushed past, walked bould to the bar an'
briskly called for three jorums of whusky. Tom, obliverous—
for he hadn't seen—handed out the dhrinks, an' the
sthranger, natural as you plaze, imptied one, wiped his mouth
with the back of his hand an' started for the door, carrying
the two other jorums. Tom, of course, follyed out to see
who was in the road, and then he clutched hould of the
three others, an' the four, grippin' aich other like lobsters
bilin' in the pot, clung, spacheless, swaging back an' forth.

An' sure 'twas no wonder, for they saw the sthrange
man lift the two cups into the naked air, an' they saw
plain the two jorums lave his hands, tip themselves slowly
over until the bottoms were uppermost—not one dhrop of
the liquor spillin' to the ground. They saw no more, for
they aich gave a different kind of roar whin Darby turned
to bring back the empty vessels. The next second Tom
Grogan was flying like a hunted rabbit over the muddy
petatie-field behind his own stable, whilst Wullum
Broderick an' Garge McGibney were dashin' furious afther
him like Skibberberg hounds. But Mrs. Grogan didn't run
away, bekase she was on her own thrashol', lying on the
flat of her back, and for the first time in her life spacheless.

Howandever, with a rumble an' a roar, the coach with
its thravellers wint on its way.

The good liquor supplied all which that last sight lacked
that was needful to put our three hayroes in good humour
with thimselves an' with aich other, so that it wasn't long
before their throubles, bein' forgot, they were convarsing
sociable an' fumiliar, one with the other.

Darby, to improve his informaytion, was sthriving to
make the best of the sitiwation be axin' knowledgeable
questions. "What kind of disposition has the banshee, I
dunno?" he says, afther a time.

"A foine creachure, an' very rayfined, only a bit too
fond of crying an' wailing," says Shaun.

"Musha, I know several livin' women that cap fits," says the knowledgeable man. "Sure, does she do nothin' but wail death keens? Has she no good love-ballads or songs like that? I'd think she'd grow tired," he says.

"Arrah, don't be talkin'!" says Shaun. "'Tis she who can sing them. She has one in purticular—the ballad of 'Mary McGinnis'—that I wisht ye could hear her at," he says.

"The song has three splendid chunes to it, an' the chune changes at aich varse. I wisht I had it all, but I'll sing yez what I have," he says. With that the head began to sing, an' a foine, deep singin' woice it had, too, only maybe a little too roarin' for love-ballads:

> "Come all ye thrue lovers, where'er yez may
>   be,
> Likewise ye decayvers be land or be sea;
> I hope that ye'll listen with pity to me
> Since the jew'l of me life is a thraitor."

"Here's where the chune changes," says the head, lickin' his lips.

> On goin' to church last Sunday me thrue love
>   passed me by,
> I knew her mind was changed be the twinklin'
>   of her eye;
> I knew her mind was changed, which caused
>   me for to moan,
> 'Tis a terrible black misfortin to think she
>   cowld has grown."

"That's what I call rale poethry," says Darby.

"There's no foiner," says the King, standing up on the sate, his face beaming.

"The next varse'll make yez cry salt tears," says Shaun. An' he sang very affectin':

"Oh, dig me a grave both large, wide, an' deep,
An' lay me down gently, to take me long sleep
Put a stone at me head an' a stone at me feet,
Since I cannot get Mary McGinnis."

"Faith, 'tis a foine, pittiful song," says Darby, "an' I'd give a great dale if I only had it," says he.

"Musha, who knows; maybe ye can get it," says the ould King, with a wink. "Ye may daymand the favours of the three wishes for bringing her what yer bringin'," he whuspered. "Shaun!" he says, out loud, "do ye think the banshee'll give that song for the bringing back of the lost comb, I dunno?"

"I dunno meself," says the head, jubious.

"Bekase if she would, here's the man who has the comb, an' he's bringin' it back to her."

The head gave a start and its eyes bulged with gladness.

"Then it's the lucky man I am entirely," he says. "For she promised to stick me head on and to let me wear it purmanent, if I'd only bring tidings of the comb," says Shaun. "She's been in a bad way since she lost it. You know the crachure can sing only whin she's combing her hair. Since the comb's broke her woice is cracked scand'lous, an' she's bitther ashamed, so she is. But here's Croaghmah right before us. Will yez go in an' take a dhrop of something?" says he.

Sticking out his head, Darby saw towering up in the night's gloom bleak Croaghmah, the mountain of the ghosts; and, as he thought of the thousands of shivering things inside, an' of the onpleasant feelings they'd given him at Chartres' mill a few hours before, a doubt came into his mind as to whether it were best to trust himself inside. He might never come out.

Howandever, the King spoke up sayin', "Thank ye kindly, Shaun, but ye know well that yerself an' one or two others are the only ghosts I 'ssociate with, so we'll just step out, an' do you go in yerself an' tell the banshee we're waitin'. Rayturn with her, Shaun, for ye must take Darby back."

With that the two hayroes dayscinded from the coach, an' glad enough was Darby to put his brogues safe an' sound on the road agin.

All at once the side of the mountain ferninst them opened with a great crash, an' Shaun, with the coach an' horses, disaypeared in a rush, an' were swolleyd up be the mountain, which closed afther thim. Darby was blinkin' an' shiverin' beside the King, when sudden, an' without a sound, the banshee stood before them.

She was all in white, an' her yellow hair sthrealed to the ground. The weight an' sorrow of ages were on her pale face.

"Is that you, Brian Connors?" she says. "An' is that one with you the man who grabbled me?"

"Your most obadient," says the King, bowin' low; "it was a accident," says he.

"Well, accident or no accident," she says, savare, "'tis the foine lot of throuble he's caused me, an' 'tis the illigant lot of throuble he'd a had this night if you hadn't saved him," she says. The banshee spoke in a hollow woice, which once in a while'd break into a squeak.

"Let bygones be bygones, ma'am, if you plaze," says Darby, "an' I've brought back yer comb, an' by your lave I ax the favour of three wishes," says he.

Some way or other he wasn't so afeared now that the King was near, an' besides one square, cool look at any kind of throuble—even if 'tis a ghost—takes half the dhread from it.

"I have only two favours to grant any mortial man," says she, "an' here they are." With that she handed Darby two small black stones with things carved on thim.

"The first stone'll make you onwisible if you rub the front of it, an' 'twill make you wisible again if you rub the back of it. Put the other stone in yer mouth an' ye can mount an' ride the wind. So Shaun needn't dhrive yez back," she says.

The King's face beamed with joy.

"Oh, be the hokey, Darby me lad," says he, "think of the larks we'll have thravellin' nights together over Ireland ground, an' maybe we'll go across the say," he says.

"But fairies can't cross runnin' water," says Darby, wondherin'.

"That's all shuperstition," says the King. "Didn't I cross the river Ryan? But, ma'am," says he, "you have a third favour, an' one I'm wishin' for mightilly meself, an' that is, that ye'll taiche us the ballad of 'Mary McGinnis.'"

The banshee blushed. "I have a cowld," says she.

"'Tis the way with singers," says the King, winkin' at Darby, "but we'll thank ye to do yer best, ma'am," says he.

Well, the banshee took out her comb, an' fastening to it the broken ind, she passed it through her hair a few times an' began the song.

At first her woice was purty wake an' thrimblin', but the more she combed the sthronger it grew, till at last it rose high and clear, and sweet and wild as Darby'd heerd it that Halloween night up at McCarthy's.

The two hayroes stood in the shadow of a three, Darby listening and the King busy writing down the song. At the last worrud the place where she had been standing flashed empty an' Darby never saw her again.

I wisht I had all the song to let your honour hear it, an' maybe I'll learn it from Darby be the next time ye come this way, an' I wisht I had time to tell your honour how Darby, one day havin' made himself onwisible, lost the stone, and how Bothered Bill Donahue found it, and how Bill, rubbin' it be accident, made *himself* onwisible, an' of the turrible time Darby had a-finding him.

But here's Kilcuny, an' there's the inn, an'—thank ye! God bless yer honour!

The Ashes of Old Wishes

All day long big flakes of soft, wet snow had flurried and scurried and melted about Darby O'Gill's cottage, until, by twilight, the countryside was neither more nor less than a great white bog. Then, to make matters worse, as the night came on that rapscallion of an east wind waked up, and came sweeping with a roar through the narrow lanes and over the desolate fields, gleefully buffeting and nipping every living thing in its way. It fairly tore the fur cap off Maurteen Cavanaugh's head, and gaily tossed that precious relic into the running ditch; it shrieked mockingly as it lifted poor old Mrs. Maloney's red cloak and swirled that tattered robe over the good woman's bewildered head, twisting her this way and that till she was so distracted she had to go into Joey Hoolighan's for a sip of hot tea and a soothering bit of fresh gossip. Then growing more uproarious the blackguard gale, after swooping madly around and around Darby O'Gill's cottage, leaped to the roof and perched itself on the very top of the chimney, where for three mortal hours it sat shouting down boisterous challenge to the discontented man who crouched moody and silent before his own smoky hearth.

Darby heard the challenge well enough but wasted little heed. A shapeless worry darkened the lad's mind. Ever since supper, when Bridget and the children went to bed—the better to get an early start for midnight Christmas

Mass—Darby and Malachi, the yellow cat, sat opposite each other in the glow of the smouldering turf. There's nothing can equal in its comfort, the comfortableness of a contented cat.

Lately Darby had taken great satisfaction in talking to Malachi. The cat proved to be a splendid listener—never contradicting any statement however boastful, but receiving all his master's confidences with a blinking gravity which was as respectful as it was flattering.

"This is Christmas Eve, Malachi. I suppose ye know that. I'm going to tell ye a great saycret. Be all the tokens I ought to be a happy man. Well, you'll be surprised—I am n't! I'm far, far from it! Everything in the world is growing mouldy. Nothin' tastes as it used to taste. Have ye noticed the flavor of the petaties lately, Malachi, or the tang of the bacon? No, to be sure, how could ye?" Darby discontentedly scratched his head with the stem of his pipe and heaved a deep sigh. "Heigh ho! oh, what petaties we used to get when I was a gossoon! The way Bridget could bile cabbage in the ould days would be a model for a quane, so it would. But, now—well, we won't disparage her. There's nothing I put into me mouth has the right smack to it. There's something or other I want bad, Malachi, and—whisht!" —he bent over— "and this is me saycret: I dunno rightly what it is I want, but whatever it is, I'll never be rightly happy till I get it."

Darby had often claimed that Malachi, with a blink of his green eye, could tell the unspoken word in a man's mind. Sure, every one knew how, at the first breath of a rise in Bridget's temper, the wise old lad would, with one nimble spring, land on the cottage roof, and there, safe from the broom, he would crouch peering over the edge of the thatch till the storm went down. So now, visibly impressed with the great secret, Malachi turned his back to the fire and began thoughtfully stroking his left ear. While the cat was thus engaged, the peaceful quiet of the hearth was rudely broken by a sudden shaking of the door and a rattling of the latch, as though nervous fingers were striving to lift it. Darby in alarm threw back his head to listen. Could it be a wraith? No! it was only the wind. Baffled in its attempt to open the door the ruffian gale then began flinging white dabs of soft snow at the black windowpanes—for all the world like a blackguard boy. At last, with an exultant shout, it leaped to the cottage roof again and, whoop! down the chimney it came.

"Poof! bad cess to the smoke an' bad luck to the wind! if they haven't the two eyes stung out of me head. I'd wind the clock and you and me'd go to bed this minute, so we would, Malachi, if I didn't know that Brian Connors, the King of the Fairies, would surely pay us a wisit the night." Malachi's back stiffened immediately, and with quick, indignant switches of his tail, he swept the hearthstone where he sat.

"Oh, I know ye don't like the Good People, me lad, and you may have ye're raisons. But you must admit that the little man has never failed to bring us some token for Christmas since first I met him. Though, to tell the truth," he added, a sudden scowl furrowing his face, "for a man who has the whole wurruld in his pocket the Fairy gives— Oh, be the powers, Malachi! I came near forgetting to tell yet me dhrame. I dhramed last night I was picking up goold suvereigns till me back ached. So, maybe the King'll bring me some traymendous present—Oh, millia murdher, me sight's gone entirely this time. Conshumin' to the minute longer I'll stay up—phew! ugh! ugh! ugh!"

The great puff of bitter pungent smoke which blinded the lad's eyes also sent him off into a fit of coughing. He was still choking and gasping and sweeping the water from his swimming lids when, happening to look up, whom should he spy through the blue smoke, calmly sitting on his favorite stool on the opposite side of the hearth, but the little Master of the Fairies himself. As usual the King's gold crown was tilted rakishly to one side, his green velvet cloak was flung back from his shoulders, and he sat with one short, pipestem of a leg dangling carelessly over the other. Put into a scale, he might have weighed, crown and all, about as much as Malachi.

"The top of the avenin' to ye, Darby O'Gill," piped he, "an' the complyments of the sayson to you an' yours."

At the first sound of the fairy's voice, Malachi, with tail erect, trotted out of the kitchen.

"The same to yerself," coughed Darby, rubbing his eyes, "an' if it isn't axing ye to go out of yer way too much, King, I'll thank ye afther this to come in be the dure or the windy, and not be takin' thim short cuts down through the chimbley. You nearly put the two eyes out of me head, so ye did."

"Oh, faith, Darby, me sowl," laughed the King good-naturedly, "the Christmas present I've brought ye'll put the two eyes back again, and brighter than ever."

The discontented look on Darby's face changed at once to a red glow of pleasure. He expected a bag of diamonds or a crock of gold at the very least. Still he strove hard to conceal his delight, and said as carelessly as he could:

"What is it, King darlint. I'll go bail your present's a grand one this time at any rate."

"You may well say that, me lad, for I've brought ye," chuckled the King, clasping his knee and leaning back comfortably against the chimney corner— "I've brought ye a jug of the foinest potteen in all Ireland ground."

Darby's jaw dropped to his chest. If ever hope took a cropper it was then. "Th-thank-ye kindly, King," he stuttered; and to hide his bitter disappointment the poor fellow began poking viciously at the smouldering turf.

The evident chagrin of his friend was not lost on the Master of the Good People, and the quick-tempered little King flared up instantly.

"Why, thin, bad manners to you, what ails you the night—you and your sour looks? So my present isn't grand enough for you, and the loikes of you. Maybe it's the pylosopher's stone or maybe it's riches or—"

Darby himself was thoroughly aroused. He felt slighted and belittled. Hammering out each word on the hearth-stone, he replied:

"You're right, King, it's riches I want! It's riches; an' that's the laste ye might be afther givin' me."

The fairy's eyes snapped threateningly. "Haven't I tould ye ag'in and ag'in that I'd never rune ye an' spile ye by givin' ye riches? Haven't—"

"We hear ducks talkin'! No sinsible man, King, was ru'ned or spiled be riches. Besides there's other things ye might give me."

The little King's lip curled. "Oh, ye ongratefull omad-haun! just to punish ye I've a mind to—" he hesitated and looked steadily at Darby. "By jaymine I will—I'll give ye any three wishes you make this night, barrin' riches. I won't break me wurrud on that score."

So great and so sudden was the offer that for a moment Darby's mind floundered helplessly. Meekly subsiding to his stool again he peered from under anxious brows, and asked doubtingly, "Do you mane it, King?"

The King frowned. "I do mane it; but the consequences'll be on your own sore head."

Darby thoughtfully regarded the fairy. Then putting the poker carefully back in the corner said:

"Don't be vexed with me, King agra; sure I've lots of throuble. I'm a very onhappy man. I don't know why it is, but I'm feelin' turrible. So by your lave, if it's perfectly convaynient, I'll take the favors of the three wishes."

"Out with them then! What do ye want?"

"Well, first an' foremost, King, I want the he-licks-her of life, that Maurteen Cavanaugh the schoolmasther was readin' about. I want to live forever."

The old King reeled and almost fell off the stool.

"Be the four fires of Fingal, Darby O'Gill, if you don't flog the worruld. But go on, man alive, what'll ye be wantin' next"

"Well afther that, if it's not too much throuble, ye may make me as comfortable an' as well off as the rich Lord

Killgobbin." By putting the wish this way Darby cleverly avoided a direct request for riches.

The King shut his lips in a grim smile, and slowly wagged his head.

"I will that! I'll make ye as well off an' as comfortable as Lord Killgobbin—with every vein of me heart. Go on!"

"The third wish, King, is the easiest of all to grant. Make me happy."

"That I will! Ye won't know yerself. Wait till I'm done with ye," said the King, getting up and drawing his cloak about his shoulders. "An' we'll lose no time about it ayther. We've a good dale of thravellin' to do the night, so put on you're greatcoat."

Nothing loath, the lad did as he was bid, and then waited expectantly.

"We're goin' into sthrange places, me bould Trojan," the King went on, "an' I think it best we go unwisible. Come nearer to me." With much impressiveness the little King of the Good People raised his hand and touched his companion lightly on the arm.

On the moment a strange tingling chill swept over Darby, and he began to grow invisible. First his feet faded into thin air; and even as he stared open-mouthed at the place they had been, his knees disappeared; and the next second the lad felt himself snuffed out like a tallow dip.

The King also was gone, but presently the familiar voice of the little fairy sounded from its place on the stool:

"We're goin' out now, avourneen."

"But how can I go out," wailed Darby in great distress. "Where are me two foine legs? What's become of me I'd like to know?"

"Be aisy! man, you'll not nade yer legs for a while. I'll put ye asthride a horse the night, the loike of which you never rode afore. You're goin' to ride the wind, Darby. Listen! D'ye hear it callin' us?"

Darby was still looking for some traces of his vanished legs when, without realizing the slightest sense of motion, he found himself in the open. There was a flash of black sky, a glimpse of wet weather and the astonished man was three miles from home standing beside the King in old Daniel Delaney's kitchen. It was all so sudden; he could scarcely believe his eyes. And to make matters more confusing, although Darby had known old Dan'l's kitchen since childhood, there was a certain weirdness and unreality about it now that chilled the unseen intruder's blood.

The room was almost dark, and filled with fitful fireshadows, which danced and wavered and dimmed upon the walls.

"Mark well what ye see and hear, Darby O'Gill, for this is but a shadow of your first wish—the wish to live forever. This is the ashes of long life." The King's voice was so solemn that Darby cowered, half-frightened from it.

Before the lonely hearth sat old Daniel Delaney and his wife, Julia. Half the county knew their desolate history. Ninety-two years had passed over their heads, and seventy years they had lived together as man and wife. Of all the old couples in that parish—and there were many of them—Daniel Delaney and his wife were the very oldest, and the loneliest. Twenty years ago their last child had died in America, an old man. Long before that, Teddy, Michael and Dan, soldier lads, fell before Sebastopol. And now, without chick or child, indeed without one of their blood that bore their name, the old couple waited patiently, each night mumbling the hope that maybe the morrow might bring to them the welcome deliverance.

As Darby gazed, a comprehension of the desolation, the loneliness, and the ceaseless heartache of the old people came to him like an inspiration, and his heart melted with pity.

He understood, as never before, how completely old Dan'l's and Julia's world was gone—faded into vague memories. The new voiced and strange young faces which kept constantly crowding into and filling the old fond nooks, gave to the couple a cruel sense of being aliens in an unsympathetic land. The winding lanes, the well-re-membered farms, and the crowded chapel were filled, for them, with dim specters. They were specters themselves, and the quiet waiting churchyard called ever and ever, with passionate insistence to their tired, empty hearts. Darby's eyes filled with hot tears.

"Will I be like Dan'l Delaney?" he whispered fearfully, to the King.

"Worse. You'll be all alone; Bridget'll be gone from you. Hist! Dan'l is talking. Listen!"

"Is that you, Julia machree!" an old voice quavered. "Ah, so it is; so it is! I thought it was me father sittin' there an'—an' I was a little gossoon again at his knee—just like our little Mickey. Where's Mickey? Oh, to be sure! Oh, thin wasn't me father the handsome man—and grand! Six feet two in his stockin's! Six feet two. An' to think, agra, to think, that now, in all this wide, wide worruld, only you and me are left who ever set eyes on him. Isn't it a quare worruld entirely, Julia! A quare worruld! Only you and me left, all dead, all dead!" The old man's voice fell to a whimper, and he wiped a tear from his cheek with shak-ing fingers.

"Aye, they're all gone from us, Dan'l, me lad. I was just thinkin', your father's father built this house and sthrangers'll have it soon—I couldn't sleep last night for worrying over it. All me foine boys and tendher, beautiful colleens! All, all gone. An' one gray day follys another gray day, an' nothing happens, nothing ever happens for us. Isn't this Christmas Eve, Dan'l? Little Norah's birthday?"

The old man lifted his trembling hands in an agony of regret. "Christmas Eve! Oh, Mother of Heaven! Oh, the merry-makin' an' the happiness of the childher! Marcyful Father, why can't we go to them?"

"Hush, Dan'l! For shame, man. Think how good God has been to us. Hasn't He kept us together? Mightn't He have taken you an' left me here alone? See how gentle He is with ould people. First, He crowds Heaven with their friends to prepare a welcome; then He fills the worruld so full of pains, an' aches, an' sorrow, that 't is no throuble at all to lave it. No throuble at all."

"God help them," thought Darby. The bitterness of their sorrows filled his own heart, and the weight of all their years pressed down on him.

"King," he asked, "isn't it quare that we can't always be young and live forever?"

"It's bekase you've no knowledge of Heaven that you ax so foolish a question as that," sighed the King.

Meanwhile old Dan'l would not be comforted, but was fretting, and whimpering, like a child three years old.

"Come away, come away, King," urged Darby hoarsely. "When Bridget an' the childher are in the churchyard I want to lie with them. Yez may keep the he-licks-her, King. I want none of it."

"I thought so. Now for your second wish," said the King.

The words weren't out of his mouth till Darby found himself standing with the fairy in the window recess of a large and brilliantly lighted bedroom in Killgobbin Castle. Soft, moss-green carpets an inch thick covered the floor. Slender shepherds and dainty shepherdesses, beautiful dames and stately knights smiled and curtsied from the priceless tapestries on the wall. In a far corner of the room stood a canopied mahogany bed, lace-draped and with snowy pillows. Gilded tables and luxurious easy-chairs were scattered here and there, while a great tiger skin, which gleamed yellow and black from the center of the floor, gave Darby a catch in his breath. It might have been the bedchamber of a king. Here no sound of the storm could reach.

Before a bright, hot fire of fine seacoals, sat the rich and powerful Lord Killgobbin, gray-haired and shaggy-browed. His lordship's right leg, bandaged and swollen, rested upon a low chair piled high with cushions. On a fur rug near him lay Fifi, her ladyship's old spaniel—the fattest, ugliest dog Darby had ever seen.

"Darby," whispered the King, "yonder is Lord Killgobbin, and remember I was to make you as comfortable, and as well off as he!"

The fairy was still speaking when the nobleman let a roar out of him that rattled the fireirons. "My supper! Where's my supper? Get out of that, you red-legged omandaun," he bellowed to a crimson liveried servant who waited, cowering just inside the door. "Bring up my supper at once or I'll have your heart's blood. No puling bread and milk, mind you, but a rousing supper for Christmas Eve. Be off!"

The footman disappeared like a flash, leaving the room door ajar. Sweet sounds of flute, violin and harp, mingled with gay laughter, floated up the wide staircase. Lord Killgobbin's only son was giving a Yule party to his young friends. At the sound of the music the old nobleman uttered a moan that would wring ones heart. "Oh, dear, Oh, dear, will ye listen to that. Dancing and cavorting an' enjoying themselves down there, an' me sitting up here suffering the torments, an' nobody caring a ha'porth whether I'm living or dead. Oh my, oh my! Sitting here trussed up like an ould roosther—." His lordship's eye roved around the room in a vain quest for sympathy; alas, the smug-faced Fifi was the only living thing to be seen.

"Bad scran to you! You're as hard-hearted as your misthress." Lord Killgobbin threatened the dog with his cane. But as if to show her disdain Fifi yawned in a bored way, turned wearily over and went to sleep again. It was the last straw. His lordship boiled with furious resentment, and leaning far over made a savage stroke at the dog with his cane. That was the unlucky blow! Instead of hitting the placid, unconscious Fifi, the furious old lord lost his balance, missed his aim, and gave himself a terrific whack on the gouty leg. There was the row!

Never since that day at Ballinrobe Fair, when Teddy McHale cracked his poor old father over the head with a blackthorn (mistaking the old gentleman for Peter Maloney, the family foe) had Darby heard such deafening roars, and such blood-curdling maledictions. Whether by accident or in an effort to drown Lord Killgobbin's voice, the orchestra downstairs played with redoubled vigor.

In the midst of the tumult, hurrying footsteps were heard upon the stairs, and presently, three wild-eyed footmen entered the room each bearing a silver tray. The first servant carried a bowl of thin gruel, the second a plate of dry toast and the salt, while the third footman stepped cautiously along bearing aloft a small pot of weak tea, without cream or sugar. The quiet, grim look which Lord Killgobbin threw at his terrified servants, sent a shiver down Darby's back.

With eyes half shut his lordship spoke slowly and deliberately, through clenched teeth:

"What's that ye have in the bowl, ye divil's limb ye?"

"The dicthor, your Lordship—an her ladyship, sir, seein' as it's Christmas Eve, thought that you'd like—that you'd like a—a—little change, so instead of bread an'—an' milk, they sent ye a little thin gruel, sir."

Lord Killgobbin grew ominously quiet. "Bring it over to me, my good man, don't be afraid," he cajoled.

The three footmen each keeping a wary eye on his lordship's stick, advanced timidly in a row. Nothing was said or done until the gruel was within easy grip of him, and then in one furious sweep of his left arm, his lordship sent the tray and gruel half way up to the ceiling, while with his right hand he managed to bring the cane down with a resounding whack on the head of the unfortunate footman who carried the toast and salt.

Instantly all was confusion. While the frightened servants were scrambling after the scattered trays and dishes, Lord Killgobbin reached quickly around for the coal-scuttle which stood near his hand, and began a furious bombardment. Two of the footmen managed to escape, unhurt from the room. The third, however, by an unlucky stumble over the rug, went to the floor on his back in the corner. There he lay cowering, and with the tray, shielding his head from the furious rain of coal.

"The curse of the crows on ye all," shouted Killgobbin, "You'd starve me, would yez?"

"Yes, sir—I—I mane no, your Lordship!" roared the terrified servant.

"Christmas Eve and a bowl of gruel!" (Bang, bang, bang rattled the coals on the tray!) "Christmas Eve with a sliver of toast and tay." (Bang, bang, bang.)

"Yes, sir" (bang) "Oh, me head, sir! Oh, me head, sir! Ow! wow! I'm kilt entirely, sir!"

"Me wife'd starve me—"

"Yes, sir, ow! ouch! I mane no, sir."

"Me son's in conspiracy with the docthor—"

"Yes sir" (bang, bang, bang.)

"Take that! Beef tay and dhry toast. I haven't had a meal fit for a dog in six weeks; six weeks, d'ye hear me, ye sniveling rapscallion?"

"No, sir—I—I mane yes, sir!"

"You're killing me by inches, so ye are! Ye murdherin' ringleaders, ye."

"Yes, sir. Ouch! I mane no, sir!"

Darby turned a disappointed face to the Master of the Fairies. "Thanks be we're unvisible, King. I wouldn't have that leg of Killgobbin's for all the money in the four provinces."

"Bah! Everybody's bread is butthered with trouble to about the same thickness. This is the ashes of foine living. His lordship'd thrade his castle an' all his grandeur for your pair of legs. But you've only seen his gout. The rale, botherin' trouble is comin' up the stairs now." Even as the King spoke, Darby heard the rustle of a lady's dress upon the landing.

"Come away, come away, King," he urged excitedly. "It isn't dacint to be listening to family saycrets. I forgive ye me first two wishes, an' I'll ax only for the third: Make me happy—it's all I'll ax."

"Oh, aye, the happiness! Sure enough! Truth I almost forgot the happiness. But never fear it'll have ye dancin' an' jumpin' along the road before ye raich home."

One may get a good idea of how quickly the pair shifted from place to place that night when one learns, that this last saying of the King was begun in Lord Killgobbin's bedchamber and finished so far away down the road that all which remained of the castle was a faint twinkle of lights on the distant hill.

And now the east wind, weary of mischief, had traveled on out over the sea leaving behind flattened hedgerows, twisted thatches, and desolate highways.

To Darby's great surprise he found himself and the King huddled together under the dripping eaves of a low, thatched building which crouched by the wayside.

"By Gar, King, that was a long jump we med. I'm only half a mile from home. This is Joey Hoolighan's smithy."

"Thrue for ye, Darby, me bouchal," answered the King. "I've brought ye here to show ye the only ralely, thruly happy man in this townland. Ye may take a look at him, he's sittin' within." Darby drew back thoughtfully. This was to be the last of the three wishes; and the fate of the other two made him hesitate.

"Tell me first, King, before I look; is he a married man? I dunno."

"He is not," said the King.

"Of course," sighed Darby, "careless and free. Well, is he rich? But sure I naden't ax. He must be—very."

"He hasn't a penny," replied the King, "nor chick nor child. He cares for nobody, an' nobody cares for him."

"Well, now look at that! Isn't that quare! What kind of a man is he? I'm almost afeared to look at him."

"Sthop yer blatherin', man alive, an' come over to the windy and do as I bid ye."

As he was bidden, Darby took a peep through the grimy panes, and there on a pile of turf, alone before the dying forge-fire, sat an old man. His head was bare and he swayed back and forth as he nodded and gabbled and smiled to the graying embers. With an exclamation of deep disgust, Darby jumped back.

"Why," he spluttered indignantly, "You're making game of me, King! That's only Tom, the child—the poor innocent who never had an ounce of wit since the day he was born!"

"I know it," said the king, "that's the rayson he's perfectly happy. He has no regret for yesterday nor no fear for tomorrow. He's had his supper, there's a fire ferninst him, a roof over his head for the night, so what more does he want."

For a moment Darby couldn't answer. He stood humped together, ready to cry with vexation and disappointment.

"There goes the last of me three grand wishes," he complained bitterly. "I'm chated out of all of them, an' all you've left me for me night's throuble, is the ashes of me wishes, a cowld in my chist from me wet brogues, an' a croak in me talk, so that I wouldn't know me own voice if I was in the next room. If you've done wid me now, King, I'll thank ye to make me wisible ag'in so that I can go home to me own dacint fambly."

"Not yet awhile, Darby," answered the King, "I haven't made ye happy. And ye'll not see the inside of yer house tonight until ye'll say from the bottom of yer heart that ye're ralely and thruly happy."

"Never mind," wailed the lad, "I want no more of yer thricks and dayludherin's. Ye may take away yer jug of potteen, too. An' all I want now is a sight of me own two legs to take me home to Bridget."

There was no reply. Darby waited a moment in silence and then the horrible realization flashed over him that he was alone. Doubtless the quick-tempered little fairy had taken offense at his words and had left him to his fate, invisible and helpless, on the high-road. The poor fellow groaned aloud:

"Ochone mavrone, haven't I the misfortune!" he wailed, "I'm fairly massacreed, so I am. What'll Bridget say to have a poor, hoarse voice goin' croaking about the house instid of the foine lookin' man I was. Oh, vo! vo!" he roared. "I wondher if I can ate me vittles! What'll I do with the new shuit of clothes? What'll I say to—"

"Hould on to whatever's botherin' ye, Darby, me friend. Don't be afeared, I'm comin' to ye!" It was the King's voice high in the air above Darby's head. The next instant our hero felt a touch upon the arm, and he and the King popped into clear visibility again.

Darby heaved a chest-splitting sigh of relief. "I thought you'd deserted me, King."

"Foolish man," piped the fairy, "I was loathe to have ye go home disappointed and empty-handed, but to save me life I didn't know what ye naded that'd do you any good. So I flew off with meself to your house, and Malachi, the cat, tould me that ye naded something; ye didn't know exactly what it was, but whatever it was ye'd never be happy till ye got it!"

"It's thrue for ye, thim were me very worruds."

"Well, I'll lave ye here now, Darby," the king went on, seriously but not unkindly, "and do you hurry along your way. Look nayther to the right nor to the left an' somewhere on the road, betwixt this an' your own thrashol', the thing that'll do ye most good in the worruld 'll catch up with ye. I'm off."

"Good-night, King," and Darby left alone splashed along the slushy road toward home. The lad whistled anxiously a bit of a tune as he went, all the time keeping wary eyes and ears strained for the first glimpse or sound of the expected gift.

"I wondher what it'll be like," he said to himself over and over again.

He had reached the tall hedge of Hagan's meadow and was already laughing and chuckling to himself over a sudden remembrance of Lord Killgobbin's butler roaring in the corner, when suddenly, something happened which brought him to a dead stop in the road.

Swift as lightning there darted through the lad's jaw a pain like the twang of a fiddle-string. At first Darby couldn't understand the agony, for never until that unhappy hour had one of the O'Gills been afflicted with the toothache. However, he was not left long in doubt as to its character, for the next twang brought him up to his tiptoes with both hands grasping the side of his face.

"Oh-h murdher in Irish, what's come over me! Be the powers of Moll Hagan's cat, 't is the toothache." He danced round and round in his tracks, groan following groan; but whichever way he turned there was neither pity nor comfort in the dark sighing hedges, nor in the gloomy, starless canopy.

Then a fiercer twang than all the others put together took the lad up into the air. Faster and faster they came, throb, throb, throb, like the blows of a hammer.

At last the poor man broke into a run as if to escape from the terrible pain, but as fast as he went the throb in his jaw kept time and tune to his flying feet.

"Oh, am n't I the foolish man to be gallivantin' around this blessed night pryin' into other people's business. It's a punishment. I wish I had that rapscallion of a King here now." He moaned as he reached the stile leading into his own field.

"That wish is granted at any rate, Darby asthore! What's your hurry?"

There on the top of the stile, quizzical, cheery and expectant, waited the little fairy.

"Ow—um! Is this pain in the tooth the bliggard present you promised me, Brian Connors?"

"It is. I came to the conclusion that you wor actually blue-molded for want of a little rale throuble, so I gave it to ye. Ye naded a joult or two to make ye appreciate how well off ye wor before."

Friend or no friend, if Brian Connors had been a mortal man instead of the King of all the fairies in Ireland, there would have flared a ruction out in the night covered road that both of them afterwards could not well forget. But what good to lift hand or foot to one who could paralyze them both with a flash of a wish. All the bothered man could do was to hold his cheek in both hands and grumble.

"Well, small thanks to ye for your present, King. If a man nades throuble he don't have to go thrampin' around all night lookin' for it with the loikes of you."

"Tonight ye wanted for a Christmas present three handfuls of ould ashes; before an hour is over you'll rayelize that no lord in Ireland ground got a finer Christmas present. You are like all the rest of the worruld, Darby O'Gill. You never appreciate what you have till you lose it. A man spinds his happiest days, grunting and groaning, but tin years afther they're over an' gone, he says to himself, 'Oh, wer'n't thim the happy, happy times?' If I take away the toothache will ye be raisonably happy, Darby? I dunno."

The persecuted man's spirit rose in unreasoning rebellion. "No, I won't," he shouted.

"Thin kape it. Please yerself. Good-night." And the place where the friendly little King had been sitting was empty. He had vanished utterly.

"Come back, come back, King!" howled Darby. "I was a fool. Ouch! Oh, the top of me head went that time. If you'll only take away this murdherin' pain, King, I'll be the happiest man in Ireland ground, so I will."

The appeal was no sooner uttered than the pain left him, and a soft, friendly laugh floated down through the darkness.

"You'll find the jug of potteen snug be the dure, avick, and all the happiness any mortal man's entitled to waiting for ye beyant the thrashol'—an' that's nothing more nor less than peace and plenty, and a warm-hearted, clear-headed woman for a wife and eight of the purtiest childher in the country of Tipperary. Go in to thim. Don't be fretting yourself any more over aymayaginary throubles; for as sure as ye do, the toothache 'll take a hammer or two at your gooms just to kape ye swate-minded an' cheerful. The complyments of the sayson to you an' yours. I'm off."

The King's voice, lifted in a song, floated farther and farther away:

> "If you've mate whin you're hungry,
> And dhrink whin you're dhry,
> Not too young whin you're married,
> Nor too ould whin you die—
> Thin go happy, go lucky;
> Go lucky, go happy;
> Poor happy go lucky,
> Good-bye, good-bye,
> Bould happy go lucky
> Good-bye."

The song died away like a sigh of the wind in the hedges. Then clear and sweet broke the chapel bell across the listening field, calling the parish, young and old, to midnight Mass. As Darby turned he saw every window in his cottage ablaze with cheerful light, and his own face glowed in warm response. With his hand on the door he paused and murmured:

"Why thin, afther this night I'll always say that the man who can't find happiness in his own home naden't look for it elsewhere."

The Haunted Bell

Part One

I suppose, your honor, like all the rest of the world, has heard of the terrible night of the Big Wind, but I have my doubt whether your honor ever has been tould how that unnatural storm arose from a certain wild thransaction betwixt Beelzebub and a gran'father of me own. The fact is that Sattin on that memorable night, in rage and turpitation ag'in me laynial ansister let loose the iliments of rain and wind and thunder in a furious endayvor to disthroy the whole Irish nation.

Faith so it was, and it's meself that'll be proud to relate the sarcumstances as we dhrive along.

Me gran'father, Jerry Murtaugh—the heavens be his bed!—was a carman be thrade, an' barrin' one unsignificant fault, was as good a man as ever put feet into brogues. An' that same failing was no more nor less than a daycided parshality for a game of cyards; he'd gamble the coat off his back and—this is a part of me story—he's done it.

'T was seldom that me gran'father ever lost a game, d'ye mind, for he and his thrusted comrade, Tim Maylowney, had betwixt themselves such a system of saycret signs and signals and tokens for playin' that the crook of a finger, the lift of an eyebrow, or the twist of a lip had each its well-known maning; and then again the pair had such gr-reat skill in mixing and shufflin' the cyards that a sthranger stood as little chanst ag'in the two as if he had been born blind. Howandever, me gran'father bein' a just man med it a sthrict rule never to play for more than sixpence a game. He had a pious feeling that to chate for more than sixpence a game wouldn't be honest.

You'll agree that there was a taste of excuse for this great fondness for cyards, bekase a carter's trade takes him into all kinds of distant places an' laves him many a lonely night to while away. Me gran'father often druve as far as the Killinturf hills and, in thim days, the same hills were a good fufty miles from the Sleive-na-mon Mountains. So ye see be this what a great thraveler the poor man had to be.

But, notwithstandin' his daily timptaytions, me gran'father had vartues too many to count. He could lift with his bare hands a load that it'd take two common men to budge; he could run like a hare and lep like a deer; no one ever saw the sign of dhrink on him even after he had put down a gallon; while as for fightin'—well, there was only one other man in the barony who could stan' ferninst him—his buzzum friend, Tim Maylowney.

Indade, I think there was only one mortil man on airth me gran'father was afeard of, an' that same one was me gran'mother—an' she no bigger than a wisp of hay, as the sayin' is.

Now this same Tim Maylowney bein' likewise a carter, he an' me gran'father always sthrove to manage to take their thrips together. This sometimes med it mighty inconvanient for the parish, bekase, such prime favorites were the two at home in Ballinderg that a neighbor'd be very loathe to give his job of carryin' to one carman lest be so doin' he'd be dayprivin' the other. So, for that rayson, whin the bell for the chapel was to be carted from Carrickthor to Ballinderg, ye may well aymagin how sore vexed an' perplexed was the whole parish to daycide whether Tim Maylowney or me gran'father was to have the honor of the job.

The way Ballinderg came to have a bell at all at all was this a-way:

Father Murphy of the rich parish of Carrickthor had a beautiful thraymendous new bell given to him by Lord Killinerg; so what did Father Murphy do but do-nate his ould bell—an' a grand one it was—to his friend Father O'Leary of Ballinderg. (The two clargymen long ago were collations together at the same college in France.)

But whin they came to take the dayminsions of the bell it was found to be too large for the chapel tower. Howandever, that throuble didn' last long, for the parish came together, and soon raised the belfry tower close beside the chapel itself.

Now, of course, aich of our two cronies wanted for himself the honor of carting the bell from Carrickthor. An' the only pay he'd ax or expect for carrin' the bell would be the credit it 'ud bring to himself and family and their generations afther thim til' the day of judgment. Some of the parish sided with me gran'father, others with Tim Maylowney, an' Father O'Leary was fairly at his wits' end to know which side to take. So what does the good man do but call a meetin' at the chapel steps for Sunday afthernoon that he might put the question to a vote—in that way the raysponsibility'd be on the congregaytion, d'ye see?

Howandever, whin the time for the meetin' was come, an' all the people, men, women and children were gathered in the churchyard, me gran'father, with that wisdom which the rayputable people say has always run in our family, walked firmly up the chapel steps and stood just below the clargyman, where afther waivin' his hand for attintion, he cried: "Let the bell be put on Tim Maylowney's cart," he says, "an' let me own two foine ponies, Anthony an' Clayopathra, dhraw the cart," sez he, "that'll make things ayquil, an' there will be no ha-ard feelin's." Ah, then wasn't he the saygacious man!

I needn't tell you that thim pathriotic worruds sint the multitude dancin' wild with dayloight and admayration. I'm tould that the cheerin' was heard be Father Nale himself in Ballinthubber. Through all the hurrayin' an' hurrooin' me gran'father, solemn an' proud, stood planted on the steps, his arms folded, lookin' for all the worruld like the ould ancient hayro, Hayjax, dayfin' the weather.

As Father O'Leary stood waitin' for the cheerin' to stop, it was aisy to see that a funny joke was stirrin' in the good man's mind; for he kept chucklin' to himself an' half explodin' with laughter; he couldn't spake a worrud durin' a full minute, but waited with his hand pressed ag'in his mouth keepin' back the marriment.

Even the little childher knew be this sign that a raymarkable joke was to the fore; an' half the parish was in roars at the fun they knew was comin' before the good man opened his lips.

"Me childher," says he, ketching his breath, "these two good neighbors, Jerry Murtaugh an' Tim Maylowney, are going two long days' journey to Carrickthor for us, an' two hard days' journey back ag'in expectin' no more pay than my blessing an' your thanks."

"They are! they are!" roared the parish, splittin' with laughter, poking aich other in the ribs and welting one another on the back. The women were stuffin' their shawls in their mouths.

"But they're far mistaken," the priest wint on.

"They are! they are!" ag'in shouted the whole church yard.

"We can't give them money," says his riverence, "but we'll pay them with something else which no fire can burn, no thafe can steal, an' no wather can drown, so long as the bell hangs in that tower," and for a minute he stood pinting at the tower, while, as you may well aymagine, the crowd was swaying an' surgin' with excited merriment.

"He's goin' to give them the bell itself," shouted long Pether McCarthy.

"He is! he is!" roared every one else.

"No, no, no!" warned his riverence. "Nothin' of the kind," says he. "We'll give thim for their pay—we'll give thim," says he, lookin' rougish at me gran'father— "the music of the bell."

For five wild minutes one couldn't have heard the bell itself above the jolly uproar over this good joke. Everyone was screeching and screamin' except me gran'father, who loike all great thravelers, was not much given to fryvolity. He stood one leg in front of the other, his arms still folded and not a sound out of his two pressed lips.

So in this way the matther was daycided, and then and there settled. Tim Maylowney would donate the cart and me gran'father was to give his ponies to dhraw it home.

But, ochone mavrone, if the parish had rayalized what fright and disthress was to folly in the wake of that same funny joke, 'twould have been terrified faces instead of merry ones they'd have brought home with them on that ayventful night.

However, no one foresaw the unlucky fuchure, so bright an' airly the next mornin' our two carters, sittin' side be side, in Tim Maylowney's cart, proud as two blue and yellow spotted paycocks, started for Carrickthor with Anthony and Clayopathra to the fore.

Part Two

Well, sorra thing worth mentionin' happened till the expaydition arrived at Father Murphy's house, an' there, afther much histin' and pullin' an' gruntin' and shoutin' the bell was lifted onto the cart and fastened in. The next mornin' at cock crow, with the wind to their backs, the proud beneyfactors started home.

The first days journey back passed aisy an' peaceful enough, only it was harrud work on the two hayros to be ridin' along side by side pious and saydate, mindin' their tongues for fear of sayin' wan unrayligious worrud with the chapel bell listining in the cart behind.

But black and airly their troubles began the last day of the journey. They were about an hour on the road an' had raiched Kelly's bog—me gran'father was dhrivin'—whin the left front wheel dhropped intil a rut and before one could say "Jack Robinson" me gran'father was trun off his seat and landed on his head in the ditch with Maylowney scrambling on top of him. But worse luck of all, the axle was broke, and our two pious min near suffocayted with anger.

"If the bell behind wasn't a chapel bell," says Tim Maylowney "I'd dayscribe ye in a worrud now that'd do me a power of good to mention," he says.

"Why don't ye say it to yer rotten ould cart?" roared me gran'father, comin' muddy up out of the ditch.

Tim flared up imayget at this belittling of his share of the honor. "No!" he says, "but I'll say it to the wooden-headed omadhaun with the thick fingers who was dhrivin' the cart," says he. "Or maybe I'd say it to Anthony an' Clayopathra, yer pair of common nanny goats that's pullin' the cart," says he.

"You know well, Tim Maylowney, I'm in a state of sinless grace bekase of hauling the bell," says me gran'father, thremblin' all over with rage. "But I hope I'll not be tomorrow," says he, "and thin I'll make surgent's worruk of ye, you slandherin' blaggard ye," says he.

For a minute the two stood barking at each other and there's no knowin' how the argyment would have inded if Danny O'Brien's empty cart hadn't druve up at the moment. Danny gingerously offered to bring help from the nearest smithy, and bring it he soon did. But do their best endayvor there wor four hours' delay before the cordage again got on its creaking way.

Aggrwaytin' as was this mishap, sure it was nothin' but a necessary pruperation for the rale misfortin' which was yet in store. And the place set for that misfortin' was no less a place than Paddy Carroll's public house, two miles this side of the village of Killgillam, an' tin dark lonesome miles from their own waiting Ballinderg.

The clouds had been gathering dark and threatening all afthernoon, and the night swept up with a rush and a roar. Afther only tin minutes of warning twilight the world grew black as yer hat. The stumbling horses could barely kape the road. And thin while the wind was whistling a doleful chune through the hedges, flash—a blaze of lightning flung high the hills. The two hayroes braced thimselves for the stunning thunder crash, and well they did for whin the clap came it almost bate them flat. Imaagetely afther there crashed and roared just wolley afther wolley of deafening thunder, and thin the rain, the smothering rain—Noah himself would have been dhrownded be it.

What would have become of the parsecuted beneyfacthors I don't know, only that a bend in the road brought them the first sign of cheer. Just ahead through the slantin' rain shivered low near the ground the one gleamin' yellow eye of Paddy Carroll's inn. Whin the cart jolted into the tavern yard, Phil O'Conner, Paddy Carroll's red-headed hostler boy, answering Maylowney's doleful call, led the dhraggled ponies back to the mangers, while our two disappinted hayroes, dhrenched and shiverin,' hurried into the tavern kitchen. As luck would have it the corned beef was still smokin' hot on the table and the beautiful perfume of the biled cabbage filled all the house. Tin minutes afther there wasn't a smudgin' of corned beef left in Carroll's tavern and only a fist-full of hued cabbage was for shame sake left floating in the pot. Just afther they were standin' in front of the fire shakin' the water from themselves like two dhrowned huntin' dogs and the rain was dashing furrous at the black windows, and Paddy Carroll at the bar was mixin' stiff noggins of hot Scotch, whin there broke so blindin' a flash of lightening that it med everything in the room dance green before their eyes, and in its wavering glare they saw a great black coach dash past the windy. And, be the powers, on that same instant the door swung open and if a tall dark sthranger dhressed like a lord didn' stand bowin' an' scrapin' on the thrashold.

So surprised and systounded was everybody that not a worrud was spoken until the sthranger, walkin' over and puttin' his back comfortable to the fire, says aisy and cajolin': "Landlord," he says, "I'm both wet and dhry; put some more turf on the fire to dhry me wetness, and give me a glass of your best to wet me dhryness—an' while yer about it, brew for this brace of foine scoundhrels here their heart's daysire."

While the three thravelers were sippin' their dhrink, friendly as yer plaze, an' Tim Maylowney was relaytin' the throuble they'd had with the bell, the red-headed hostler boy stuck a frightened face inside the door, an' callin' Paddy Carroll over, whispered: "The coach an' horsed must have sunk intil the ground. I can't find hide nor hair of thim!" he says, every flamin' hair brustlin'.

Without lookin' round the sthranger spoke up. "Never mind thim," he says, "I sint them on a message to the village. They'll be back for me. Glasses round, landlord, and bring us a pack of cyards. I'll play yez for another round of dhrinks, juntlemen, that is, if yez understand how to play cyards," he says polite.

Paddy Carroll came near smotherin' with laughter.

Although me gran'father wondered over this well-dressed condaysintion, he never blinked an eye but keepin' a savare suppressing frown upon the grinning hostler boy, Phil, who was juggling a round table and three chairs into place, he sez: "It's seldom I touch the cyards, sir, and never with a sthranger. I'm that narvous of bein' chated," says he; "still, as be the looks of the weather we have a heavy hour upon our hands, and as your honor seems so rayspectable a man, I'm willin' to take the chanct fer oncet."

Sure he hadn't the worruds half out of his mouth whin the shameless Tim Maylowney was already in a chair fumblin' careful and affectionate at a pack of cyards, as handy at floppin' them together as if he never had done any other sort of work in his life.

Me gran'father with a rayluctant but raysigned air, sat down to the table; but no sooner had he touched the chair than he was half up to his feet again, for, never since the worruld was creayted had been seen such a pair of ears as those which brustled on the head of the sthranger. Although they had no hair on thim, d'ye mind, they were long and narrow and thrimmed up to a point and stood out like a bull terrier's.

"Dale the cyards," says the juntleman, greatly annoyed at me gran'father's spachless onpoliteness, "I'm a Boolgarian Jook," he says, "an' where I come from all my countrymen have ears like thim." Me gran'father sat down aisy again but do his best endavors, he couldn't keep his eyes from starring at that puzzling pair of Boolgarian ears.

Fair and aisy Maylowney dealt. The little cyards from the top of the pack fell to the sthranger, an' wondherful to raylate, all the big cyards, which some way happened to be on the bottom of the pack fell to himself an' to me gran'father. I needn't tell ye that the first game was over in a jiffy, an' that the dark man lost.

Me gran'father laned over an' said in a sootherin' way: "Ye had the divil's own luck that time, sir."

"I had," says the Jook. Wid that for no rayson at all, he trew back his head and let a screech of laugh out of him that rattled the windys.

The punch was handed round steaming hot.

"Have ye a toast?" says the Jook.

"I have," says Maylowney, liftin' his glass. "Here's that we may all be in heaven tunty-four hours before the divil knows we're dead."

"I'll not dhrink it," says the dark man, frowning and layin' down his noggin.

"Whist! Tim, maybe the juntleman has a betther one," me gran'father says, cajolin'.

"I have," says the sthranger. "Such good company as this should have a friendlier toast. Here's that we three may soon meet again for better and longer closer acquaintance."

Many an' many's the time aftherwards both me gran'father an' Tim Malowney would wake up in the night and fair shake the bed with their thremblin' at the raymembrance of how careless an' free they swallyed down that toast. The two carters cooled their bowls but hot as it was the Jook threw his own down at one swolly and roared for another noggin.

To make a long story short, the second game was over as quick as the first, an' the third game was like it, but as the Jook was picking from a fistful of silver the pay for the third round of dhrinks, he seemed to be very much vexed at his misfortune.

"Here," says he, in a blusterin' voice, shakin' the handful of money undher the nose of both of them, "play me for this! I dare yez!"

For a moment you could have heard a pin dhrop. Knowing well what was in store for the sthranger, Paddy Carroll, turned his back on the room quick, purtindin' to wind the clock, an' Phil O'Conner, whustling, wint over an' begun polishing the pwether as hard as he could; but all the time aich of the two kept one merry eye over his showldher.

Me gran'father was sarchin' careful through a handful of shillin's an' pennies an' brass buckles an' horseshoe nails for a sixpence, and had just picked one out, when happening to look up he caught the scornful eye an' dishdainful smile of the dark sthranger fixed on the sixpence in his fingers.

The most raynouned thing always about the Murtaugh family has been their pride, and that same scornful smile lashed me gran'father like the cut of a whip. His face blazed red with raysentment and without a worrud he planked down in the center of the table buckles, nails, money an' all—a matther of eight shillin's and threepince ha'penny.

Tim Maylowney scraped anxious every pocket, but, sarch as he would, all he could find was five shillin's; he flung them to the table with the air of a lord.

"I'll put all this ag'inst the two of ye," the dark juntleman says, careless houlding up a fistful; "I haven't time to count it," says he, lettin' a silver rain of shillin's an' sispences slither through his fingers, until it hid and covered the threasure of the two carmen, nails, brass buckles an' all. There must surely have been at laste four poun' tin in the pile. Paddy Carroll let fall the key of the clock and Phil O'Connor for want of breath stopped whustlin'. So much money had never been bet on a game of cyards before in that tavern.

Well, me gran'father, his heart in his eyes, was watchin' Tim Maylowney fumblin' and fixin' careful the cyards (for it was Tim's dale oncet more), and the juntleman with eyes shut was lighting his poipe with a sthraw, careless an' slow and paying not a bit of attention to the game, whin me gran'father's conscience plucked him by the sleeve, and it whispered, "Ye're playin' for more than six-pence, and ye're chatin," says it.

Me gran'father turned fierce on his conscience and he says to it, "Blur an' ages! I'm not chaytin! Isn't it Tim Maylowney that's daleing the cyards! Lave me alone! Are ye my conscience or are ye Mr. Tim Maylowney's? That's what I'd like to know." Without another worrud he took up the cyards which had just been dealt to him, an' rai-sin' his right elbow as high as his showlder (a habit he had while runnin' the cyards over betwixt his forefingers and his thumbs), whin sudden every dhrop of blood in his body rushed up to his head, for tare and 'ounds, there wasn't in his hand a single cyard higher nor the noine spot of clubs and—hearts were thrumps, and Tim him-self, the artfulest dealer in Tipperary had dealt them to him.

He flashed a surprised and indignant glare over at Tim Malowney. But Tim sat looking at his own hand, with jaws dhroppin' and eyes bulgin', starin' as though he were looking at a ghost.

A sickening fear pressed down on me gran'father, and he spread two fingers on the ind of his chin, which was a signal to Tim: "What is the highest cyard in yer hand?" and Tim, with the bewildered face of a man who had been trun from his horse an' is just pickin' himself up off the ground, crooked the third finger of his left hand, and that signal meant: "The highest cyard in me hand is the noine spot of spades."

But lo and behold! the sthrange jook smiling and ca'm led out with the ace of hearts and follyed it with the quane; an' he lathered me gran'father's noine spot of clubs with the knave, an' he murdhered Tim Malowney' noine of spades with the ten of thrumps. It wasn't a game at all— it was cowldblooded murderous robbery, that's what it was.

An' while the juntleman was pullin' over the pile of silver me gran'father, slow an' careful, raiched undher the table with his foot and med such a savage kick at Maylowney's shins that, if Tim hadn't guv a quick hist to his two legs, faith an' there was one carter who would have wint on crutches for the rest of his life. Before me gran'father could thry it ag'in the sthranger spoke up jolly an' cajolin': "Oh, well, what's a few shillin's that I should beggar the loikes of you for the loikes of thim! Now listen! I'll give yez yer revenge. I'll put up every penny I've won from ye ag'inst—let's see—what have yez? Oh yes," he concluded, "ag'inst the hats on yer heads. Come, be quick, shuffle the cyards!"

It's no lie I'm tellin' ye! The sthranger won the hats on their heads; an' afther that, without losing a game, the jackets on their backs, their weskits, the brogues on their feet, and every stitch the two could afford to lose an' still go dacint.

And when the pair had put the clothes they had lost in a damp pile on the floor beside the sthranger and were sittin' miserable and shamefaced as a couple of plucked geese, aich in only his undershirt and a pair of knee breeches without stockings or brogues, what does the juntleman do but roar out laughing. "Ho! ho! ho! but yer a foine lookin' pair," he screamed, and the rafters shook. "Haven't yez anything else?" says he. But the carters shook their dhroopin' heads.

"Think now," cries the jook, "haven't yez any debts comin' to you? What do ye get for cartin' the bell outside?"

Me gran'father and Tim Maylowney exchanged one quick glance.

"Never mind what it is," says the sthranger ginerously. "Be me sowl, I'll put everything I've won against yer wages for cartin' that bell."

In spite of his crushing misfortin' a grin spread over me gran'father's woebegone face, and without another worrud the three hammered at it again, an' in less than a minute by the clock the last game was played and the sthranger had won. The last cyard was barely on the table when the jook rose, lookin' very tall an' grand, and he says: "I'll not take yer clothes, though they're mine be right, nor yet yer money, but the music of the bell." (Now mind, no one had mintioned that to him, however he knew.) "The music of the bell," he says, "is mine and that I'll keep."

As he spoke there came the swirl and dash of horses in the road outside, and the great shining lamps of the same coach flared past the windys. With his hand on the latch, the jook turned about. "I'll see you all ag'in some time," he says, "and whin that day comes"—he guv a most ojus smile— "be the powers we'll have great goin's on together."

With that—an' it's the thruth I'm tellin' ye—he disappeared through the door without opening it at all, and an unconthrollable shiver an' shudder doubled up everyone

in the room, for by that wondherful disappearance it was
aisy known who they had been daleing with.

The rain was over an' the moon had come out in the
sky, an' nothing was left for me gran'father an' Tim but to
hitch up Anthony an' Clayopathra an' purceed on their
lonesome heavy journey back home.

I'll have yez to aymagine their turror an' disthress. It
was three o'clock in the mornin' whin they druve undher
the belfry at Ballinderg. Leaving the car with the bell still
on it undher the belfry, me gran'father led his tired ponies
home. An' it was the sore an' sorrowful luck they brought
to Ballinderg. It's little ayther of the two benefactors slept
that night.

Part Three

Well, anyway it happened, the next day in the
afthernoon was no less a day than Saturday, an' the
counthryside gathered about the black, solemn-looking
bell where it lay in the cart. The big clapper was wrapped
thick in fold after fold of cloth for fear that by accident it
might give a sthroke or two, and Father O'Leary had
daycided that its first sound should call the people to
church Sunday morning.

Afther much histin' an' "hu'hing" an' "ho-ho-ing"—even
a long line of women an' little childher put their hands to
the ropes—the bell was lifted up to the crossbeam, where
Joey Hooligan, the smith, hammer in hand, sat straddling
the beam, ready to rivet the treasure to its place. And
whin Joey's last blow was sthruck an' the bell swung free
an' clear, a proud and joval shout roused the listening
fields. Be-gar, ye'd think some one had freed poor ould
Ireland!

"Me childher," says Father O'Leary, turning about an'
the glow of a dozen wax candles seemed to be shining

from the inside of his head through his face, "the wish that I have carried in me heart for thirty-one years is rayalized to-day. Ballinderg has a bell! And I appint Jerry Murtaugh and Tim Malowney to the honor of ringing the bell to call yez all to church tomorrow morning. For," says he with a sly smile, "since they own the music of the bell, by rights they should have its first bestowin'. Don't mind yer clocks, my childher, but start when ye hear the chime."

Everybody crowded round me gran'father an' Tim Maylowney slappin' thim on the back an' sthrivin' to shake their hands. The hayros tried to be cheerful, but in spite of all their strained laughin' an' cajolin' a heavy brooding fear kept scorching their hearts about the dark sthranger an' the music of the bell.

That night me gran'mother noticed her husband Jerry's throubled face at supper an' waited for him to explain. As he gave no worrud she misdoubted he'd lost his money gambling, so she waited till the childher were in bed, thin she says to him quite an' aisy: "Where's all yer money, Jerry, agra?" Me gran'mother was surprised an' a thrifle disappointed when the good man dhrew from his breeches pocket eleven shillings tinpence—not a shilling missing. Afther takin' every penny away from the parsecuted man, what did she do but whirl in to cross-question him like a Dublin lawyer. She accused him sarcastic of every crime on the calendar, in the hope that she'd at last hit on the right one. It's little he'd ever say to her in rayply but from the look on his face one might think he was under sentence for murder, and weather permittin' would be hung bright an' early in the mornin'.

Little sleep did me unfortunate gran'father get that night ayther. An' every time his eyes close, he was back on the instant in Paddy Carroll's public house. There was the dark sthranger again, but now, d'ye mind, covered with hair like a black goat, and he had a spiked tail on him as long as a carter's whip. The jook was always sitting at a table, shuffling a pack of cyards an' darin' me gran'father to play another game. For answer at last me gran'father was siddlin' over to give him a good belt, when some one grabbed hould of the poor man an' tould him to get up, it was time to be off to the chapel and ring the bell. "An' what's all this talk ye're havin' in yer sleep about Sattin, an' Paddy Carroll, an' the chapel bell?" axed me suspicious gran'mother.

Afther boultin' in spoonful of stirabout, me gran'father, with a face as long as your arrum, started off to the chapel an' the wrinkled, worried visage Tim Maylowney brought along with him when the two met at the crossroads didn't elevate me gran'father's feelings in the laste.

"You haven't a minute to lose," cried Father O'Leary from the chapel steps. His smile was like a May day. "Isn't it a beautiful morning?" he says, sthriving to be ca'm, "now to it, me lads, an' give us a ring that'll be heard over the mountain in Father Nale's parish."

Throwing down their hats, the two carters took a good clutch on the rope an' pulled with all their might. And now came the first sign of the dark sthranger's worruk. For though the great bell swung gaily enough to and fro, the sorra sound came out of it any more than if it wasn't there.

"Marcy on us, but that's quare," says Father O'Leary, coming forward. "Let me thry a hand with you."

An' thry he did. An' the three swayed an' swayed an' see-sawed up an' down till they were red in the face, but the glowering bell only rolled and swung above their heads, sullen and silent as one of the tombstones near by.

"Go into me stable and bring the ladder," panted Father O'Leary. "That rapscallion, Joey Hooligan, has done something amiss with the clapper. 'Tis his fault," says his riverence, mopping his forehead. Only too well the pair of carters guessed whose fault it was.

Well, the ladder was brought an' put ag'in the beam; and while me gran'father stidded it with both hands, Tim Maylowney mounted it to find out what was wrong. He'd climbed about half way up whin, crack, goes the ladder in two in the middle, an' down comes Tim on the top of me gran'father, an' the two went thumping to the ground.

"The divil's in it!" yelled me gran'father from somewhere undherneath Tim and the ladder, and at thim worruds— tis the truth I'm tellin' ye—the bell gave one loud jovial clang an' thin stopped short. As the two benefactors struggled to their feet you may well believe every hair on their heads stood up with fright like brustles on a brush.

"One of yez go for that bliggard Joey Hooligan," says his riverence; "and tell him to bring his tools an' a ladder. As it is we're tunty minutes late," says he, lookin' first rueful at his watch, thin at his broken ladder.

So off me gran'father hurries to the smith's house half a mile down the Kilcuney road, and as luck would have it—or maybe as Beelzebub had managed—Joey was away; he had gone over to doctor for a cracked heel, Cornaylia, Mrs. Regan's cow; an' she lived a half a mile across the fields.

In the meantime the whole parish of Ballinderg was sitting impatient within their doors wondhering what was keeping the bell.

A dozen of the neighbors had gathered around Mrs. Morrissey's clock to time the bell, bekase it was the most raynowned and rayputable clock in the whole parish.

Mrs. Morrissey was lookin' rayproachful at the clock, blamin' it for being fast, and the systounded clock was ticking as plain as plain could be: "Oh murdher! oh murdher! what's the matther with the infudels, why don' they go to church?" whin Tim Maylowney came galloping breathless and frightened to the door.

"Out, all of yez," cried he. "The bell's broke. Scatter among the neighbors and warn them off to church. Ye're half an hour late."

'Twas in this way the bell scored its first great victory; it made everybody in Ballinderg late for church that Sunday morning."

Part Four

You may be sure the neighbors needed no second warning. Scatter they did, an' pretty soon the whole parish came sthrealing along one afther the other like Darcy's cows. Winding up the hill they came to where poor Father O'Leary stood despairing undher the belfry.

"It's a punishment, me childher," he says piteous, fumbling with his withered hands. "Take warning! It's a punishment for me sin of pride and glorification over the grandeur of the things of this worruld. Oh, what'll we do at all at all!—Is that you, Joey Hooligan, you bliggard? What have ye done to the clapper of the bell? Ye've spiled it, that's what ye've done," he cried out to the smith, who was hurring up the road with me gran'father, an' they carryin' a ladder betwixt thim.

"I haven't spiled it," says Joey stoutly; "whin I fastened the bell up yesterday the tongue wagged back and forth as free an' ready as the tongue of"—he looked about for a comparison— "as the tongue of Mrs. Morrissey there. Stand aside an' let me put up the ladder till I have a look!" says he.

You may believe me or believe me not, an' wouldn't blame yez a thimbleful if you didn't—bekase foive hundred men, women and childher that day rayfused at first to believe their own ears—but it's the truth I'm tellin' ye. Joey Hooligan had no sooner put his foot on the first round of the ladder than the bell without a hand to the rope began—not ringing, mind you, but chiming. An' not exactly chimin' ayther, but playin' a chune to the open eyes an' gapin' mouths of Ballinderg.

It was the purtiest chune ever heard. Stirring an' sweet an' urgent. Some way it med one think of the beating of drums an' the clashing of swords, an' of sojers marching out to die.

"Oh," gasped Father O'Leary, "the Marshal Aise." He covered his eyes with his hands to shut out some vision, an' his face wint gray as the stones.

"The Marshal Aise! the Marshal Aise!" The word was picked up and tossed from one person to another to the furthest varge of the crowd. Sure wasn't that the identical song Father O'Leary heard in the sthreets of Paris whin he was a student there? They played it while they were massacreein' the 'ristocrats an' the clargy.

"Oh, God, have marcy on their sowls!" half whispered the good man. "I can see now the gentlest an' the bravest being dragged up to the headsman; an' two of the best an' the thruest friends I ever had smiled good-bye to me from the crowded tumbril!"

Overcome with the raycollection, the priest stopped a moment, and thin lifting to the sky his two hands, cried: "Oh, may the deep curse of Heaven"—he caught himself quick: "What am I sayin'? A minister of God! May God forgive them an' me too."

Lookin' wistful around he saw me gran'father's white scared face with the big dhrops of purspuration standin' on it.

"Don't be frightened, Jerry, agra," he says, thremblin'. "There's nothin' at all shupernatural about the bell. We live so far out of the worruld here that we know nothing of the wonderful invintions that are springing up among men like new grass in the meadow. I make no doubt this is one of thim; an' that there's some hidden conthrivance up above the clapper we haven't noticed, an' don't undherstand, that makes the bell ring so. I'll ask Father Murphy about it tomorrow. Oh, mush, mush, you rose-grown hedges an' vine-dhressed hills of France, how far away you've flown! God help us! Come in to yer prayers, good people," he says, broken, "come in to yer prayers!"

'Twas a sober an' a solemn crowd that afther church wandhered home in groups together debaytin' an' disputin' as they wint, for the mystification of the congregation led to thraymendous disputaytion.

But nayther me gran'father nor Tim Maylowney joined in the argyfyin' crowds, for well they knew that Sattin by

means of the bell, had timpted even Father O'Leary himself to the sin of hathred an' rayvenge. Off to thimselves
together the two slunk, like men who had committed a
saycret crime. When the pair were well out of hearing of
anyone else, me gran'father says, bitther: "Well, Maylowney, ye done it this time. What with yer love of the
cyards, and yer fondness for pickin' up with sthrangers
ye've been the complate ruinnaytion of my reputation and
the reputation of Ballinderg."

The tongue of Malowney was so hot with indignaytion
at the whole blame bein' trun on him this a-way that all
he could do was to sputther: "Why, thin, bad manners to
ye for a slandherous bosthoon! Weren't ye with yer winks
an' yer nods as deep in the mud as I was in the mire?"

"That's nayther here nor there," says me gran'father,
coolly waving him away. "Wasn't it you that first planked
yerself down at the table before I had a chanst to daycline
the jook's inwitation? An' isn't it you that is always a
timptation to play with. sthrangers, for if ye weren't along
how could I chate thim? It's you that knows well how aisy
led I am."

"But heigh-ho, cryin' over spilt milk'll do no good. We've
only now to save ourselves an' our repitaytions. Do you,
Tim me dacint lad, dhrive down at break of day to Paddy
Carroll's an' warn him not to breathe a blessed worrud of
what's happened. He's as bad off as we are. Wasn't it himself as had Beelzebub for a customer, an' wasn't it him as
let the pair of us he timpted?"

"I would go willingly," answered Tim, "for I make no
doubt the bell'll begin its depredaytions foine an' airly
Monday mornin', an' what we've just heard will be only a
flay-bite to what'll happen thin. But," he sez, rubbin' his
chin rueful, "you remimber me cousin, Nellie Grogan, is
to be married the morn, an' it's needful that all her
relaytions should be there to give her reyspict—she's had
such har-rd luck with her young men, poor girl. I needen't
tell you that when three years ago Ned Kerrigan

disappinted her and slipped off to be a sojer two days before the weddin'; 'twas a cruel blow enough, but whin
young McCarthy the year afther took the Quane's shillin'
within a week of their marriage, the poor lass almost lost
courage. Now, thin, thanks be, she's within a day of her
weddin' to Shamus McCormick, it will never be said that
I, the most rayspected of her relaytions, will rayfuse to
ornament the occasion. No, I couldn't think of it; besides,
Mrs. Maylowney 'ud be sure to prevent me from goin' away,
no matther how much I wanted to," he sighed.

So the long an' short of it was me gran'father consinted
to go to Paddy Carroll's, with the undhersthandin' that
Tim should be waitin' for him in Anthony and Clayopathra's stable in the evening to make known all that had
happened during the course of the day.

At that the two down-cast conspyrators separated aich
to put in the longest Sunday afthernoon of his life.

Every minute of the day his conscience was a burnin'
coal in me gran'father's chest, an' to add aggrawaytion
an' turpitation to his misery, the poor man couldn't cross
a foot or crook an elbow but he'd feel me gran'mother's
two suspicious eyes boring a hole in the middle of his
back.

Worse than all he dhreaded the night bekase of an
unforchunate habit he had of talkin' in his sleep, and well
he knew—for she'd often done it before—that me gran'-
mother would lay wide awake as an owl to catch every
whusper. Women haven't the laste taste of honor about
such things. But go to bed he did and at last into onaisy
slumber he fell, but not for long. When he caught me
gran'mother asleep and before the sun had a chanst to
shake his scarlet jacket above the hill, me gran'father with
Anthony an' Clayopathra wor well on their way toward
Paddy Carroll's public house.

Part Five

Tim Maylowney was right in his prophesying. Bright and early Monday morning the bell began its divilment, and of course, who should it commence on but Pether McCarthy, the most sinsitive man in the County Tipperary? So suspicious of intintions to insult him was Pether all his life, that one couldn't safely raymark the toime of day in his presence without danger of having the sayin' caught up as an underhanded reyflection on Pether himself or on some of his raylations.

But sure, nobody ever thought of insultin' the poor man, for the only thing that could be whispered against his char-ak-ther was a rumor that an uncle of his father's down in the County Cork—the McCarthy's were all ab-originally Corkonians—was thransported to Van Di'man's Land for stayling sheep.

So now in the early mornin' as the honest man started for his worruk in the fields, the black wuzzard up in the belfry tower spies him, an' what does the ould targer do but sthrike up playin' an ancient well-known chune called "The Sheep-Stayler's Lament."

Well, at the sound poor Pether stood pathrayfied in his thracks. Could it be that Father O'Leary himself was makin' game of him? He gave one wild, horrified look at the belfry up on the hill, hesitated an instant, thin turned ag'in an' hurried back to his house. The unmannerly rap-scallion of a bell kept time to his steps with the beat of the chune, an' never let up till the door closed behind Pether—when it stopped suddint! McCarthy waited a little, thin cautiously opened the door, but no sooner had he stuck out his head than the maylodious sthrains of "The Sheep-Stayler's Lament" was heard in every field and cot-tage for two miles around. That squelched him. The poor lad ventured out no more till he spied from his windy some two hours afther, the wedding purcession of Nellie Grogan windin' up the hill to the chapel. Bad as was the thratemont Pether McCarthy rayceived, it was bread an' treacle to the outrageous welcome that awaited the poor bride.

At the head of the purcession be course walked Nellie and the groom, while close behind marched Tim Maylowney and his wife, Honoria. In spite of having to wear a neckerchief that was stranglin' him, Tim, the poor man, was thryin' to look happy an' unconsarned, though 'twas himself had the feeling that there was trouble enough an' to spare watching for thim all in the belfry on the top of the hill.

But if Tim was unsartin an' worried, not so with his cousin Nellie, the bride. She laned on the arm of Shamus an' smiled up at him proud an' happy as a June rose.

The neighbors stood in the doorways along the reoad waving good wishes at the happy pair, never so much as mentioning to each other the two miscrayants who had run away and left the disappinted bride behind them, all for no better rayson than for the bit of temper that was born in her.

Jokin' an' cavortin' an' with ribbons flyin', the happy party arrived at the foot of the hill lading up to the churchyard, and as they did, the runny-gate in the tower broke loose.

An' what chune of all paralyzin' chunes did the desparaydo sthrike up loud an' rollickin' but "The Girl I Left Behind Me!"

At first ye'd think a piece of the sky had fallen, so great was the sudden wondher. Howandever, no one sthopped, but they marched timidly on while the bell kept playing the insult gay an' cheerful, almost spakin' the worruds:

> "They dhressed me up in scarlet clothes,
>   They used me very ki-i-ndly,
> But I'll never forget the purty little girl,
>   The girl I left behi-i-nd me."

Maylowney stood it as long as he could, but at the churchyard gate he halted an' shook his fist at the bell. Whether 'twas bekase the party were enterin' the churchyard, or bekase of Tim's dayfiance will never be known, but, as Tim did so, the bell changed its chune into the mournfullest toll that ever was heard. Every toll'd raise the hair from yer head—'twas that fearsome.

Flesh and blood could stand no more. With wild shrieks and yells the purcession broke an' run for their lives. Shamus didn't run though hard he thried. Mrs. Maylowney, cool-headed woman that she was, had stepped up an' caught him by the arrum; an' while she grippin' him on one side an' Nellie on the other, what betther could he do but race up to the chapel and inside with thim? An' so the day was saved for Nellie.

Outrageous as was all this, sure it was only the beginning of the troubles for Ballinderg. The wuzzard insulted half the parish. He played "The Rogue's Mar-rch" for Wullum Duff, the schoolmaster, keepin' time to his steps whether fast or slow: "Rum-ti-tum-rum, Te tum rum-te-rumpty rum, Te-tum," an' whin at last Wullum, beside himself with mortification, broke into a mad run, it med no difference, the music kep' time with him just the same. The schaymer played "The Divil's Hornpipe" even for pious ould Mrs. Donovan as she limped slowly by on her cane, an' sthrive as she would an' thry as she could, she had to keep step to it.

The consthernaytion an' fear an' excitement that day were so great in Ballinderg that be foive o'clock in the afthernoon there wasn't a sowl to be seen abroad. Everybody was indoors listening to find out who'd be scandalized next, when sudden the bell sthruck up glorious an' beautiful: "Lo, the Conquering Hayro Comes."

On the minute every door and windy flashed open, so great was the curosity to know who it was that the ould targer, of a barbariyan would be showin' such honor and rayspect to. Me gran'mother stuck her head out with the rest, an' what should she see comin' bobbin' along the brow of the hill but Anthony an' Clayopathra, an' sittin' ca'm an' peaceful behind thim,—me gran'father!

Me gran'mother waited for no more, but throwing her shawl over her head, hurried off on her way to Mrs. Maylowney's for informaytion an' advice—there was always great sociology betwixt the two families—an' who should she meet up with in the lane hastenin' down to see her on the same errand but Mrs. Maylowney herself?

"It's comin' up to your own house I was, Honoria, to spake to ye about me husband, Jerry," sez me gran'mother, afther the time o' day was passed betwixt thim, "an' to ink-wire whether yez have obsarved anything out of the common about yer own honest man Tim, I dunno."

Mrs. Maylowney trew back her head, an' liftin' her two hands guve the air a hard push.

"Arrah, thin, don't be talkin'," sez she, "wasn't I on me way to ax the same question of yerself? Isn't me heart broke worryin' over him, an' ain't me two eyes almost fallin' out of me head from watchin' him? And as for scoldin' and beratin' him, I get no comfort out of it at all, at all, for he won' answer back and I have a fear on me that I can't express, that Sattin himself is in the bell above an' that our brace of foine husbands have more than a little to do with it." Me gran'mother hilt her apron to her mouth an' shook her head despairing: "Oh, oh, sorra's the day! what'll we do at all, at all?"

Now that was a foolish question entirely, for what did anyone do for miles around who had a fear or a heartache or any sort of throuble but bring that sorrow up to Father O'Leary; an' there be the same token did the two good women take thimsilves, though sore ashamed they were to turn informers that a-way ag'in their own husbands.

Manewhile, Tim, as good as his worrud, was scrooged waiting in the stable ag'in me gran'father's return; an' whin at last the ponies had been fed an' dhressed down, with dhry lips Tim towld me quakin' ansisther, faithful an' complate, all the outrageous doin's of that raymarkable day, an' sittin' down on the tub beside me gran'father, his chin in his hands, he wound up his conversation be sayin': "Oh, begora, this'll be a lesson to me the remaynder of me days. I'll never touch another dhrop of dhrink ag'in so long as I live, an' I'll never look at another cyard till the day of me death, an' as for bad company"—he groaned, clinchin' his two fists.

"As for bad company," me gran'father says, thinkin' gloomy an raysentful of Sattin, "I'll never meet—Oh, be the powers!" he says, jumpin' up, "is it me ye're callin' the bad company, Tim Maylowney?"

What answer Tim would have med will never be known, for at the instant a shadow darkened the stable door, an' lookin' up, who should they spy standin' solemn an' savare before thim but Father O'Leary himself? The pair thried to splutther a civil greeting, but for rayply his riverence crooked a finger, first at me gran'father, thin at Tim Maylowney, beckonin' thim to folly. An' the two culprits, like retrievers at heel, follyed the clargyman up to his house. Only oncet on that doleful journey did me gran'father spake an' thin it was to whusper a warnin' to his comerad: "Whatever he does till yez, kape yer tongue in her head."

"No fear," whuspered Tim, an' his voice was as hoarse as the say.

Whin they arrived at the priest's house, the first thing Father O'Leary did was to put me gran'father into the study, turn the kay in the door, an' thin, takin' Tim be the showlder, he led the unfortunate man into a room across the hall.

The clargyman pushed Tim into a chair, an' sitting himself in another close ferninst, with hands on knees, Father O'Leary fixed an eye on Tim that dug to the very bottom of the squarmin' wictim's over-flowin' sowl.

For foive long minutes not a sound was heard except the craklin' of the twigs on the hearth.

Tim, perched on the edge of his chair, wondhered if this was going to last forever. He twisted his cap round and round in his finger, coughed polite into it, and looked out the windy; he put the cap on his head, quick snatched it off ag'in and dhropped it on the floor; stared despairin' at the pictur of Dan'l O'Connell over the mantel, and wished that he had the courage of that great man, but all the time feelin' himself skewered be Father O'Leary's raylentless eye. Whin there was no more strength or courage left in his body than there is in a suckin' pig, he says in a wake voice: "It's gettin' dark, an' it's goin' to rain, I think I'll be goin' home."

Father O'Leary nodded stern an a-cusing, lanin' back in his chair, spoke slow and pinted: "I heard yer whuspered promise to that bliggard Jerry Murtaugh, as we came along, an' I'll not ask ye to break it; but tell me one thing only," says he, "was it your fault or was it his?"

"It was Jerry's fault, yer riverence," says Tim, givin' a great gulp of raylief at gettin' out of it so aisy. "Sure, your riverence knows well that I—"

"That's enough," says Father O'Leary, rising: "do you stay in that chair an' never lave this room till I call you."

You may aymagine the condition of me gran'father sittin' alone in the study during all this while, sore disthracted to know what was goin' on in the room across the hall. He strained his ear to listen, but divil a sound could be heard, and he'd half med up his mind that his comerad Tim must be sthrangled dead whin the door opens and Father O'Leary pops in on him. "Jerry Murtaugh," says the priest, lookin' sore put out, "it's surprised an' scandalized at ye I am! To think of me blamin' the poor lad across the hall whin all the while 'twas your fault."

"My fault!" yelled me gran'father, jumpin' to his feet, "who said it was my fault?"

Father O'Leary nodded stern an a-cusing. "I've Tim Maylowney's word for it," he said, "what have you to say ag'in it?"

Me gran'father let such a roar out of him that Tim
Maylowney concludin' thin an' there that his comerad was
bein' kilt, lept out of the windy an' raced down the Kilcuney
road, an' never stopped till he raiched home.

"Did the slandherin' villain say the loikes of that?" says
me furious ansisther. "Now listen to my side of the story
and I'll have ye to judge."

An' what does me gran'father do but up an' tell the
whole thransaction from beginning to end, just as it happened.

As Father O'Leary listhened he passed from onbelief to
inkerdulity, from inkerdulity to wondher, an' from wondher
to conwiction, an' thin he put three pinances for their terrible sins on Tim Maylowney an' me gran'father. An' these
punishments wor to last them for the rest of their natural
lives. The first pinance was to give up cyard playin'
complate an' intirely; the next was that they should taste
no sthrong dhrink save and except one noggin of punch
to be dhrunk on Saturday night, aich beside his own wife
an' ferninst his own fireside. These two were hard enough,
you'll agree, but the third and last was the killin' pinance
entirely, and it was no less than that they must save their
money and not to spend it foolish.

"Oh, thin, ye're the flinty-hearted man, Father O'Leary,"
cried me gran'father whin he heard the pinance. "Why don't
ye turn me into a chiney image at once and have done
with it? To think that I must suffer this away, an' the
black schoundhrel that is to blame for it is swingin' free
up in the tower, makin' game of us all."

"Ha!" says Father O'Leary with a wise nod, "lave him
to me! Tomorrow morning I'll fix that lad. I'll fasten him a
presner in the bell till the day of judgment, and every time
the bell rings the clapper'll pelt him betwixt the two
showlders. It's a sore back the schaymer'll have on the
last day, I'll warrant ye," chuckled his riverence.

Well, the worruds weren't well out of his mouth when
there came a crash of tunder an' a flare of lightening. Me

gran'father waited for no more. With a hurried "Good-
night, yer riverence!" he took the road in his hands. There
was barely time to raich his own good door whin the
memor-iable Big Wind began to blow.

Sure the worruld knows how it tore up threes be the
roots, whirled houses through the air, an' druv saygoin'
ships up on the Kerry shore, where it left them perched
up on the rocks like so many say-gulls.

You understand of course that all this was bekase
Beelzebub, furious with the disappintment at bein' driven
from the bell, was sthrivin' to daystroy the Irish Nation.
An' the fear of Father O'Leary's threat was on the vagobone
too, for next mornin' the bell was gone an' the neighbors
say how in the night inwisible hands must have carried it
through the air, an' thin dashed it down upon the great
flat rock in Hagan's meadow; for there it lay broken into a
thousand pieces, an' the stone itself was busted in two.

That was the last of Sattin and the bell.

But as for me gran'father an' Tim Maylowney, they kept
their pinance well. Howandever, they had made special,
d'ye mind, two pewther noggins which held a full quart
aich, and these the two hayros'd sit an' sip side be side
on Saturday nights. Many's the winther evening I've seen
them there, an' many's the toime I've heard them tell this
story beside that same fire.

The Sheep Stealer

We have no raley criminal crimes now down in this part of Tipperary. We believe that locks on dures bring bad luck. There doesn't hang a lock on a dure in the townland of Ballenderg but one, and that an ould ancient padlock half the size of ones head with a rusty kay sticking out of it as thick as me finger, that lies in the clasp of the latch on the forge dure of Joey Hooligan, the smith. It hangs there yet as a wondher and as a curiosity.

If any art or object ever brought bad fortune to a man that same lock dhrew down ill luck in the Hooligan family, and at the same time spiled the repitation and siled the glory of the town of Ballenderg. Where he got it I don't rightly raymimber, but me mind some way misgives me that he took it for pay for shoeing a horse that was belonging to a thraveling tinker.

More than twunty years ago, the night of Christmas Eve itself above all nights in the year for such a unhappy thing that the crime was purpetrated, and if yer honor cares to listen, I'll till yez the story from beginning to ind, while the pony is dhragging us up this long hill ferninst us.

There's some do be saying to this day that the faeries wor mixed up in the thransaction, but as I'll aylucidate to yez now, the Good People had no more hand in that same crime than yerself or me-self or the pony there. It's many a charge of stealing cattle and butther and fowls is left to

the Good People, so that I believe hardly half I hear agin
them any more. Maybe as I grow old I'm getting shuperstitious. I don't believe half the ghost stories I hear these
days ayther.

Well, as I was saying: If a person steal a cow or a horse
or money or anything like that, the guilt and the disgrace
of it rests only on himself and his childher. Many a dacint
man has committed murdher. Mild as I look this minute,
taking all the length of me days together, I dare say I've
kilt in cowld blood no less than fifty people. I've kilt Jimmy
Carroll that keeps the public house in Carrickton not less
than tin times in the last two years for slighting the feed
in me horses manger and for putting rain water in me
own whiskey. Of course, it's only in me own mind I've kilt
them, but Father Cassidy says a sin of the intention is as
black as a sin of the hand and the only difference is that
in the one case the police aren't botherin' you. Well, to me
mind that makes a raymarkable dale of difference.

There was a great thraveler once tould me that in some
parts of England a man is counted great by the number of
sheep he has purloined, but in this counthry of Ireland to
steal a sheep is the most dayspicable, unforgivable crime
mentioned in the tin commandments. It lasts as a rayproach on his daycendents down to and including his
fourth cousins, and his ancestors must hang their heads
at the mention of his name back to the time of the flood.

If the ould saying stands thrue that the darkest hour
is just before the dawn, doesn't it as often come out that
the merriest, lightest-hearted minutes turn into the sudden forerunners of black misfortune?

Well anyway, that's how it came about that the merriest night in the lives of Joey Hooligan, the big giant smith,
and of his wife, Nancy, and of his eight purty childher
changed to a miserable and bitter memory on Christmas
morning twunty years ago.

That night the four rooms in the cottage glowed with
candles. Nancy had been moulding them in all sizes during

a month past. A big candle stood in every corner and one as tall as Nancy herself and as thick as yer wrist beckoned and laughed at every windy. A fire of sea coals in the big grate sent a thousand gleams cavorting and glinting to the dishes on the dhresser, to the shiny tin pans on the walls and intil the eyes and hearts of the childher as they romped and roared and galloped about the cottage.

Joey like all big strong men was slow of speech and solemn of mind. "Nancy," he whispered to his wife, "I'm so happy tonight I'm almost afeared."

The center of all the play and divorsion was Blackie, the pet lamb. Sure it's almost like one of the childher, the young baste carried on. They put a nightcap on the black head of him, and you could hear Joey himself roaring half a field away when Poudeen showed how much the lamb raysembled long-faced Julius Callaghan, and when they put a fur cap over the sheep's ears the childher rowled helpless on the floor laughing and shrieking at the way Blackie raysembled solemn-faced Maurteen Cavanaugh, the schoolmasther. Well, it was nothing but fun and noisy merriment for the childher and hugs and twistings and caresses for Blackie till Eileen, the youngest of the childher, worn out from very happiness dhropped asleep undher the table. That was a sign that the happy Christmas Eve was spent. Joey tied the cord about Blackie's neck.

The smithy fronting the road stands as ye may see half a stone's throw from the cottage, and it was in a box filled with sthraw hard by the forge fire that the little pet med his bed.

"Isn't Tim Malowney, the carman, coming to ye early in the morning for a shoe to go on the horse's foot?" asked Nancy.

"Bad manners to him, but he is! Christmas morning and all," answered the smith, stopping on the threshold. The lamb was frisking and bunting at Joey's knees in its hurry to be off to bed.

"Wait a bit!" called Nancy. "He'll be opening the forge
door in the morning before you're out, and that villain of
a sheep'll get away and keep us the whole day hunting
him, as he did last fortnight."

Joey nodded and stepped into the dark, but he called
back: "I'll twist the kay in the lock so Malowney can't be
opening it."

The sheep darted from the smith's hand into the shop
at the smithy door, and Joey stood for a minute to look at
the wondherful night. He was the kind of man who felt
things instead of thinking them. A sift of snow, dhry and
light as flour, had just begun to fluther down from a sky
that hung so low that one'd aymajine he could almost raise
up and touch it with a long stick. A pack of blaggard grey
clouds were hunting a frightened grey moon to its shelter
on the Slieve-na-mon mountains. Joey looked up and down
the clear road. Everything waited still as death, except
that far as sound could raich the dogs were barking. He
raymimbered afterwards how for a second the shadow of
a man seemed to stir just undher the big oak across the
way. Afar over the fields happy lights still twinkled in
neighbors' windows. When he looked back to the oak three
again no shadow stirred at all, so he blamed the ould age
in his eyes.

Then he turned to padlock the closed dure. But the
kay bekase of the rust wouldn't budge for all the famous
strength of the Hooligan fingers. For a full minute he
tugged and he twisted; he bit his lip and he braced his
heels, but bad manners to the creak the kay gave. "I must
get the wrench," he muttered. It was only till all the
strength of his great arm got on the wrench that the kay
turned and the dure locked. While he worked there crept a
queer uneasy feeling in his bones that some one very evil
or very miserable was watching him. He took the wrench
with him intil the kitchen for use on the morrow's morn.

It was a sthrange, wondherful thing for Joey Hooligan,
the smith, not to be able to sleep. He hadn't his like in

seven counties for snoring. Most times his thrumpeting
would be rattling the tin pans on the walls while Nancy
wouldn't have finished threatening the giggling childher
into quiet. But tonight of all nights for some hidden rayson
Joey couldn't shut an eye. Long afther the cottage was so
still that the click of the clock sounded daystinct as the
hit of a hammer, he rowled and he turned his head as hot
as a new baked loaf of bread.

Once he could have sworn that sly fingers thrifled with
the dure latch, but listening close the sound didn't come
again. The head of his bed lay right up against the windy
sill. At last, just as the worn out man was beginning to
doze something tapped softly on the windy pane above
his head. He lifted himself to his elbow and parted the
windy curtains. Nothing at all!

The full moon stopped in her flight shimmered down a
flood of sphlendor.

Already the snow had stopped filtering down. Only a
half inch or an inch or so had fallen, but it covered quiet
and sparkling the meadows, the glistening branches of
the trees and the far roofs of the neighbors' cottages. The
restfulness and the beauty stole soothering in on him, so
that he must have fallen asleep as he looked, for it seemed
to him only a few minutes afther that Nancy poked him in
the ribs and said:

"Get up, it's late. Tim Maylowney'll be at the door. Get
up till I fix the gifts and the breakfus' for the childher."

With no one on the outside to push it along, a new
idea thraveled a long hard journey before it was able to
get undher the thatch of Joey Hooligan's great tangle of
black hair. His long leather apron hung on a nail that was
in the wall just over Blackie's bed. The smith stood a
minute thumbing with his stiff apron strings, all the time
staring down at the empty sthraw, mind ye, and never till
he'd just turned to give a pump at the bellows did he hould
his hand to say:

"Tare an' ages, what's become of Blackie?"

Then for another few minutes he stood pumping the bellows and searching with puckered brows under the shelves and benches into the shadowy corners of the room. "Well, on my sowl I think the baste is gone!"

"Now that's quare," he says, "I shut the dure careful when I came in so he couldn't scoot past me. He couldn't melt away like a crock of butther, could he?"

At that in his heavy way the puzzled man began to rayson.

"I'd say maybe," he went on, "that he broke a pane of glass and jumped out the windy, but how could he since there never was a windy in the smithy from the hour me gran'father built it? Then how could be break a pane of glass in the windy if there wasn't any glass or any windy?"

He bent peering afther the curl of blue smoke that was darting up the wide chimney.

"If it was coming into the place Blackie was, I'd say it's down the chimney he might have lepped, even if he hed be smothered in the live coals that wor laying all night on the forge hearth. But as for climing up the chimney, I'd dayfy any baste in Ireland to do it. No it must be the dure. But who in Ireland's ground could have twisthed the kay in that dure!"

The new idea be this time had got well in its home behind Joey's puckered forehead.

"I'll have a look at the dure," he said "and the thracks in the new fallen snow'll till what way he wint."

Only an inch of snow lay on the ground. Except the marks of Joey's own brogues not a trace or a thrack of human or of baste showed in the soft white carpet. Hands locked behind and body bent, Joey was searching about outside the smithy, when his wife, Nancy, came too. One by one the childher came out and joined the search. Out in the high road not a wheel had passed during the night, nor lay there a footstep of man or baste or even of fowl.

Blackie had never come out of the forge on his four visible feet, nor had any flesh and bone feet carried him.

What had come to him? Of all the mysteries of the world, was there a bate of this one?

"Go into yer horseshoeing. Here comes Malowney. Say nothing—it's no use looking farther. Don't yer see who took him?" Nancy whispered, pulling at his sleeve.

But Joey, the smith, lifted his great fist to the sky and shook it at the clouds.

"Now may the curse"—he was beginning to say when his wise wife put her hands on his lips.

"Are ye mad, Joey Hooligan?" she warned. "Don't anger them. Don't ye know well that it's one of the childher itself they might be taking next for spite. They have the lamb—they're welcome. Maybe they have more nade for it than we. Good luck to them!"

My, but the Hooligans were sore-hearted!

For a good week the parish searched high an' low, but nayther hide nor hair of the baste was ever seen again. So complete, so suddint, an' so mystarious had been the taking that the wisest heads in the townland settled down to the unanswerable conclusion that no human thief at all had taken Blackie, but that the poor little crachure had been a-pro-pryayted be the Good People. Not that anyone was bould enough or foolish enough to say as much aloud. As everyone knows, if the fairies carry away a cow, or a pig, or say a couple of ducks, the laste said the soonest mended. If you go raising any ructions with the Good People maybe out of spite it's one of yer childher they'd next be afther taking with them to their home in Slieve-na-mon.

Howandever, one stormy morning, a matther of five or six weeks afther, when a crowd of neighbors purty well filled the smithy and they idling the time with their pipes and their jokes and their chat, Joey, himself, suddenly laid down the horse's hoof he was houlding and rubbing his hands hard and scowling around at them, said a thing that they spread afther over the scandalized barony. No one at all had been speaking of the misdaymeanor of taking Blackie, but Joey broke in:

"I've an idea in me head," he says, "that the thief who stole my sheep never rode the wind at all" says he, "but walks in two brogues and something in the back of me skull tells me that one day I'll lay me two livin' hands on him an' when I do, God help him!"

And Pether McCarthy looking at the width and the thickness of Joey's two grimed hands says afther him: "If ye do, God help him. But 'tis in the heart of Slieve-na-mon mountain yer sheep is being hid."

And Joey in the folly and foolishness of his madness burst out with a saying that sent a chill intil the heart of everyone who listened: "Then the curse of the crows light on them that took him and them that has him—man or immortal," says he.

For a good many weeks follying afther, the women of Ballenderg would sigh anxious at each other when anyone of the Hooligan childher'd be passing down the village street, and of a Sunday morning the crowd of men gathered at the chapel steps would blink owls eyes together and grow talkative as the stumps of dead threes when Joey jined in on the crowd.

Well, as the saying is, that throuble passed as all throubles must, an' it was a good foive months after that dismal Christmas Day before Joey Hooligan heard anything more of the sheep stealin'. But whin he did get worrud of it, the bewildherin' news started the sleepin' mysthery into a roaring blaze.

This is how it came: One May mornin' the smith was alone at his worruk, whustling a chune, when who should come fast galloping down the road an' dhraw up slap dash at the forge door, but Terror, Father Cassidy's black hunther, and on Terror's back sat Father Cassidy himself.

"Come out, Joey Hooligan! Come out, me dacint man!" cries the priest, his voice hoarse with aggytation.

At the call the towering smith came to the door and stood there in his apron, gawpin'; for the priest's face was in a blaze of excitement an' the good man couldn't couldn't sit quiet on the horse's back.

"Hould out yer hand, me lad," says the clargyman. "Stretch it over here," he says.

An' thin', whin the smith put over his great dusty paw, Father Cassidy dhropped intil the hard palm a fistful of shinin' silver.

A minute the good man stammered, for the words seemed hard set to force themselves from behind his teeth, while Joey with wrinkled, bewildered forehead stared from the shinin' silver in his grimy hand to the face of the priest and from that to the snorting excited nostrils of Terror and back again to the clump of money.

"There's the pay for yer sheep an' with it two crowns more than the pay," says his riv'rence. "The thief who stole Blackie sinds it an' he humbly axes yer forgiveness, an' he begs God's pardon, too. I charge ye on yer conscience not to breathe a whusper of this to a livin' sowl," cautioned the priest. "Tut, tut, ye're to ax no questions," he says.

Joey Hooligan has a powerful mind, as everyone knows, only it worruks slow, as I tould ye; so Father Cassidy was off and away down as far as the Widdy Deegan's before the truth had wormed itself full length intil the smith's hard head. But, whin the lad at last rayalized that no fairy at all had taken Blackie, but that some sneakin', murdherin' hound of a rapscalion had stole his little colleen's pet lamb, an' that all the heartaches of his childher were med be some red-handed, unfeeling robber, thin it was that a wild fury sayzed the big smith, so that the surge of blood in his head dhrove the sight from his eyes. What was the money! Musha, wasn't he just crazy! He was fair conglomerated.

Smashin' his apron hard upon the floor, the lad charged down the road follyin' Father Cassidy, shoutin' abuse an' wituperation ag'in the thief as he ran. You'd think to see him that 'twas ould Nick himself that was in it. All he wanted of Father Cassidy was to get from the priest the name of the malayfacthor. And so hot was this purpose in his heart that he paid no attintion to the people he mat up with on the way, but with his head lowered, he rushed heedless past thim down the road like a mad bull. Some thought the smith had gone daft, but Bothered Bill Dono-hue, the tinker, who had seen Father Cassidy ride away from the forge, spread the rayport that Hooligan was only doin' a hard pinnance put upon him by the priest, for not putting all the nails complete in the horse shoes. Maurteen Cavanaugh, the schoolmasther, shook his head sorrowful and said: "I always thought there was some kind of saycrit villany in that Joey Hooligan."

Well, anyways, the time I'm tellin' ye of, Joey ran on till he was half way up to the mountains. There the lad's breath failed him an' he sat down upon the stone be the lonely roadside, his head in his hands. Bime-bye the an-ger cooled a bit so that little by little he began thinkin'. Sure it wasn't long thin till he raymimbered how the clargyman had put it hard on his conscience not to ax questions. At that raymimbrance he wondhered an' he pondhered, an' he mumbled an' he grumbled. But at the ind of all his osculaytions an' pondherations, he was only left where he began. His mind, so to speak, was up agin a stone wall, an' the mysthery having woke from its sleep famershinger than ever was once more atin' its fill from the core of the smith's big warm heart. So up he rose an' home he wint, an' the next morning found him at his worruk as before.

Not a word did he say to the childher, not a whisper to Nancy, his wife, although night and day for a fortnight she was twisting his heartstrings this way and that to find out the throuble that was on him. Many's the neigh-bor wondhered at the sourness that had come over Joey, the smith, for to hide his feelings Hooligan would sing and whustle or take offence where there was no cause.

But thry what he would,—sing, whustle or quarrel— through four long weeks the bother stayed fretting at his

mind, an' 'twould maybe have been there till this good
day had he not been forced to bring a cow an' two fat pigs
up to the fair at Clonmel.

At that time the fair at Clonmel had such a grand
repitaytion for fun an' jolity that Joey wint early; an' afther
sellin' the cattle an' gettin' a good price for them, he turned
his attintion from the haggling of the cattle-buyers as was
only natural, to the wondhers and divarsions of the fair.
Whilst so bint an' inclined, he was sthrollin' about here
an' there, amusin' his idle eyes with the sthrange sights,
whin what should he see as it was coming out and standin'
at the door of a brown tint, but a Wuzzard. And Joey
stopped ferninst him and stood wondhering and pulling
his whiskers. Now ould Mrs. Casey could read taycups to
make yer hair stand, so, if she wasn't a witch herself she
had daylins with them; and the beggar woman, Sally Foley,
would put the black blight on the petaties if ye didn't give
her the fill of her fist of coppers. To his sorrow Joey knew
both of thim well, but in all his born days before he'd
never met up with a Wuzzard. Still and all be rayson of the
pictures he had seen and the tales he had heard Hooligan
knew without being told that this was a soothersayer.

This sthranger was certainly the most mystarious
lookin' crachure, man or mortial, ever seen before in
Tipperary. At a fair whin one person stops to look at a
strange sight another pushes up, then another and another, so while Joey was takin' his full of a look, a crowd
the size of a funeral swayed this way an' that, every mouth
spachless and every eye poppin' wild.

Over a round red face that was fringed by redder
whuskers, the Wuzzard wore a tall peaked cap, an' he had
a long red dress with silver moons an' goold stars sprinkled
all over it. He talked haughty and commanding, and you
could hear him half the fair away.

"Yer Past, Prisint, an' yer Fuchure," he was sayin'. "The
hidden saycrits of yer life rayvealed for a bit of silver! Come
on, good people! Me fadder was a Aygyptian an' me mudder

was a African. I'm the siventh son of a siventh son of a
siventh son," he says. "Is there any saycrit yez'd like
diskivered; is there anything yez'd like to know what yez
would do?"

An' then an' there ferninst the brown tint Joey straightened stiff as a gun, for a pro-ject shot intil his mind with
a swiftness that no other pro-ject had ever displayed itself there before in Joey's whole life.

Although Hooligan knew well that the loikes of thim
forchune tellers sell their sowls to Sattin for the power of
foretellin', yet the smith was mortial hungry to find out
the name of the thief that stole Blackie, so, he rayson'd
with himself this away: "Well, if he's sold his sowl that
was before I met him, and since he's lost anyway I can do
him no harm."

"I'll tell yer past for nawthin', an' thin if yer satisfied
with the strength of me power, I'll tell yer prisint an' yer
fuchure for eight pince," bawled the soothersayer lookin'
hard with his little yellow eyes at Joey.

At thim worruds, though feelin' all the time in the
marrow of his bones that this raysonable offer was only a
timptaytion from the divil, Joey began to argyfy with himself agin, and he says:

"Bedad if Sattin has informayshun to sell, an' I pay
him square an' honest for that same informayshun, sure
there's no fayvors granted on ayther side. He gives me
what I bargain for, an' I pay him for what I get. Thin,
there's no bones broke," says he.

There was always an irrayligious sthreak in thim Hooligans.

Thinkin this away, the smith was standin' as I've tould
ye, with one hand deep in his pocket, feelin' for the money,
and his brows knitted, whin suddin the Wuzzard stretched
out a hand an' touched Joey on the showider.

"Come in, me poor man," says the maygician. "I see
plain the throuble that's wound up on the inside of ye.
An' 'tis me that can unwind it."

There was something so confidential and at the same time so cock sure in the way the Wuzzard spoke, that the smith hesitayted no longer.

Although his conscience could have been heard acrass the lane hollerin' at him, an' although he was a good dale frightened, still without a worrud follyed Sattin's immissary intil the booth, an' the Wuzzard pulled shut the flap of the tent. Thin the two sat on stools just ferninst aich other. The smith's big hand thrimbled a little whin the maygician took it up an' began peerin' intil the hard, black, horny palm.

"I'll begin on yer past an' yer prisint," says the wise man; an' with that he shut both of his two eyes. Joey waited anxious for the first worruds an' whin they came they were so wondherfully thrue that the smith blinked with a-stonishment.

"Yer a smith!" says the Wuzzard.

"My sowl," gasped Joey to himself. "He niver before in all his life seen me, an' I niver till this minute set eyes on the soothersayer."

"Ye have niver been very rich," says the Aygptian, thriumphant.

"Look at that now! No more have I," gasped Joey.

"But if ye were only rich ye'd be a raymark-able man," the Wuzzard says, solemn. That capped everything. Joey had always and ever since childhood said that same thing to himself, but no livin' sowl before had ever a-greed with him. That one bit of informaytion alone was worth more than the eight pence.

"Ye've had throuble," wint on the fortune teller.

"I have! Lots of it," cried Joey wagging his head pitiful.

"An' yer wife is sometimes onraysonable with ye," the Wuzzard says.

The cowld pusperation started out on Joey's forehead. "Say no more," he says, growin' hoarse. "I'd give fi' pounds if only Nancy could hear ye say thim worruds. Here's the eight pince?" he says. "Ye know me past like a book. Niver mind goin' over me prisint, I know that as well as ye do yerself. Unfold me fuchure," says the smith.

Joey could hear the crowd whuspering and sniggering just outside the tent door, but so entranced was the smith with wondher that he gave them no heed.

The soothersayer opened his eyes wider an' as he glared intil the smith's hand, wint on talkin'. An' he spoke hollow:

"Ye'll get a letther," says the raymarkable man, "an' ye'll go on a journey," he says hurrying; "an' some of yer wife's relaytions'll take down sick, an' ye'll be rich some day, but 'tis little good that'll do ye, for ye'll not live long afther; an' yer wife'll be a great dale happier in her next marriage than she's been in this one. I think yer wife's name is Nancy," says the siventh son, suddenly frowning gloomy up at Hooligan. "At laste there's a Nancy in yer hand," he says.

For a moment the smith was nonplushed, as well he might be; his face grew crimson. Thin he broke out:

"Do you mane to tell me," he says chokin' "that me wife,—Nancy's her name sure enough—do you mane to tell me that Nancy'll marry agin afther I'm dead and gone?" Joey widened his palm and frowned down into his own hand the same as if he could read the signs himself.

"I'm only tellin' what I see plain in yer hand," says the soothersayer, cowld an' savage. "Don't crass me," he says. "Give me back yer paw. It isn't the likes of ignerant smiths that has the saycrits of the fuchure," says he.

Joey was still for one bitther minute, thin he bridled up. "Tell me," he says, "is the man she's to marry a little wirey fellow who wears a hairy cap?"

The Wuzzard bent back Joey's fingers till they cracked and peered down a long time.

"I see in yer hand a hairy cap on the head of a little wirey man," rayplied the forchune teller at last.

"Once more; answer me this: Is the little villain a schoolmasther?" axed the smith.

"He is, no less!" answered the Wuzzard imaget.

"She rayfused Maurteen Cavanaugh, the school-masther, six times before we were married," says the smith, grittin' his teeth, "I'll go home now an' bate the life out of him," says he, startin' to get up.

"Have sinse," says the Wuzzard, putting out his hand. "He has yit not an idee of what's comin', nor has Nancy, nor will they have till yer dead a year an' a day. There'd be no satisfaction in batin' a man onless ye towld him what ye were batin' him for, would there? An' if ye towld the schoolmasther, ye'd be the mock of the counthry. No, no, no, I have a betther way nor that," says the Wuzzard, taking out of his pocket something that was like a snuff-box. "I have an enchanted powdher here that I med spe-cial for the Imperor of Boolgaria, on just such an oc-casion as this. Now for four silver crowns I'll give ye enough to make Nancy hate the schoolmasther all her life an' even afther."

With hand dipped far intil his pocket and one leg stretched the smith strove to cogitate. The wise man mintioned four silver crowns in the same disrayspectful tone of voice in which he might say "four little petaties."

But, so far as Joey was consarned—an' the smith was be no manner of manes a stingy man—thim worruds gave him a toothache in his heart. Though four crowns would almost buy a foine young pig, the pain was not for the loss of the money alone, mind ye, but it came mostly from the needcessity of spindin' a sum like that for any such shuper-flous purpose. Howandever, he answered nothing at all just thin; he only sunk a little lower on the stool, flinging one leg dayjected over the other an' his chin hur-ried in the folds of his new cravat.

The Wuzzard leaned over an' spoke confaydential. "This same powdher med the Quane of Swuzzerland thry to pizen the King of Rooshia—Ah thin, wasn't that same King of Rooshia a divil among the girls!" says the maygician, smilin' roguish an' pensive. "Many's the time he sint for me to ate dinner at his house. If I'd known 'twas again him the powdher was to be intended, I'd never have sowld it to the Imperor of Boolgaria." He dhropped Joey's hand and propped his head on his own hand, his elbow on his knee.

"That's the way the Royalty used to be cutting up. Poor people never know how lucky and contented they are."

"The Boolgarian slipped a taste of that same powdher into the Quane of Swuzzerland's punch one night whin we were all at a christening, an' it thwisted her feelings the other way altogether. Before that she used to be langwidging afther the Rooshin."

The Wuzzard sighed raygretful. "Blessings be on thim ould happy days," he says, shakin' his head, "whin me an' the Royalty used to wandher in one crowd from place to place, seekin' nothing but divarshin, an' we all as sociable an' as common in our ways an' talk with aich other as, saving yer prisence, a flock of geese." At this his voice broke into a sigh. "Hi ja!" says he.

The longer the Aygyptian talked about Kings and Quanes an' high s'ciety, the smaller four crowns grew in Joey's eyes; they dwundled and they dwundled till whin the Wuzzard stopped an' hung his head sorrowful undher thim happy raymimbrances, a silver crown seemed about the vally of a copper fardin.

Straightening himself up, the smith said: "The price is not so onraysonable if the enchantment does its worruk," says he. "An' I'll take the chanst," he says. "But if it fails— if it doesn't purvent me widdy marryin' that man—begorra if ye'll ever crass me path ag'in, I'll make surgents worruk of ye. Mind that now," says he.

"I give ye lave," says the Wuzzard, thumping his knee umphatic.

Well, what could Joey do but count the four crowns out of his leather bag, an' so disturbed was he about Nancy and the schoolmasther that after he had safely stowed away the powdher in the bottom of his leather purse, he was actwilly goin' out of the tint without axin' one worrud of Blackie, whin the bleatin' of a sheep which was bein' dhrove past outside, called to his mind the ould misfortune; so the lad turned hurried, an' sat himself down on the stool ag'in.

"I want ye to tell me," he says flusthered, "who was the blaggard that sthole me pet lamb last Christmas eve night," says he. "I must hate someone or me heart'll bust inside of me. Sendin' me back the price be Father Cassidy, as he did, won't save the thief, nor the axin' of me pardon be the same manner and manes won't relayse him. Tell me his name, for salt won't save him."

"I saw all that in yer hand the first minute" sneered the maygician.

"Then why didn't ye tell it?" cried Joey, turnin' hot on the soothersayer.

"Ax yerself why I didn't," says the Wuzzard, high an' lofty. "I only agreed to tell yer own past, prisent an' fuchure for eight pince. There was no bargain I can raymimber of to go over your farm an' tell the past, prisent an' fuchure of all your pigs an' cows an' sheep. I'd like to see meself," says the Wuzzard; "shame on ye!" he says.

Joey wasn't what ye might call light-footed at an argyment, so he could think of no answer. All the same, he had a dull hurt feeling that in some way he was being chated. So he threw a surly grunt and an ugly eye at the Aygyptian.

"None of yer black looks, me man," says the forchune teller, swaggerin' his head. "Fair worruds will sarve ye betther here, me lad," he says.

Joey at that let a growl out of him that sounded like an impty barrow goin' over the stones, an' begorra at the sound of it the soothersayer put on a friendlier face an' spoke more modified.

"I'll tell ye what I'll do," he says, confidin' "just so as to sind ye away satisfied. There's some questions I'm forbid to answer. The powers that have me in conthrol won't let me tell all I know. But, barrin' such things as I'm forbid

to dischlose, for another shillin' I'll answer any four questions yer amind to ax about the forchune of yer sheep. An'
loathe enough am I to tell a baste's forchune at any price.
It takes all me power—I haven't the strength of a cat for
hours afther," he says.

Still sour-faced an' sullen, Joey took another shillin'
from the leather bag an' tossed it at the Aygyptian, sayin'
threatenin' as he did so: "Now go on. Tell me the past,
prisent an' fuchure of me sheep an' tell it thrue," he
growled.

The Wuzard must have been a fighting man himself,
for afther he got the last shillin' in his pocket he brustled
up, an' this time looked Joey square in the eye, an' the
look he gave was so study an' so belittlin' that the big
smith felt himself rayly growin' kind of cowering.

"Raymimber I'm only to be axed questions," says the
maygician. "But I don't mind tellin' ye that yer sheep has
no prisent or fuchure—it only has a past. It was kilt an'
ate long ago. That's why ye got back the money instid of
the baste. But ax yer four questions an' ax thim all at
once," says he.

Joey wrunkled his brows an' for awhile puzzled hard.
Then he says, says he: "First an' foremost, tell me the
name of the man that sthole me sheep. That'll be the first
question. Thin ye'll unfold to me how he managed to get
the baste away so quick an' complete. Thirdly," he says,
"ye'll expatiate why the thief sint the money back be Father Cassidy, or why he sint it back at all. An' lastly, ye'll
tell me, since there's a thief in the parish, why it is that
he niver stole anything before nor since. Do that an' ye'll
take a powerful load off me mind," says he.

All this time the Wuzzard, his chin in his hand, was
watchin' Joey with hawk's eyes, an' whin Hooligan had
finished, the wise man picked up the smith's hand, an'
afther peerin' intil it a full minute, began bending the palm
an' slapping it an' twisting the fingers till Joey cried out
with hurt.

"I niver saw anything so mystarious," says the Wuzzard. "There's one thing I can't make out for the life of me. Was the sheep stole at night or in the daytime? Yer hand don't show which it was."

With that Hooligan, growin' impatient, up an' touldt the time of night it all happened, an' in tellin' that relayted everything else he knew consarning the sarcumstances.

The last worrud wasn't out of his mouth before the Wuzzard, with a groan, started up from his stool.

"Wait a minute," he says whusperin'; "I must make a saycret incantaytion." Saying this, he went behind a black curtain which hung acrass the back pa-art of the tint. The cloth was left a little dhrawn an' what did Joey see inside, sittin' on a box, but skilliton's bare head, an' around the head was laid a row of bones.

The smith was staring, horrified, when the maygician, afther his saycrit incantaytion, came out and sat down again. Joey caught a quare, sthrong smell coming from the soothersayer. 'Twas something like the smell of whuskey.

"I find," says the maygician, "that I'm forbid to tell the name of the purloiner, but I'll give ye such a thrue dayscription of him that ye can go from the door of this tint an' lay yer hands on his showldher.

"Listen: First,—he's a near neighbor; that's why he got the lamb away so quick an' so complate. Next, he's an honest man, that's the rayson he niver stole before nor since. He's a rayligious man, too; ye may know that be the way he ran to Father Cassidy.

"Lastly, an' be this sign ye may know him best of all, he's powerful proud; so a-mazin' proud that rather than let his hunger be known to the kindly-hearted neighbors about, he'd commit sheep-stealin', the most disgraceful of all criminal crimes. Don't be too hard on the unfortinit sowl, for I tell ye his need was great that black time. And now," says the Wuzzard, getting up and guiding Joey gently toward the door, "afther that dayscription ye're a dull man if ye can't go out an' lay yer hand on him."

Bekase Joey didn't like to admit himself a dull man, an' bekase, too, the maning of things always came to him not sudden, but afther awhile, the lad was contint to ax no more questions, bein' sartin sure that the name itself would drift in on his mind during the journey home.

Ye may believe what ye like, but the wondherstruck, satisfied look on the smith's face as he marched out of the maygician's tint into the waitin' crowd, med the Aygyptian's fortune that day.

Howandever, sorra mind did Joey mind the stares of the pushin' crowd, an' just as little attintion did he give to their impident questionings, but showldhering his way through the throng, he welted his brogues down the sthreets of the town an' out intil the quiet counthry lane. The spring twilight was just settlin' down over the white of the hawthorn bushes and the new green of the meadows. As he wint along, his thoughts were thrippin' an' throwin' aich other.

Instead of one mysthery to dale with, now Joey Hooligan had two; that about his wife, Nancy, an' Maurteen almost smothered the first. Oh, how he longed to grip his two hands in the schoolmasther's hair. But no, he must kape that throuble covered in the bottommost hole of his heart, for very shame sake if for nothing else.

While thinkin' of Maurteen, another idee popped up sudden an' startlin'. Was it Maurteen that stole Blackie? No, that couldn't be, bekase the thief was a rayligious man. Was it Father Cassidy, thin? Surely no, for where was the needcessity! The clargyman might have anything Joey owned an' welcome just for the axin'. So in that way the boy wint on, casting a blot of the char-ack-ther, aich in his turn, of every man, woman, and child in the parish, except one, an' that one fillin' the soothersayer's day-scription best of all.

I think that one man would have escaped suspicion altogether if be a sthrange chanst the smith hadn't spied on the road not a quarter of a mile in front, a stooped, slender figure hurrying along in the same di-rection as Joey himself was goin'.

"Begorra, there goes Dennis Egan, the scholar. Oh, be the powers—." The smith stopped stock still in the road and began scratchin' his head with both hands. "But no," he mutthered, "it couldn't be the loikes of him any aisier than it could be the loikes of Father Cassidy. Though it's mortial proud an' big feelin' he an' his family are, sure enough. Didn't a score of the boys hear him give back talk to the priest himself at the last illection? Wirra, wirra," says Joey, growin' throubled, "an' he's a rayligious man an' a near neighbor, too."

The onwelcome suspicion worried the smith greatly. Now ye know the scholar an' his family were what ye might call rayfined people, an' hilt thimselves shuparior to most others in the parish; yet they had had great friends with the Hooligans, though in a lofty kind of way. Indade, fifteen years before that the scholar an' his wife had conday-scinded to stand sponsors for Joey's first born—Dan'l O'Connell Hooligan.

"No, no, it can't be him," Joey argyed to a blackbird that was darting back an' forth in front of him. "He never was in needcessity. Though, by tunder, come to think of it, last summer the blight did come upon their corn! He never raised many petaties," says Joey to the bird, anxious, "yet the scholar couldn't be in want for all that, for didn't he sell every hoofed an' horned baste on his place an' turned them intil money the Ayster purvious; so that he must have a hatful of goolden suverings in the house. Am n't I the dunder headed Omadhaun to ac-cuse such a man. But the scholar is a wise man," he says ag'in, "an' I wondher if 'twould be presumin' to go an' tell him what the soothersayer dayscribed to me," Joey says. "I have no manner of doubt but what he will name the criminal imaget," says he to himself.

Filled brimmin' up with thim thoughts, an' growin' excited at the good chanst of at last finding out the name of the mystarious thief, Joey broke intil a sharp trot an' catchin' up with the scholar, dhropped intil step at his side.

Never before had Joey noticed how ould an' haggard the proud man's thin, shaven face was growin' an' how slow he walked—it even seemed that Dennis was hanging back a little to let the smith pass. Without even bidding the time of the day, Joey tapped the scholar on the back. "Dennis Egan," says Joey, "I've found out who stole Blackie." The proud man's face tightened so that Joey thought that the light sthroke on the showldher must have hurt him.

"He's one," wint on Joey savage, "who was too proud to beg, an' he's so rayligious an' so rayspectable," says the smith, sarcastic, "that no one misdoubted him."

Egan's cheeks turned gray as ashes an' he tuned to moisten his lips with his dhry tongue. Hooligan noticed these things at the time, but he didn't put them intil their right places until long afthward.

"His conscience is throublin' him now," says Joey, givin' his stick an angry shake, "but wait till I'm done with him. I'll kill him first an' have him thransported afther," says he.

Thin it was that Egan spoke an' whin he did, a-stonishment at his sthrange, wild worruds knocked the big smith spachless. Not that Joey understood rightly even then, but the scholar's look was so pathryfying.

"Oh, God in Hiven, your blow has fallen!" Egan cried, standin' still in the road an' spreadin' wild an' wide his two stiff arrums. "Oh, Father of marcy, be pittiful to me an' to me innocent childher; an' to her!" he says with a dhry sob.

Joey stood gapin'; the first thought in his mind bein' that there was a dangerous sickness among some of thim up at the scholar's. Next, Egan turned fierce an' sudden on the smith.

"Wait before you sthrike, Joey Hooligan. You'll never know the need I was in, man. Me patities an' me corn runed—you know that—an' me money in the bottom of the say."

"Why I—I—I—thought ye were rich," gasped Joey, the thrue idea beginning to bore its way intil his head.

"An' wasn't I!" says the scholar. "I had scraped together every livin' thing I owned an' sowld them an' it med foive hundhred pounds, an' I sint it till me cousin, Dan McTighe, in Claremorris, an' he too had foive hundhred pounds, an' we put the money intil cattle an' Dan tuck them to England an' sowld them there."

"My, oh my! That was a thousand pounds!" says Hooligan.

Egan wint on talkin' fast an' dusperate, mindin' one for all the worruld of a wild baste in a thrap. "Comin' back, Dan's ship wint intil another ship in the channel, and—I've wisht a hundhred times since that I was rowling calm beside him at the bottom of the say."

Joey hadn't time as yet to rayalize in full or get vexed consarnin' Blackie; besides, everything was swirling about in a whirlpool of a-stonishment. "But what of the thousand pounds?" was all he could say.

"There was more," says Egan, "more; there was a profit. Well, the hopeless days closed in, an' little be little we dayvoured what was left at home, till black, naked hunger came at last to sit in the chimney corner that niver before had known anything except comfort an' plenty. But a still bittherer pain crept in an' sat beside the hunger, an' that was the dhread which we all felt that some of the neighbors we'd so often lorded it over—God knows with how little rayson—might find out our sitiwation an' pity us. Father Cassidy I avoided most of all, bekase of the hot worruds we'd give aich other at the illiction."

The two were fronting aich other now in the dusk, and the scholar's arms had sunk to his side. "My, oh my, but weren't yez the foolish people!" says the smith.

"One night," Egan wint on, not mindin', and his voice came dhry and broken, "I left home to walk down to

Claremorris, hoping that me cousin's family might spare me a little, though I knew 'twas little they had left. I thramped on foot three days an' one night, only to find them as bad off as me-self. Back I came without asking them, an' was four days on me journey. Ye may guess I was foot-sore an' heart-sore, and on the last day I was sick an' wake from the hunger. Christmas Eve I dhragged meself past your own good house an' I saw the bright lights in your windys an' heard the happy laughin' of your childher, an' inside with them the dog barkin' in his play— an' I goin' home to carry to me own famishing ones only disappointment an' dispair."

"I'm ashamed of ye—," Joey started to say, but the other stopped him.

"Yerself stood fumbling at the door of the forge, and lest ye might be a witness to me misery I stopped behind the oak three till you wor gone."

"Wow—," shouted Joey, hitting one fist intil the other.

"An' as you bent over the lock I saw what I thought was the dog run out behind ye intil the road. Sure now I know it was the sheep."

"Tare and Ages,' cried Joey again, "of all bastes in the worruld a sheep or a lamb have the laste reliableness," he says.

"A little way down the road I heard somethin' follyin' behindt, an' lookin' back I saw it was a young sheep that was throttin' along afther. I swear to ye be the sowls of the parents I have dishonored that I had no thought of taking it then. I only hurried on till I came within sight of me own house. Not a light shone out in welcome. The cottage stood there lookin' dark and huddled as me own sowl. I listened at the door but there was no sound from within. A shuddering dhread that the wife and childher might be starved an' dead turned me faint an' sick an' I was afeared to lift the latch. Me head was a bit dizzy, too, from the wakeness I think. So I studied meself with a hand ag'in the house— this away—an' creepin' around to the windy I looked in."

He stopped a second, broke be the raymembrance. The big smith lay a gentle hand on the man's shoulder. "Go on," says the smith. "It's a lucky hour we met the night. What yer sayin' will lift the load off yer sowl. Go on! no livin' person'll ever get tidings from me. God help ye and fergive ye as I do with all me heart."

"The wife an' childher lay in their beds cuddled up to-gether for the warmth, an' alive. Thank God! At that sight me heart began to beat once more. I laned on the windy-sill prayin' to Hiven for to know what worruds to greet them with when I'd go in.

"But worruds wouldn't come. An' as I kneeled down with me forehead hid upon the sill there came a soft cry from behindt, an' lookin' round I saw the black pet lamb which had followed afther.

"You'll never know,—God only knows, how farvint I called up the last bit of strength to fight ag'in that timp-tation. But 'twas no use. Only this I'll tell ye that I ray-mimbered in that instant, an' the raycollection was like a touch of hot iron: that never before had one of me name or breed done a mane or dishonest act. I was to be the first. So 'twas with the feelin's of a murdherer that I slipped through the back door an' from the kitchen stole out the sharp knife." The scholar glanced frightened over his showldher an' his eyes were like the eyes of a man who is seeing a ghost. With a hand at his throat he gulped a couple times an' thin wint on.

"The thrusting little crachure touched this hand with cowld wet nose an' follyed where I led it out intil the middle of me own field, an' there in the darkness—." He could go no furder bekase of the sobs that were chokin' him, so dhrawing the collar of his coat up over his eyes the poor man gave way to a perfick hurricane of crying.

As for Joey,—the smith had no feelin's at all but those of smothering pity mixed with a sort of guilty onasiness that be some way or other, he himself had done some-thing undherhanded.

Two or three times worruds of comfort got as far as the big man's lips, but there they lay jumbled and useless at the ind of his tongue. So for a while he just stood in the road ferninst the other, twishting his heel restless an' givin' little coughs.

Whin he did spake at last it was to say:

"Have sinse, Dennis Egan! Sure many's the dacint man before you turned sheep stealer. I may do it meself yet. We niver know what we'll do till we're thried," he says, awkward. "Come on home," says he.

'Twasn't just what Hooligan said nor the gentle touch laid on the cryin' man's arrum that roused the scholar, but 'twas the friendly sootherin' sound of the smith's rough voice. At any rate, whin Dennis began talkin' ag'in he stood with hands clasped together an' his arrums twitchin' narvous an' his head bint like a little boy that had just got a batin'.

"Ye were ever the foine-hearted man, Joey Hooligan, dull as ye are," he says. "I'll never forget that Christmas mornin' how whin I knelt in the chapel you came in an' knelt down beside me, an' how I shrank from ye as though I was a leper. There was God Himself lookin' down at both of us an' you kneelin' honest an' brave, an' I, with me pride an' me honor, an' me courage withered like a winther's reed. I couldn't stand it long, but crep' out intil the air to wandher about all day, a vagabone an' a thief, afeared of the sight of even me own childher."

"Don't mind telling any more," says the smith, striving to save himself from the pain of listening. "Come on home, now. It's dark." He took Egan by the arm and led him down the road. But the scholar's heart must get relief from its bursting load, and he kept talking as they went.

"'Twas a bed med of livin' coals I slept on that night, an' just at daybreak I arose an' wint where I should have gone at first, up to Father Cassidy. Oh, may the Saints pursarve him! He helped me with money, an' he helped me a hundhred times more be the things he said. An' afther that day an' every day he helped me ag'in. He gave me the quarther's rint, he bought me the petaties an' the corn for seed, an' whin the letther came from the lawyers sayin' that the Englishman paid poor Dan McTighe for the cattle not in money but in papers dhrawn ag'in a bank, an' that there was siven hundhred an' fifty pounds waitin' for me to dhraw out, 'twas Father Cassidy—"

Joey stiffened with amazement, and wheeled the scholar to face him in the road. "Don't tell me," he gasped. "Did yez get it?" says he.

"I did," says Egan, "an' there ye know the whole miserable story. An' there's yer stick in yer hand an' here's the thief, an' if ye'll bate me good an' plenty I'll feel betther than I have felt for many a day. Only I beg of yez, for the love of God, not to tell on me," he axes pitiful.

The idee of batin' a man worth sivin hundhred pounds was reediculous, not to say irrayligious, so Joey, with one hand in his pocket, an' his brow in deep ridges, answered:

"As ye say, Dennis Egan, I'm a dull man, an' I can't think quick, an' I can't give raysons for what I do. Only now I have the feelin' that someway I'm in the wrong. That God borryed from me to whom he'd allowed plinty, an' give it to you that had nothing at all, an' that I took pay an' dhrove a harrud bargain with Him to whom I owe everything. I may be wrong, but I think I'll have nayther luck nor grace so long as I carry about with me the price of that sheep. Ye must take it back, Dennis Egan," he says, slow an' airnest.

But the scholar, with hands lifted, shrank from him. "No," he says. "The only comfort I have is that I med amends. Don't dayprive me of it," says he.

"Well," says Joey, "may God forgive ye as I freely do. We'll away now with the money to Father Cassidy an' ax him what we'll do with it. But have no fear of me tellin' on ye, Dennis," says he.

An' so they both together wint off to the priest's house, but what he did with the money I never heerd.

An' be the same token no one ever heerd this story that I'm afther tellin' ye, till two years ago whin the Egans wint to live in England. Thin it leaked out someway.

But Joey Hooligan is still throubled in his mind about his wife an' Maurteen Cavanaugh; for although he put the brown powdher in her tay faithful, an' with every eye in his head as big as the taycup watched her swally it, still he's afeared it mightn't worruk well. She med a wry mouth, to be sure an' spluttered "Bad cess to it I must have put salt in me tay." But she looked and acted just the same afther takin' it as before—not a ha'porth of difference. So when he comes sudden acrass Maurteen in the road it always gives Joey a turn. An' whin Nancy buys a purty new dish or a thing like that, Joey, sly, an' as if be accident, breaks it so that be no chanst Maurteen'll get the use of it; and the smith wears his best shuit of clothes on the slightest oc-casion, so that they'll be well used an' spint whin he dies.

One resolution is set firm in Hooligan's mind: whin he will feel sure that death's comin' on he'll call his eldest son to his bedside an' say:

"Dan'l O'Connell Hooligan, I charge ye an' put it on yer conscience that if ye ever see that little sneakin' Maurteen Cavanaugh spakin' civil to any faymale member of this family, ye'll throunce him; an' if he ever crasses this thrashol' when I'm dead ye'll bate the life out of him."

An' 'tis a consolation for the smith to know that Dan'l never had any great fondness for the school or the schoolmaster.

Bridgeen and the Leprechaun

"Outside of France the month of May is not the month of May," Victor Hugo says. Surely, surely the great poet never saw the break of May in Ireland. If on the May day we are talking about, he had walked down the winding road from Ballinderg by little Bridgeen Daley's side, and with her had kept his eyes and ears awake, looking in the ditches and under the hedges for the leprechaun, the little fairy cobbler, he would have changed that saying entirely, I'm thinking.

On either side of the narrow lane pressed the bursting hedges, dazzling pink and white, while beyond, in the fields over every hillock and upland surged riotous crowds of laughing, yellow buttercups and golden-hearted daisies. And the violets—every green leaf hid a purple cluster! And the perfume—but sure one can't talk about the perfume of the Irish violets, because it gives one such a lonesome, longing heartsickness to think about them there! The linnets and the blackbirds contended desperately with one another as to who should give the heartiest, merriest welcome to the spring. And above all hovered the kindly sky, as grave, as blue, and as tender as Bridgeen's own eyes.

But back in the village of Ballinderg it was little about blackbirds and linnets the people were thinking. Little Mickey Driscoll, who never before in all the troubled days of his short life had resented any honestly earned cuff on the ear, today leaned disconsolately against the shady side of the thatched cottage, weeping torrents of indignant tears into the short skirt of his brown linsey frock.

A few feet away, on an upturned tub beside the open door, sat his subdued and commiserating father, too wise for any open expression of sympathy or comfort, but nodding and winking covert assurances and beckoning to the lad with coaxing, compassionate fingers.

"Come over here, Mickey avic," he whispered. "Don't cry, ahager. Where did she slap ye? Oh, my, oh, my, on the two little red legs of ye! What did ye do, allanna?"

"Naw-nawthin', da-daddy; I—I—only dhrew wan finger down, that a-way, on sisther Eileen's white dhress to see if it would make a mark," sobbed the heartbroken child.

"Oh, isn't that the turrible thing," soothed his hypocritical parent, "to larrup ye loike that just for wan weeney bit of a sthreek. Oh, husheen, husheen; no wondher yer heart's in tatthers!" He drew the little lad between his knees and smoothed his tumbled yellow curls.

Daniel Driscoll and his weeping son Mickey were not the only victims of feminine oppression in Ballinderg that Saturday afternoon; they but typified the general state of affairs, for in every cottage an anxious, flustered woman was bustling back and forth from dresser to clothespress and from bedroom back to kitchen, and woe betide any unfortunate man or child or four-footed beast that got in the way of her flying feet!

On each side of the winding village street the male portion of the community, apprehensive, subdued and biddable, sat smoking their pipes under the projecting thatch of the cottages. The air was tense with expectation. Today no child loitered on an errand. At the first word of command there was a flash of bare legs, a swish of red petticoat, and he was shot across the street from threshold to threshold with the speed and precision of field gun practice.

And who could blame the busy mothers for their feverish perturbation! Wasn't the archbishop himself—not the bishop, mind you, but the archbishop—coming down on the morrow to the humble village chapel to give confirmation to the children. Don't be talkin'! Wasn't Father Cassidy the clever man entirely to get such an honor for Ballinderg?

But, oh, dear, the bother of it! What with the grandeur of white veils and wreaths for the girls and brand-new suits for the boys—shoes for a good many of them, too— the parish was fairly turned upside down and made bankrupt, so it was.

Late in the afternoon, Father Cassidy, tired and happy, having put the last touch to the decorations in the chapel and the last bunch of wild flowers in the altar vases, went cantering home along the gravel country lane on his black hunter, Terror. He passed through the village and had almost reached the Ballymore crossroads when he spied just ahead of him a slim, bare-footed little girl, trudging wearily along and carrying in her clasped arms a pair of brogues almost as heavy as herself.

"It's Bridgeen Daley," he muttered. "The kind Lord look down on that houseful of motherless children." Father Cassidy reined in his horse beside her. "Is that you, Bridgeen?" he called. "Come here, asthore. Oh, I see, ye've been to Neddy Hagan's to get yer father's brogues mended. I'm greatly afraid all this grandeur will be the ruination of us at last."

The little girl bobbed a curtsey and raised a pair of timid blue eyes to the priest's face.

"I hear everyone saying, allanna, what a grand little mother you are to the brothers and sisters since—your poor mother was taken away from you; and it's pleased I am and proud of you."

The ghost of a smile flickered a moment over the child's sensitive lips. Wasn't it the grand thing entirely to be praised like that by such a great man as Father Cassidy! But it's little he knew the trouble Bridgeen had with those same brothers and sisters; indeed she was strongly tempted to tell him of the goings on of Jamesy. Musha, why shouldn't she tell him? When Daniel Casey, the tailor, went wrong with the drink didn't his wife, Julia, call in Father Cassidy to put corrections on Daniel? And didn't it work wonders?

As if reading her thought the priest bent low and looked almost deferentially into the innocent, blushing face. "I suppose it's great trials entirely you have with them, acushla?"

Thus encouraged, the colleen broke forth: "Jamesy's the worst, sir," she cried. "Even Paudeen the baby is more biddable—and Jamesy four years old yesterday and ought to have more sinse. But nothin' plazes him, yer riverence, but pokin' at the fire. Whin I go home now I'll warrant it's hunkerin' in the ashes I'll find him. If yer honor's riverence'd only stop in and give him a spakin' to"—there was a little catch in Bridgeen's voice as she realized her boldness— "I'd—I'd take it kind."

Father Cassidy shook his head in sorrowful surprise. "Dear, dear, will you look at that now! I wouldn't have believed it of Jamesy, and him four years old too. Wait till I lay me eyes on him! However, 'tis of yourself I'd like to be asking. Are you all ready for the confirmation tomorrow? Have you yer white wreath and veil?"

Bridgeen's eyes dropped instantly, and she fell to digging in the turf with a bare toe. "No," she half whispered, and her head dropped lower and lower.

Wasn't it a terrible thing to be the only girl in the chapel before the archbishop without a white wreath and veil. But, ochone mavrone, the pennies which her mother and she had so carefully hoarded for them, had gone a fortnight ago to buy the makings of a sober brown shroud with which to cover a quiet breast.

"Never mind, mavourneen," said Father Cassidy. "I've a plan. On your way home do you be looking carefully under the hedge as you go along, and who knows but what you may meet up with the leprechaun. Do you know what the leprechaun is, Bridgeen?"

"Yis, sir—I mane, yer riverence—he's the sly, wee, fairy cobbler that sits undher a twig makin' shoes for the Little People; and if ye can only find him and kape yer eye on him the while, it's three grand wishes he'll give ye to buy his freedom."

"True for you, Bridgeen, but remember what a cunning trickster the lad is; if he can beguile you to take your eyes from him for a second, he's gone forever; don't forget that. I'm on now. Do you take the lane and hurry home, asthore, and I'll take the road and keep an eye out for him myself, an' whichever of us finds the leprechaun first will go and tell the other."

There was a laugh in Father Cassidy's eyes as he nodded good-day. Then something tinkled on the road at Bridgeen's feet. She stopped to pick it up. Wonders! It was a bright silver shilling.

"Thank you kindly, yer riverence," she gasped, but Father Cassidy was already galloping away down the road, laughing softly to himself.

Look at that now, Father Cassidy himself to be talking of the leprechaun. Why, then, in spite of what the schoolmaster said, there was truly such a little fairy man, dressed in a green cloak and red cap. It was no lie at all Tim O'Brien was telling. Dear, dear, wouldn't it be the grandest luck in the world if one could only—

"But sure what good if I did meet up with him?" thought Bridgeen. "Isn't it too frightened to spake to him I'd be, let alone clever enough to make the like of him a prisoner? But the wishes! Oh, if I only could."

Bridgeen had heard a hundred times how years and years ago it was a fairy thrush that had coaxed Tim O'Brien out of this same lane—in troth, almost from this same spot—across the fields to the fairy rath, where, Tim declared, he saw the leprechaun. Now, a thrush which had followed Bridgeen from the village, whirring in short flights along the top of the hedge, stopped on a branch just above her head and began singing fit to burst his swelling throat.

And indeed 'twas he that had the fine, friendly song with him!

At first it's little heed the child gave to the bird, for the priest's last words had raised a solemn wonder in her mind; for now, after what Father Cassidy had said, there could be no danger in asking from the fairy cobbler the favor of three wishes. Neither could it be wrong for one to search for the little fairy; didn't the priest himself bid her look carefully under the hedges and didn't he promise to do that same? Well, wasn't it a queer world entirely!

By this time she had reached the stile into Hagan's meadow, so she seated herself on the lowest step to think up the three best wishes and to rest her arms from the heavy brogues.

Wouldn't it be the grand fortune entirely to meet the leprechaun? She turned a dozen wishes over and over in her mind. There was the wreath and veil for herself of course, but then on the other hand there were potatoes and meal for next week, and barely enough turnips for the cow, and the turf down to the last row, and oh, so many needed things; but, above and beyond them all, one impossible, shining wish.

However, Father Cassidy had bidden her to hurry home, so, putting aside the pleasant wishes, Bridgeen slowly picked up the brogues from the grass where she had laid them and arose to go. As she did so she cast anxious eyes at the big red sun which was already sending slow-creeping shadows across the fields. And lo! as she looked, there arose sharp and clear before her the great dead tree off at the foot of the blue hills, the tree that marked the fairy rath where Tim O'Brien once had seen the leprechaun.

"Why couldn't I go there looking for him?" The colleen trembled with excitement. "But it would be dark before I could go to the fairy fort and back again," she thought, shrinkingly.

And the distant tree towered so gloomily, so lonesomely, so silently, that Bridgeen hesitated, with her foot on the

stile. But only an instant did she pause, for the friendly
thrush which had followed her down the lane from the
village, rose out of the hedge near by and with a coaxing,
beguiling trill darted away across the meadow toward the
fairy sentinel tree.

"I do believe he's calling me," she whispered.

The cheery note of the thrush took much of the lonesomeness out of the gathering shadows, and Bridgeen,
with an answering cry in her throat, quickly hid her
father's brogues under the stile and without so much as a
glance behind followed the bird's flight.

Eager and brave enough she ran across the fields after
the twinkling brown speck which, with many excited calls
and soft, coaxing trills, lured her straight as a sunbeam
through the cool, damp grass. Out of the meadow over
the upland Bridgeen sped; down from the upland into the
moor she flew. An astonished curlew sent up a reproachful cry, and the moor hens, indignant at this untimely
intrusion, fluttered angrily out of the bog.

The wind beating against the girl's face as she ran
blurred the sight of her wide, blue eyes; and by and by,
because of a throbbing in her temples, the line between
earth and sky began to waver unsteadily up and down.
Then, too, a mysterious, shadowy form, invisible, but never-
theless strongly palpable to her excited imagination,
peeped out of the ditch after she had passed, and she
knew that another strange shape crouched hidden in the
rushes.

But, in spite of all her fears, a new, wild hope lent
fluttering courage to her heart and gave such strength of
speed to her bare, brown feet, that before Bridgeen realized how far she had traveled, the gray, withered sentinel
tree flashed up from the ground in her path and stood
towering high above her head.

With a quick clasp of her hands and a frightened little
gasp, Bridgeen stopped short and looked timidly around.
Well might she hesitate! Just a few yards beyond the tree,

shadowy, dark, and dumb, crouched the low green mound which was famed through all the countryside as the leprechaun's fairy fort.

There was not a man in the barony, let alone a child, foolhardy enough to venture to this spot after dark; and yet here was Bridgeen standing alone in that very place, with the sun fast disappearing behind the mountains.

To gain a moment's courage, she turned and looked in the direction of the village. It seemed miles and miles away, and a soft, white mist was creeping low along the meadows, cutting her off from the world of living things. There was not a cricket's chirp to break the throbbing silence. Even a curlew's cry would have brought some comfort with it. As she listened a chilling sense of utter loneliness fell upon her, and a nameless dread reached out and touched her like a ghostly hand.

Overcome by a shapeless fear she turned to fly from the awesome spot, when clear and cheery from a leafless bough above her head the same thrush began to call. Bridgeen paused, wonderstruck, for the bird was now chirping as plainly almost as spoken words: "The leprechaun! The leprechaun!"

'Twas like a friend's voice in her ear and brought with it the recollection of the importance of her mission. She hesitated no longer. Stealthily and still half afraid, she tiptoed her way over to the shallow ditch which ran about the enchanted place and, with many a shuddering glance, stepped slowly down. There was nothing there save Mayflowers, ivy and daisies.

It was in this very ditch that Tim O'Brien had seen the leprechaun; Bridgeen remembered that well. Her heart beating like that of a captured bird, the child stood, with parted lips and panting breast, wondering whether she should go to the right or to the left, when the twigs stirred on the bank above her head and, glancing quickly up, she saw through the fringe of leaves two round, golden eyes peering down upon her.

For one horrified instant Bridgeen stared fascinated at the eyes, and the eyes, fixed and unwinking, glared back at her. All power of motion deserted the child. Then a smothered cry broke from her lips. At the sound of her voice a pair of slim ears popped straight up above the eyes, and a great brown rabbit rabbit sat up on his haunches and listened for a moment, greatly surprised. Then, as though reassured, he coolly turned and with a saucy whisk of his fluffy tail, scampered out of sight.

With a quick laugh of relief the nervous colleen wiped her lips with her apron and crept on her way round the fairy rath. She looked eagerly under every bush, and behind every clump of rushes, but found no sign of the leprechaun. After making the circle, so tired was Bridgeen and so disheartened that she sat herself down to think. But lo and behold you, she had hardly time to settle herself comfortably, when from somewhere behind her came the tack, tack, tack of a little hammer!

She listened, every sense alert. There could be no mistake. From behind a sloe bush not five feet away the sound came tinkling clear as a bell—tack-tack-tack-tack.

"Surely," said Bridgeen to herself, and she trembled at the thought, "it must be the leprechaun!"

Then quietly, oh, so quietly, she stole over to the sloe bush and peeped cautiously behind it. There, in truth, was a sight of wonder. Seated on a flat stone and partly hidden by the grass worked a frowning little bald-headed cobbler, not the height of Bridgeen's knee, hammering and stitching with all his might on a dainty wee slipper, the size of your thumb.

While Bridgeen stared, the fairy, frowning deeper still, began singing in a high querulous voice:

Tick, tack, tickety, tack!
I've not a breath to lose;
Bad manners to their dancing,
But they're cruel on their shoes!

The quane plays on her silver pipes,
The king lolls on his throne.
But underneath the hawthorn three
I mend and moil alone."

He stopped singing. "All the rest of the world spendin'
their lives in fun and jollity!" he muttered. "Wirra, wirra,
I'm fair kilt with work, so I am." With a vicious bang of
the little hammer he started again:

"They trail their robes of shiny silk
Wear many a jeweled ring;
Id make them careful of their brogues
If I could be the king.
They ride the wind from cloud to cloud
'Mid wonder and delight,
But I must stitch the satin shoes
The quane will wear tonight.

The mist is on the spangled fields;
I'm perished with the frost!
If a mortal's eyes falls on me,
Tare an' ages, sure I'm lost!
He may ask for love and beauty;
Sure they always ask for wealth;
Much good in love or beauty—
Huh! I'd rather have me health."

Tick, tack, tickety, tack—Suddenly, as if stuck by a
pin, he sprang to his feet and turned, shaking his tiny
hammer at Bridgeen. "What's the worruld comin' to," he
shouted fiercely, "whin one of your age comes gallopin'
and cavortin' over the fields to torture out of a poor ould
man the favor of three wishes, you young r-r-rob-ber?"

"No, no Misther Leprechaun, not that at all," Bridgeen
hurried to say. "I don't want to force yer honor to do anything. I came only to beg from you one little wish. See, I

will take my eyes from you, so that you may go away if you like; but, oh, it would be kind of you, indeed, indeed it would, to hear the wish before you go."

"Do! Take yer eyes from me! I dare ye!" snapped the little man.

And indeed turn away her head she did; but when she looked back to the rock again, there still sat the little cobbler much as before, only now there was a friendlier light shining through his big spectacles.

"That was the daycintest thrick," vowed he, thumping the rock with his fist, "that I've seen a human crachure do in foive hundhred years—I mane whin ye turned yer head, mavourneen. Be raison, I've a gr-reat curiosity to know what this one grand thing is that ye'd be after wishin' for. It's a crock o' goold, no doubt," he said, peering.

Bridgeen shook her head sadly and threw him a wistful look.

The leprechaun dropped his chin into his hand and stared quizzically. "It's a coach an' four thin, I'm thinkin'," he ventured.

The sad, wistful look deepened on Bridgeen's face.

The leprechaun puzzled a moment in silence and then spoke up quickly: "A-ha, I have it now! If it isn't a purty red dhress wid green ribbons, an' a hat wid a feather as long as yer arrum, thin I'm fair bate out!" exulted he, clasping his knee in his hands and leaning back.

The little girl still hesitated.

"Millia murdher! Isn't it that ayther? Out with it! Spake up!" he encouraged.

Bridgeen nervously plaited the corner of her apron in her fingers and answered: "It isn't any of thim things I want at all, at all," she hesitated. Then, boldly, "Of course, I need a white veil and wreath and dress for my confirmation tomorrow."

"Oh, my! Oh, my!" broke in the leprechaun. "The wreath and the veil and the purty white dhress! Oh, dear! Oh, dear!"

"Still," Bridgeen continued, "It isn't for thim I came to ask you."

"Tare and ages, what is it, thin? Ye're makin' me narvous! I niver saw such a quare little colleen."

"A fortnight ago last Monday"—and Bridgeen bit her lips to hide the tremble— "my mother died; and oh, how can I live longer without her!"

The leprechaun slowly wagged his head and clucked his tongue sympathetically.

Bridgeen faltered, "I know she's in Heaven as Father Cassidy says, and that it's cruel and wicked to wish her back to life again; but I know, too, that even if she is happy with the angels she still must miss little Paudeen, the baby, sometimes—and, Misther Leprechaun, the one wish I have is that you'll let me see my mother for a minute, just for a minute, won't you?" Without realizing the boldness of it, she stretched her hands out to him, all the pleading of the world in her eager eyes.

The little cobbler shook his head sadly. "What good 'ud that do?" he sighed.

"If you only knew how my heart aches and aches for a sight of her when I go home and find her not there! You don't know what a terrible thing it is to be without your mother, Leprechaun, do you?"

"I don't," he answered, wiping his eyes with the corner of his apron. "I never had a mother, but I can aymagine. I wish I could bring her to ye, acushla, but it's beyant me power, I'm sorry to say. Ye see, she's a blessed sperrit up in Heaven and we fairies are only onblessed sperrits down here, ye undherstand; an' it's little the likes of her'd have to do with the likes of us. But maybe the talk I'm talkin' is too deep for ye, colleen. It's tayology," he said with a grand sweep of his hand.

The last hope was gone. Her head sank forward in a despair too deep for tears. "Never again! Oh, mother! mother!"

The leprechaun had pushed his spectacles high on his forehead and was vigorously wiping his eyes with his sleeve. "Stop, mavourneen," he said gruffly, ashamed of his weakness. "Now maybe it isn't so bad as all that. Whist now!" He paused a moment in deep thought, and a grim, determined look stole over his odd little face.

"I'm goin', Bridgeen Daley," he said, getting up and tightening the strings on his leather apron. "Sthop yer cryin' an' dhry yer eyes. I'm off. I may get insulted an' I may be malthrated, and at the very laste I'm sure to have an ackerymoneous argymint. Howandever, what I can do I will do, and what I can't do I won't do, but I'll sthrive my best endayvors; so do you go and sit again undher that withered three, and we'll see what'll happen. Don't be afeared, for if a thousand fairies were there ferninst ye they'd not harm a hair of yer purty head. But whatever ye do, stir not a stir, and spake not a worrud till the shadow of this three raiches yondher hazel bush. Good-by, I'm off!" And flash! he was gone.

Bridgeen went and sat under the tree as she was told. Presently she noticed how the stealthy shadow of the tree crept nearer and nearer the hazel bush. At last, the quivering tracings of the topmost branch, reaching out eager fingers, touched the bush.

Bridgeen caught her breath and glanced around for some sign, but for the moment there was none. The only moving things she saw were two belated bees, which, rising heavily laden from the sweet-briar bush at her side, buzzing and tumbling, started for home; and in the grass at her feet a busy little brown spider was measuring off the outlines of a net and stopped now and then to listen, one slender arm lifted. The colleen looked reproachfully toward the white stone upon which had perched the leprechaun. There it still shone dimly amongst the swaying rushes.

"The time is past and she isn't here. Oh, I wonder if she'll come," grieved Bridgeen.

As if in answer to the thought the rushes bowed low to the ground and over their heads swept a cool wind which lifted the curls on the child's brow. Or was it the wind? Was it not rather soft, caressing fingers that were smoothing the brown hair back from her forehead

Bridgeen started to her knees with a sobbing, laughing cry of "Mother! mother! My own mother!"

For there, bending over her, was the white, gentle face she loved best in all the world. Never before had the child seen so much tenderness and peaceful happiness shining in the dear, patient eyes. Crying and laughing, Bridgeen flung herself into the arms outstretched for her.

"Bridgeen asthore, acushla machree!" Though the voice was as soft as the voice of the wind, it still held the same lingering tenderness that had soothed and comforted a thousand griefs and sorrows. And wonder of wonders, slowly about her shoulders closed the remembered pressure of her mother's arms.

And now, with her head once more in its old place upon her mother's breast, all the cares, all the heartaches were forgotten.

"Your lonesome cry brings me thus visible to you, allanna!"

"Oh, mother, I've wanted you so much!" murmured Bridgeen with a sigh of measureless joy and relief.

"But don't you know I am never away from you, asthore? I've felt every tear that you have shed, and every grief of your heart has been a pain to me."

"Oh, if I had only known that, mother, I wouldn't have grieved. I thought you were away from us entirely," cried the child.

"Listen, Bridgeen, and mark my words," the mother warned, "for the time is short and I've many things to tell you."

And then, with faces close, the two talked earnestly about many important things—how willingly Bridgeen must obey her father; how careful she must be to keep the stirabout from burning in the morning; but, above all, how watchful she must be to keep her brother Jamesy away from the fire. The colleen promised faithfully not to forget. And so they talked on lovingly, happily together.

At last the mother said: "It is the children's bedtime, and you must be my own brave daughter and go to them. Keep well in your mind what I have said; be cheerful and contented, for we are not separated. And listen, mavourneen!

"Tomorrow—the morning we had so long hoped for and planned for together, the day of your confirmation—though you will not see me there, still I'll be kneeling happy at your side."

"Mother, I'll be contented and happy always now, indeed, indeed, I will."

"Now hurry home, mavourneen," the mother whispered. "Run straight on without looking back. Have no fear, and remember!" Bridgeen felt a kiss on her forehead, and she knew that her mother was gone.

So, her happy heart filled with satisfied longings, without once turning her head, she ran out into the fields, her spirit growing lighter and lighter at every step.

On and on Bridgeen hurried, picking up her father's brogues as she passed the stile; and she never tarried till she came to her own door.

There she found waiting for her, all bristling with excitement, Kathleen, Norah, Jamesy and Paudeen, and they were carefully guarding a long, white, pasteboard box, held jealously between them.

"Oh, Bridgeen, Father Cassidy was just here, an' he said he met the leprechaun, an' he left this box an' said he'd skiver Jamesy for pokin' at the fire, an' for us all not to so much as lay a finger on the knot of the cord till you came home." It was Kathleen who spoke.

With shaking fingers and amid eager proffers of help from Kathleen, Norah, Jamesy, and even little Paudeen, the string was untied and the lid lifted. And what do you think was in that same box?

Why, nothing else but the prettiest white dress and veil and wreath ever worn in the parish of Ballinderg.

The next morning the good old archbishop leaned over Bridgeen Daley where she knelt.

He thought that in all the years of his life he had never seen so happy a face.

And do you wonder that to this day Bridgeen will listen to no doubting or unkind word spoken of the leprechaun?

The Monks of Saint Bride

There was a decent bit of a man, yer honor, named Michael Bresnahan, who till a few years ago lived over in that little fisher village under the cliff, and he had a good sensible lump of a woman for a wife, named Katie.

No one could say a word against Katie—she was thrifty, she was clean, she was hard-working—only she used to be faulting Michael, and faulting him, and faulting him. If the decent man happened home of an evening with a sign of a little drop of drink on him, one would think from the way Katie went on that it was after robbing a church he was.

Well, one day Michael said to himself that he'd bear it no longer, so he up and went to his wife's relations, especially her sisters' husbands, to ask their advice about what he should do. They pitied him, indeed—sure no one could do less—but all the counsel they could scrape together to give the unfortunate man was just the kind of encouragement relations always give.

"Arrah, God help ye, me poor man, don't I know, and bear it the best ye can!"

Well, there wasn't much comfort in that, so Michael put in the next day going around asking the neighbors what he'd do with Katie, and everyone freely gave the advice the neighbors always give under such circumstances: "Musha, God help ye, me poor man, and ye're a fool for standing it!"

Now taking public advice on family matters soon grows into a pleasant habit with anyone, so, after Michael had exhausted the cottages on both sides of the village street, he took the road in his hands, and was making his way down to Haggarty's public-house at the crossroads when who should he meet up with, ambling along on the gray pony, but his Reverence, Father John Driscoll.

"This is me chance to get in the first word before Katie sees his Reverence," he thought.

And what does the blundering lad do but stop the priest in the middle of the road and there make his bitter complaint. That was the rock Michael split on, for the clergyman, without a word of warning, up with his whip and hit Bresnahan two rousing welts over the legs, and then when the poor man took to his heels Father Driscoll galloped after, at every jump of his pony larruping Michael down the road and calling his such heart-scalding names that the very crows wouldn't pick his hones. You'd pity the state he was in after, and he sitting by the hedge rubbing his smarting legs.

"There don't seem to be any rale appreciation of a good man in this worruld," he whimpered.

That same night Michael made up his mind to do something tremendous; so bright and early the next morning the desperate man slipped from the blue tea-pot on the dresser the last shilling in the house, and taking the road in his hands again off with him to Ballinderg to get the grand advice from Shiela McGuire, the fairy doctor. It's she that was the deep knowing crathure.

And the advice that Shiela gave him would raise the hair on your head:

"Hand me the shillin'! All Souls' night'll be here soon and whin it comes d'ye go up to the monastery of Saint Bride an' help the monks an' they'll help you."

If one goes to the Fairies for counsel and afterwards doesn't follow what he's bid, it's certain sure he'll find himself twice as bad off as ever before.

When Michael heard that same advice the cold sweat broke out on his forehead, for no man in five hundred years had ever been bold enough to face the monks of Saint Bride.

Where are the monks of Saint Bride, is it, yer honor? Why, God rest their souls, they're dead hundreds of years! That old ruin up on the cliff is where the monastery used to be. Troth and I must tell you of the monks of Saint Bride, or you'll never be able to rightly appreciate the terrible thing that happened to Michael Bresnahan that Hallowe'en night.

So you see that high bare cliff beyant?—Aill Ruahd they do be calling it—well, in the days when the five kings ruled over Ireland—and many a year ago that was—Black Roderick O'Carrioll with three hundred of his fighting men lived perched upon the very pin point of the hill. Right opposite, on that other bold headland where you see the ruins lying tumbled, dwelt the far-famed Monks of Saint Bride. And just as you see it now, between their stout old monastery and the castle of the O'Carrioll, the blue sea curved in like the half of a cartwheel.

Barring these two habitations there wasn't another strong house within forty miles; but only the cottages of the cowherds and of the swineherds and the low mud huts of the kerns.

However, it's little the O'Carrioll cared for near neighbors, and it's little he bothered the monks with his visiting, and as for the monks, it's far from being sorry the holy men were to have the O'Carrioll keeping that way to himself.

A fierce proud man was Black Roderick, and the greatest pleasure he took in life was in leading a hundred or two of his spears over the walls of some nobleman's castle and leaving its roof glowing blood red against the midnight sky.

But though half the province of Leinster, hated and feared the O'Carrioll, it wasn't that way at all with him in his own household, for, whatever was the reason, with all his stern, cold ways, there was many a man-at-arms who sat at the chief's table that would willingly have laid down his life to serve Black Roderick. But if the chief himself had any great liking for his men, he wasn't the one to be making much talk about it, and indeed they used to be saying that there was but one mortal man that he showed any fondness for and that same his only brother, the yellow-haired, pleasant-faced young Turlough. And it was no wonder for him to be fond of the lad the way he was, for a brighter minded, comelier young fellow there wasn't to be found in the seven counties. Indeed, it's more like father and son the two men were than like brother and brother.

All their days they lived that way together, with their foraging and their games and their hunting, and their feasting, happy and contented enough, I dare say, though it's little enough attention the two paid to prayers or to fasting or to any other pious thing. Nor at Christmas, nor Easter, nor on any other holy day did either of the two go next or near the monastery chapel of Saint Bride.

In that way they kept their lawless lives, living to themselves, for themselves and not caring a ha'porth for Heaven or the crack of a finger for Hell. Sometimes on dark nights when the torches would be glimmering on the far cliff, the old Abbot would sadly shake his head, "Let them see to it," he would mutter. "What can anyone expect from the likes of that but misfortune on earth and torment hereafter."

Well, the misfortune came at last, and when it did, a bitter, burning, incurable misfortune it was.

One black midnight the holy monks were awakened by a great noise of confused shouting and cheering passing along the road in the valley below them. And what should the good men see but the flare of a hundred torches held high by O'Carrioll's men above a dim crush of hard-driven cattle.

"The O'Carrioll is home from his raiding," said Brother John. "I wonder who this time was the unfortunate that felt the edge of his sword."

"God rest his soul the night, wherever he lies," sighed Brother Andrew. "And isn't it the marvel that Heaven has spared the heartless spoiler so long!"

While the monks stood wondering what depredation Black Roderick was after doing, there suddenly fell a hard rapping upon the convent gate, and a voice strident as a trumpet startled the monastery: "Open, open I say! 'Tis the O'Carrioll bids ye!"

Straightway there buzzed a hurried consultation among the brown brothers at the gate. While some were for letting him in, others brought staves and scythes and one hid a sword under his robe.

However, at last the drawbridge was let down, indeed, and the gate was opened, as needs must be, and then two shadowy horses crossed the wide moat and stumbled into the abbey court.

First of all plunged the O'Carrioll himself on the tall black horse that people used to be saying could fight as well as his master. And the figure of a woman is what Roderick carried in front of him, and she wrapped in his wide cloak; and at the black steed's haunches, on a panting white mare, rode Turlough, the brother, and by the strange wild look on his face the monks thought at first that maybe it was a deep wound that was on him and that it was for a leech the two men were coming.

"Quick, Sir Abbott," cried the dark man, "out with your book and marry the both of us here, for when this lady crosses my threshold I wish her to go as my wife. That much I'll do for her father's daughter." So saying he dismounted and helped his burden to the ground and standing beside the girl lifted her hand in his and then sternly waited.

And Brother Paul was telling the next day how when Black Roderick took the lady's hand young Turlough's face went deadly white and the lad's fingers made a sudden stealthy reach toward the sword hilt at his side; and sure everyone saw how the colleen (it's little more than a child she was) tottered and would have fallen if the O'Carrioll himself had not held her up.

I never rightly heard the truth about the three of them, but I think there must have been something before that time between Turlough and the young colleen. Who was the lady and how came the friendship between herself and young Turlough was, you may be sure, more than a nine days' wonder at Saint Bride's.

One morning a rumor reached the monastery that the colleen was the O'Coffey's daughter, and that she had been stolen out of the West, but that couldn't be true because the O'Coffey's daughter was being reared in France; and after that some pilgrims were saying that the lady might be the child of the O'Donavon from Munster, but if that were true, half of Ireland would have been in arms against the O'Carrioll. Even Black Roderick wouldn't have dared the O'Donavon. So one way and another, the matter was bothering the friars at their beads and distracting them at their vespers till they could get no good of their prayers.

News traveled slowly in those old days, and he was a bold man that journeyed far from home. So that weeks went by and no word drifted through the monastery walls about the bride, when lo and behold, one morning about three months after the wedding, an astonishing thing happened: The Lady O'Carrioll herself, and no other, came riding across the drawbridge again. This time, however, she rode hurrying alone up the winding path, her mist of brown hair streaming in the wind and a look of terror frozen on her white face. At the same time rushed galloping in furious pursuit Lord Roderick O'Carrioll.

"Open and let me in," she called to the warder. "I claim the protection of this holy place."

And the draw was let down to her when they heard that cry, but when she rode over the bridge the O'Carrioll already galloped at her heels, and when they drew bridle in the midst of the crowd of curious friars one horse's head tossed beside the other horse's head.

The man's eyes gleamed on her like coals of living fire, and what he said was:

"Is it to escape you thought you would! Return to your house and to your duty, shameless woman!"

The Lady O'Carrioll didn't answer him then, but slipped quickly down from the horse, and it's on her two bended knees she went before the abbot.

"I claim your protection! Save me, Sir Abbot," she implored.

The old monk looked in stern amazement from the dark, threatening brow of the angry man to the death-white checks of the girl at his feet.

"Stop where you are, O'Carrioll," was what he said as the chief dismounted, "and come not a foot nearer, for, though I'm a priest of God, now if you so much as lift a finger to this woman it's little help that sword you're striving to draw will be to ye then."

At that the abbot turned, and it's what he called to the warder:

"Brother John, raise the drawbridge." And while the bridge was clanking up a score of stalwart monks armed, some with staves, some with spears, and two or three with naked swords, crowded hurrying up and grouped themselves around their abbot.

"And now, Roderick O'Carrioll," demanded the soldierly old friar, "what means this rude pursuit?"

"By the cross it's what it means, that she is a disobedient wife," haughtily replied the O'Carrioll, and it's more than that you shall not know."

"It's more than that I shall know indeed," said the abbot; "for unless you swear by the cross on your sword-hilt never to harm a hair of the woman's head, it's not one foot she'll stir beyond this gate. And if your men shall try a rescue 'tis your own corpse they'll bear away."

"Most willingly do I take that oath," spoke the O'Carrioll, "though it's not through any dread of this nest of scurrying brown mice. An O'Carrioll never did anything yet through fear; but I'll take the oath you say to ease the fears of this woman. Unworthy as she is, I love her."

And straightway, holding up the gold hilt of his sword, he swore by it blunt and plain like a soldier to keep her safe from any hurt or harm or shame that might come through himself or through another.

The lady dropped her tear wet hands from her white face and unassisted rose to her feet. Not a word did she utter but the proud hopeless look of her eyes would wring one's heart.

And the two rode silently away together.

"Now may God forgive us all," cried Brother Andrew, the youngest of the monks. "We've done a craven thing to let him take her from this shelter."

"Not so," answered the Abbott, "it's safer for her to go. The man will keep his oath."

The monks of Saint Bride never saw her again and for two months it's little they heard of her, and then a dark rumor crept over the valley. And when two cowherds stood together out on the lonely hills they whispered the rumor to each other, and when any two men were alone together in their currach on the ocean they talked of it, and it's what they said:

"The O'Carrioll has reddened his hands with his wife, and he has reddened his hands with his brother Turlough that she had the love for, and the both of them are lying beside each other cold and dead at the bottom of the sea."

At last one day a fisherman found a lady's blue cloak washed up between two rocks, and it was the Lady O'Carrioll's gold embroidered cloak they were saying. They brought that cloak to the monastery. Now when the abbot of Saint Bride heard this thing and of the way the sword oath that had been put upon the O'Carrioll was broken, it's great indeed the wrath that was on the good man, for such treachery never had been heard of before in all Ireland.

The evening of the day that the blue cloak was brought to him he called all the monks together in the chapel, and there they consulted one with the other what was a just and worthy punishment to put upon the O'Carrioll. It was the turn of midnight before they decided that and went to their cells. And then on the morning of the morrow, just when the great round sun was reddening the foreheads of the hills, they all gathered again on the east turret of the monastery, and when the abbot found that they were all about him he fronted the castle of the O'Carrioll and raised his oaken cross. Then he cursed that house, and he cursed the chief of that house. And it wasn't the O'Carrioll alone he cursed, but he banned him and all who cleaved to him with the curse of sleepless nights, which is the most agonizing of all curses, and he doomed them with the curse of friendless days, which is the most terrible of all curses, and he cursed them with the blight of a quick-coming death, which is the surest of all curses. And he put excommunication upon the lord of the castle, so that he would be banished from out of the ways of living man.

And the abbot sent Brother Paul and Brother Philip over to the castle, and the two holy Friars repeated to the O'Carrioll and to his retainers the terrible curse and the words of excommunication.

So no wonder it is at all, at all, that quick and heavy that curse fell. For from that day out the kerns began to steal away from Black Roderick's land, the way they were afraid of the curse; and the fighting men deserted him, at first by twos and three and then by scores; and then the women of the house crept away in the night; so that presently he that used to be counting five hundred spears was left with but a dozen or so of the old retainers.

And that is how Black Roderick's power went from him, so that he was forced at last to pay tribute to the O'Driscolls that he might save the roof of his castle from the torches of the MacDonoughs. And that's the way, too, it befell with him when the red plague came sweeping up from Ath Cliath, as they used to be calling the city of Dublin then, and it leaving in its track no living man, woman, or child.

One morning six men lay dead in the castle of the O'Carrioll and within the hour the master of the house, in the way that he would be ready if his own turn came, sent a quick messenger over for one of the monks of Saint Bride to come and shrive him. But the abbot sent a stern answer back, and it's what he said:

"Let Roderick O'Carrioll come himself to this monastery, and on his bare knees make public confession of the murder of his brother, and of his wife, and full acknowledgment of his other crimes, and then let him humbly take on himself the penance I'll impose,—and it's no light penance that will be either; and let him not be sending here for a priest again, for it's to the chapel he himself must come, and it's my own tongue and no other that shall ask the forgiveness for him, and until I do that same it's unshriven he will be, and it's neither ease for his body, nor rest for his soul, he may expect in this world or in the next."

When the frightened messenger went back and told that, it's what the O'Carrioll answered:

"It's a hard saying, that is, and the curse they put on me I send back to them, and let it be laid against their souls that as I am innocent of the crime they say, they shall pray for me until I am blessed, whether in this world or in the next!"

The words were no sooner out of his mouth than he felt the sickness of the plague on him, and he turned to the serving-men and what he said was:

"The hand of death is on me now, and after all I'd wish to die at peace with God, and I'm not guilty of the crime they lay against me, so put me on the litter there and carry me with what haste you can to the monastery of Saint Bride. And when they hear what I have to say it's well I know they'll shrive me then."

And the serving-men were loath to go, for the night was on, and it was All Souls' night, and wild with the wind, and the thunder, and the rain. But for love of the old times they took the master up between them at last, and it's how they carried him out into the darkness, and down into the valley, and by every short way toward the monastery.

By the time the serving-men had readied the path on the edge of the high cliff, which was half way between the two places, they were as frightened as four shivering hares, and they set down the litter to rest themselves. When they did that there sprang across the sky a long flame of green lightning, and when it was over a man of them said:

"We need go no further, the O'Carrioll is dead!" And they crossed themselves then, but not one of them dared say "God have mercy on his soul," because of the curse that was on him. Then one of them said, "What shall we do with him now?"

And the waves were leaping up against the rocks, the way they were striving to drag the men down into sea.

Then the oldest of them answered, and what he said was: "The sea is calling for him, because he cannot be buried in the consecrated ground. We shall bury him in the sea."

So they flung him far out over the cliff, and the strong waves of the green sea leaped up to meet him as he fell, and there was his grave.

At sunrise, on the morning of the morrow, the red plague stalked into the monastery of Saint Bride, and the first token of its presence was when it put its hot breath upon the old abbot himself so that he withered within the hour. And it's the dying that was burying the dead from that hour on, until the last friar of them all, with his spade in his hand, tumbled, stricken into a half-filled grave.

Then the loneliness and bleakness of desolation settled down on miles of hills and leagues of plains.

For three times ten years the deer browsed under the castle walls, and the badgers dug their lairs in the dry monastery moat; and then the O'Broders sent their herds and their cattle and their swine down into the fat grass lands which for so long had lain fallow. But for years after that no one had the courage in his four bones to take shelter in the castle, or the monastery, for fear of the sickness and the misfortune that was on the two places.

But after a time there came an old swineherd of the O'Broders—Brown Shamus he was called—and on winter nights he used to be driving his pigs into the castle yard and to be building a great blaze on the hearth of the hall the way he would be sleeping in the warmth of it.

One night as he sat huddled before the fire, with his chin on his knees, there fell a hard rap on the hall door behind him. Brown Shamus never turned his head, for he'd often heard sounds like that before at night in the castle, and he had seen strange shapes, and well he knew that it's from the grave they were, and what he'd do then was to be shutting his eyes and striving not to be thinking of them. In that way they never bothered him.

But the rap came again, and after it a blast of cold air. By that Shamus knew the door was open. He turned around then, and what he saw was a very old man and a very old woman, and they were perishing with the cold. At that Shamus began on his prayers, for he made no doubt but what it was two spirits standing ferninst him.

Then the old man, seeing the fright that was on Shamus, spoke up, and it's what he said:

"Have no fear, swineherd of the brown beard, it is I, Turlough O'Carrioll; and this is the Lady O'Carrioll, my brother's wife, that has come back with me."

At that the terror was all the greater on Shamus, for he was sure the two had been dead at the bottom of the sea those forty years. But when they drew nearer to the fire, and he heard the fall of their shoes on the stones of the floor, he knew by that it was living creatures they were, for the others that used to he coming and going there, made no sound at all on the stones.

And sure enough, Turlough O'Carrioll it was, coming back after all these years, and his brother's wife along with him. Instead of being murdered and killed, as the report was out, they had taken a currach at night, and had slipped away to foreign parts, where they lived together until the hour I'm telling you about. And the pride of Black Roderick O'Carrioll, and his bitter shame, and maybe a bit of love for the both of them as well, had kept their flight and their crime secret—even when the dark man was excommunicated, and cursed, and forsaken on account of them, he made no sign. Sure you can never tell what good or evil thing is working hidden inside the mind of a man.

How long Turlough and the Lady O'Carrioll remained living it's not very sure. It may have been one year, or it may have been two years, but it wasn't very long. At any rate, the two of them died, and were put in the one grave, and that was the end of the world for them, and they came back no more. You may see the wide brown stone flag that covers them to this day in the churchyard of the monastery, for they were lain in consecrated ground.

And wouldn't it have been a good thing, too, if Roderick O'Carrioll, and the monks of Saint Bride with him, could have found untroubled graves in consecrated ground? But an unjust curse is a dreadful thing. And through five hundred years, as sure as the night of All Souls came, the friars of the abbey, and the lord of the castle, made bitter penance for their sin.

The dead make no account of time, they say—and, indeed, why should they?—and so one generation followed another generation, and the story of the curse came down with the years, and the weary penance kept still unfinished.

By and by the lonely castle of the O'Carrioll melted away in the sun and the snow. One by one its great stones were rolled down the mountainside to build the fishers' village of Killgillam, which was growing up on the ribbon of sandy beach below—the same village that I was telling you about, where Michael Bresnahan lived.

But no man proved hardy enough to take a single stone from the haunted abbey, for fear of the bad luck it might bring him. So it, too, crumbled away in the sun, and in the storms, but the gray rocks that tumbled lay where they fell.

And many's the strange whisper that went around about things that were seen at night on the top of that lonely hill. And I myself knew a very truthful old man, who once lived in that village, and his name was Thomas O'Deegan, and this is what he told me:

One All Souls' night when he drifted out on the bay alone, fixing his nets, and the wind fluttered in sweeps down from the face of the cliff, he heard the sound of many voices chanting together, and it was the litany for the dead they were singing.

Now it's in the prayer book, as every one knows, that the living may pray for the dead, and the dead may pray for the living, but the sorrow of it is that the dead may not pray for the dead. It's a queer way that is, but they do be saying that there's a stranger thing still and I'm greatly bothered sometimes to know the reason, and it's what it is: Though the dead cannot pray for the dead, if one among the living say a prayer for the departed, then the dead may join his prayer to that same living prayer, and so as it makes one prayer they'll both be heard.

And this was the penance that was put on the monks of Saint Bride:

Once a year, upon All Souls' night—the night O'Carrioll died—they were to come out of their graves, every one, and to pray for the dead man's soul, and this until the day of judgment, with no release unless some living voice would join itself to their dead voices.

And it was a punishment put upon Black Roderick, too, for his red deeds, that his soul should attend them there and find no ease until it felt the blessing of the Abbot of Saint Bride. And so the useless prayers went on through all the generations, for sure what man in all the country felt brave enough to climb that lonely road at midnight on Hallowe'en?

So by this time your honor will understand the hard task that Sheila McGuire put upon Michael Bresnahan: He must go alone, d'ye mind, at midnight of All Souls', to the ruined monastery and there face the unhappy spirits of the monks of Saint Bride, and join his living prayers with their own, over the body of Black Roderick.

On the way home from Ballinderg, after seeing Sheila, Michael turned over and over in his mind, the advice the fairy doctor had given him, and it's what he decided at last:

"Well, after all, I think I'd better try to stand the faulting of Katie for a while longer, and if the worst comes to the worst," said the persecuted man to himself, "maybe I'll stop a trifle of the drink for peace sake." With that he tossed the matter from his mind and decided to do the best he could with Katie.

Be that as it may, one afternoon not long after, as the lad was on his way home from the village of Ballyslane (where he was after selling a fine cow to his uncle, Ned Corrigan, who kept the public house by the bridge), he took for a short cut home the path along the cliff. When he reached the top of the hill there fell a queer weariness on him, maybe from his journey and a bit of a weakness as well, so he stopped to clear his wits and to rest awhile on the sunny side of the old abbey. In that way maybe he could with a clear head meet Katie. Trouble never stayed long at a time with the lad. As he sat comfortably reclining with his back to the wall and smoking his pipe, the boy could see far down below him the little village straggle lazily along the yellow beach. About a stone's throw out from the edge of the green cliff stood his own white cottage, with the gray nets drying on its roof, and he could make out, too, Katie moving around in the thumb-nail of a garden, with one of the children clinging to her petticoat, and it's what he thought:

"Oh, wouldn't I be the foolish man to be going down there now the way I am with the sign of the drop of drink on me after the hard warning about the public houses she was putting on me when I went away this morning! No, no, Michael, take my advice, be a wise lad, and do you go in there now to the old chapel, where no one will he seeing you, and take a matter of forty winks or so, the way you'll have a sober and a clear head going down to her while it is still in the light of the evening."

So saying, Michael rose, stepped carefully over the fallen arch stones that blocked the doorway of the ruined chapel, and, after picking out a soft green mound for a pillow on the sunny side of the wall, laid himself down and fell asleep. But sure, it wasn't forty winks nor forty hundred winks the poor man took. The afternoon shadowed into evening, and the evening darkened into night, and Michael says he was sleeping like one of the cold stones when, suddenly, something like the skim of a bird's wing, or the brush of a garment passing across his face, startled every vein in his body, and he was wide awake at once and sitting up.

The full moon was sailing swiftly out to sea through a bank of fleecy clouds, and it took a wondering second or two to place rightly in the lad's mind the tumbled, roofless walls, and the tall broken arches of the ruin. And it's ghostly and solemn enough the place was, too, in the moonlight, with the sighing of the wind in the yew trees, and the whispering of the restless ivy on the walls, and far away the lonesome chirping of a cricket.

As Bresnahan hesitated, round-eyed and breathless, suddenly from the gaping tower of the abbey, soft and muffled, stole the boom of a tolling bell. Its toll was like the hollow moan of the shoal bell when the fog lies heavy on the sea—it was the mere ghost of a sound. This was strange for no mortal's bell ever was heard within six miles of the spot.

"My grief and my woe, where am I at all at all," he began "and what's this awful place?" The jump of his heart up into his throat took the breath from his lips, for the truth flashed into Michael's mind that this was the ruined abbey on the cliff where he had lain down for a minute's sleep; and, O Father in Heaven, wasn't tonight All Souls' night, when the terrible monks of Saint Bride walked in their awful penance?

The tolling ceased.

"The saints preserve us, 'tis the abbey!" whispered Michael. "Maybe I'll be able to slip down the hill before they come." He was half to his feet when there broke from the court outside the chapel a low wailing cry that froze the blood in his heart. It was as if some one in deep torment were begging for a drop of pity.

"Remember not his iniquities," pleaded the terrible voice. "Nor let thine anger encompass him."

Instantly the mournful chant of many lips, like the swelling moan of the ocean, took up the response of the litany:

"O Lord, we beseech Thee to hear us."

Michael crouched breathless behind a broken pillar. To the day of his death the bitter beseeching of that litany rang in his ears.

"From Thy wrath and from everlasting death," wailed the first supplicant.

And then the response, growing wild and dismal as the winter wind:

"O Lord, deliver him."

"I'm lost," groaned Michael. "'Tis the monks of Saint Bride, and they're coming in." Twice he tried to look, but the courage wasn't in him, so he just huddled there, cowering. At the same time the ghostly chant kept swelling nearer and nearer, and every wild prayer for the dead, with its pitiful response, went driving through the heart of poor Bresnahan.

Presently he felt that the monks were near the chapel door behind him, and compelled by very terror, Michael glanced shrinkingly back over his shoulder.

By this time the great white moon was flinging a soft steady light over the old ruin, and clearly, through the archway of the chapel, the crouching man saw approaching a sight terrible for mortal eyes.

Marching two by two, moved a shadowy procession of brown-robed monks, and they chanting the litany for the dead as they came. The spectres walked with aims folded, and each bowed head was hidden in its cowl. There must have been fifty of them. The fallen stones along their way made no hindrance to their feet any more than if those same stones had been moon-shadows.

A few paces in front of the procession, slow, solemn, and silent, the abbot advanced alone, a tall, stately figure. Just behind him four monks carried something between them on a litter. As the abbot entered the ruined chapel, soft and low again the bell in the tower began tolling.

Michael saw that they were going to pass by within a yard of him, so he strained every nerve and sinew to move aside, but the arms and legs of the poor lad were as heavy and had as little life in them as the stones lying scattered about the ground. When the monks drew near the night air grew cold and damp and close as an open vault.

"Out of Thy great pity pardon his infirmities," chanted the abbot.

"O Lord, we beseech Thee to hear us," answered the monks.

When they were within five feet of him Michael could see the abbot's hands crossed humbly upon the sunken breast; and, oh, achone mavrone! they were the long, thin, fleshless hands of a skeleton. Then he might have put out his hand and touched the dreadful shape.

One face in all the ghastly train was visible as it slowly passed, and that one was the still white face of a dead man who was being carried by on the bier. And a terrible thing he was to see with his long silken tunic dripping wet from the sea-bring, and the heavy seaweed clinging to him.

"Merciful Father!" gasped Bresnahan; "isn't it Black Roderick himself that I'm looking at, an' him dhrownded and dead these five hundred years?"

It's well Michael Bresnahan marked that as the monks passed him by not one of them cast a shadow on the ground. And they turned neither to the right nor to the left, nor changed their pace, nor made any kind of sign till they reached the place where the old altar used to be standing. There they stopped and the four bearers set the litter on the ground. The bell ceased tolling. Even the crickets shrank into a frightened silence. Michael's breath came in faint sobs.

It was the abbot himself, then, that moved solemnly to the head of the bier, and, kneeling down as though before an altar, stretched wide his arms. He was praying there, but what he said Michael couldn't hear because the chanting had begun again. But at any rate, there they all were, the helpless dead praying for the helpless dead. Here was the chance at last for poor Bresnahan to escape. And so he made one mighty effort. With teeth chattering and knees quaking, the lad turned him round and began creeping over toward the black, gaping archway. Barely was he able to climb the fallen stones.

There isn't a doubt but what Michael, if he had had the strength, would have opened his lips and prayed aloud with the monks, for he remembered the legend well of how the tormented spirits needed only a living voice to join its prayer with their own, the way they would have rest in quiet graves, but the fear lay too heavy on the poor man, and he couldn't do that.

But just as he reached the archway the heartbroken wail rose higher and higher and more despairing, so that he could bear the sorrow of it no longer, and, turning where he stood, he bent his knees and fiercely cried aloud with the others: "O Lord, we beseech Thee to hear us."

Those were the happy words. Instantly the chant ceased. The abbot rose from his knees and flung his arms to the sky. The man from the bier was kneeling beside the abbot. A sudden glow illuminated the chapel. Michael waited to see no more.

As Bresnahan scrambled over the fallen stones of the threshold and darted down the hill with all the strength of his legs, the wail of the solemn chant for the dead had changed for the glorious burst of the "Te Bourn Laudamus." And no wonder: the curse was broken, the punishment of the centuries was ended, for the prayer of the living had been joined to the prayer of the dead. In that way Bresnahan knew that the spirits were released from their penance. And ye may not believe it, but it's as true as the Book that from that good day to this the monks of Saint Bride walk the ruin no more.

As for Katie Bresnahan, the kind hearted woman, when she heard of the great miracle that her husband, Michael, had performed that night, she quit faulting him about the little drop of liquor he used to be taking, and on account of all that had happened to him Michael grew to be a hero throughout the countryside, and was looked up to as a knowledgeable man to the day he died.

Naturally he walked happy in this new and deserved importance. There remained but one thorn in his side. Whenever he chanced to meet up with Father Driscoll on the highway the suspicious minded priest would only laugh and shake the riding whip at him. Every one else paid him his due of dignified respect.

KILLBOHGAN AND KILLBOGGAN

Once upon a time, and a black fortuned, potato-blighted time it was, there lived near the town of Clonmel, in the beautiful County of Tipperary, a sober minded farmer named Jerry O'Flynn.

Of cattle or horses or sheep or goats or any four-footed beasts Jerry had none, saving and barring a beautiful white pig which he had picked up at his own threshold on a blustery evening in April, when it was a little stray, shivering, pink-nosed bonive.

Well, that same pig grew and grew, fat and silky and good-natured, till it was the pride and the pleasure of the family to currycomb him, to wash him, to feed him, and to rub his fine broad back. And when the time came for him to go the way of all pigs, Jerry's thatched roof covered as sore hearted a family as dwelt in all Ireland. However, the piteous law which compels the strong to prey upon the weak, was in this instance considered to be inexorable; so, the evening before the day of execution, Jerry repaired to a secluded spot behind the high, black, turf stack, and there, with his own unwilling hands, arranged the grim paraphernalia for the morrow's tragedy.

When this dismal work was finished, the honest fellow had not enough courage left to carry him back to the cottage, there to face the accusing eyes of his children; so he slunk over to the stile in the lane and stood with his right arm thrown listlessly about the hedge post, lost in troubled contemplation of the unconscious and confiding victim who stretched himself luxuriously in the grass at his master's feet.

So preoccupied was the lad with his bothersome thoughts, that he failed to notice the hasty approach of good-natured old Mrs. Clancey, and he answered her cheery "God save ye" with a half-frightened start.

"I've come to tell ye, Jerry agra," the excited woman panted, "that there's a letther—a big blue letther—from Amerikay—waitin' for ye down in the town; and the postmasther (bad cess to him) wouldn't let me have it to bring to you. He even rayfused to open it for me, so I might bring ye the news who it was from. The curse of the crows light on him!" She spoke with such hearty bitterness as to suggest a keenly disappointed curiosity.

"Thank ye, and thank ye ag'in for your throuble, Mrs. Clancey! You're sure the letther was from Amerikay?"

"Oh, faith I am; the postmasther hilt it up, an' more than a dozen of us saw the postmark."

"My, but that's quare," muttered Jerry. "I have no one in Amerikay who could be afther sending me a letther barrin' me Uncle Dan, and Dan's dead an' gone, Heaven rest him, these two years. I'm bilin' to know who the letther's from, but I can't go afther it the morrow bekase" (and he sighed deeply) "we've set that day for the killin' of Char-les, the pig there. And it's a red-handed murdherer I feel meself already, Mrs. Clancey ma'am."

Well, at these words, strange as it may seem, Cha-rles gave a startled grunt, rose to his fat haunches, and threw a look of such resentful surprise from under his white eyelashes, first at Jerry, and then at Mrs. Clancey, that the old woman, with a muttered "God save us, will ye look at that now," shrank back a pace from the stile.

"I wouldn't kill that pig, Jerry O'Flynn," says she, with a wag of her forefinger. "I wouldn't kill that pig if he was as full of goold suverins as the Bank of England, Ireland and Scotland put together, so I wouldn't!"

The smouldering trouble in Jerry's gray eyes deepened, and he sucked hard at his empty, black pipe.

"And why wouldn't ye, Mrs. Clancey, ma'am? What raisons have ye agin him?" asked Jerry, peering anxiously at her from under the rim of his old caubeen. Mrs. Clancey deliberately folded her arms in her shawl, and came a step nearer the stile.

"Well, first and foremost," says she, "he is a shupernatural baste, and there's a knowledgeableness in the cock of his white eye when he turns it on me that makes me shiver, so it does. Look at him sittin' there now! Look at the saygacious twisht of the tail of him. I'll warrant he ondherstands every worrud we're thinkin', let alone sayin'—conshuming to him."

Jerry threw an apprehensive eye over his shoulder at the pig who now sat with his back toward them solemnly twisting his tail first this way, then that. But for all his seeming indifference there was such a subtle suggestion of listening in the twitch of the beast's ears and the hump of his broad shoulders, that Jerry placed a cautious hand to his mouth when he whispered: "Do ye think so, Mrs. Clancey? No, no, it's only just the natural cultivaytion of the baste. Though I'll not deny that Char-les has sometimes the look of a Christian on him. Then, again, his ways are so friendly and polite that it goes sore agin me heart to lift a hand till him, so it does. Sure, pigs have feelings as well as you or I, and you wouldn't like to be kilt yourself, Mrs. Clancey, I'm thinkin'."

The unhappy personal comparison offended Mrs. Clancey's ever sensitive dignity, so with head askew and tight lips she replied, "If I wor a, pig, which Heaven forbid, I hope I'd be philosopher enough to be satisfied with me station in loife. Pigs were born to be kilt; how else could they be turned into things needful! 'Tis the least they can expect."

"Thrue fer ye!" apologetically sighed Jerry. "And to substantiate what ye're sayin' there's the rint long due, an'

Christmas almost on top of us, and the childher needin'
shoes, an' herself fairly perishin' for a bit of a bonnet; an'
look at him! there sits tay, an' bonnet, an' shoes, an' rint,
an' lashin's an' lavin's of tabacy; and here am I wid an
empty poipe, too tindher-hearted to transmogrify the baste.
What'll I do all, at all?"

"Faith, I dunno, Jerry me bouchal. It's beyant me,"
replied Mrs. Clancey, turning to go. "But"—and a sudden
thought halted her— "tomorrow is market day at Clonmel,
and if that same Char-les wor my pig, I'd have him half
way there before the sun stuck a leg over the mountain,
an' I'd sell him widout the flutther of an eyelid. By that
manes ye'd shift the raysponsibility onto himself. And if
Char-les is half as wise as he purtinds to be, lave him
alone but he'll take care of himself." With a self-satisfied
toss of her head and a cheerful "Good-night," the wise
woman took herself hurriedly up the road.

Jerry leaned heavily on the stile and gazed with
unseeing eyes at the brown shawl fast disappearing in
the shadows, until he was startled by two short indignant
grunts at his side. Looking quickly around, he met the
reproachful eyes of the pig gazing steadfastly up at him.

"Arrah, don't be blaming me, Char-les, me poor lad!
Don't look at me that way! Me heart's fair broke, so it is.
Haven't I raised you since you were the size of that hand?
an' a sociabler, civiler-mannered baste I niver saw. Musha,
I wisht you were a cow so I do; then you wouldn't be a pig
an' have to be kilt. Heigh, ho! Sorrows the day! come along
up with me, agra, an' we'll have a petatie."

That night long after the hearth was swept and the
childer and herself were in bed, Jerry sat with his chin in
his hands, gazing moodily into the smouldering turf. The
heavy task of the morrow drove all wish for the bed from
his mind, so the leaden-hearted lad decided to sit up until morning—the better to get an early start.

As thus he waited, the stillness of the night grew heavier
and heavier around him, broken only by the spluttering of

the ash-covered turf at his feet, and he felt the darkness of the room creeping up from behind, and pressing down upon his shoulders like a great cloak.

The expiring rush light on the old oak mantel above his head struggled feebly with the strangling shadows as it burned itself to the very rim of the tall brass candle-stick. But the contest proved a hopeless one, and so at last with one despairing spurt of yellow flame the vanquished light sank gurgling and choking out of sight. Jerry marked how its soul in one slender, wavering spire of gray smoke crept softly upward and disappeared. With a little shivering shrug, the lad drew his stool closer into the hearth. "Some one stepped over me grave sartin that time," he complained. "My, but isn't this a murdherin' shuperstitious night?"

And the turf fire at his feet—sure never before had its dull red caverns held so many weird and grostesque phantoms; an old woman with a bundle of sticks on her back glowed for an instant there, then suddenly changed and sank into a body stretched out on a low bier. And then the body rose slowly upright and stood a tall, long-faced, hunchbacked man who soon spread and spread, and then crumbled into a pack of running hounds. Jerry's fascinated eyes watched the pack until with a sharp crackle and a little hiss of flame the hounds dropped into an open sea of gray ashes. As they disappeared a sudden chill filled the whole room, and on that instant, loud and shrill, Phelim, the old black cock, crowed from his perch outside the door—a most unlucky sign before midnight, as everyone knows. Jerry flung a startled look at the clock. Its two warning fingers pointed the hour of midnight. He hastily drew himself together on the stool, counting the slow, heavy strokes and dreading he knew not what. The last chime of the old clock was yet tingling through the room, when Jerry heard (and his heart turned to jelly at the sound) a strange, weird voice calling from outside under the window.

"Jerry! Jerry O'Flynn!" wailed the voice, "why don't you open the dure?"

But Jerry never moved; he sat with stiffened hair and wild, straining eyes fixed on the black window-panes.

"Jerry! Jerry!" demanded the voice, now harsh and commanding, "I ask you once more, will you open?"

Slowly, like one asleep, Jerry arose, and step by step, retreated backward till his groping hands touched the wall behind him. There with parted, dry lips, and trembling knees he waited.

The clock had ticked five times—he timed it by his beating heart—when, without so much as a bolt being drawn, the door swung wide open, and from the blackness without what should step boldly over the threshold but Charles the pig.

Not as he was wont to come, mind you, with friendly grunt and careless swagger, but silent, and stern, and masterful. He marched into the room, over to the fireplace, and sat himself upright in quiet dignity upon the stool that Jerry had just left. Jerry never moved a muscle, but stood frozen with surprise and growing resentment that Char-les, the pig, should give himself so many airs and make himself so free about the house.

The beast never deigned so much as a side look at his master but, wriggling himself into a comfortable position on the stool, he opened his mouth, and in a gruff patronizing way began to speak.

At the sound of the strange voice all the boy's fears rushed back on him.

"Jerry O'Flynn," said the pig, "what are ye afeared of? Come over and sit on that stool fernist me, an' don't stand there shiverin' and shakin' like a cowardly bosthoon!"

"I'm not afeared," quavered Jerry as he sidled over and seated himself gingerly on the very edge of the stool. "But may I ax yez a fair, civil question?" says he.

"You may not," snapped Charles, "you're here now to do as you're bid, and not to be axin' questions."

At this unheard-of impudence, Jerry's anger got the better of his fright. "As I'm bid!" he spluttered, thumping his knee. "What do you mane? Amn't I the masther?"

"Masther! Ho! ho! Masther! Be-dad, will ye listen to that!" roared the pig. "Why you dundher-headed Omadhaun, who has been currycombing me, an' brushing me down all these months, an' who has been working for me early and late in the fields to get butthermilk an' petaties for me brakwusts, I'd like to know? Masther indeed! let me hear no more of that," grunted the pig, crossing his legs as he spoke. Jerry scratched his head in furious bewilderment.

"Tundher an' turf!" he gasped. "Thrue for ye, Char-les! I never thought of it that way. But thin, me lad, the raison ye got such grand care was because I intinded to—" He stopped short, frightened out of his seven senses by a quiet look in the pig's eye.

"Intended to what?" asked Charles calmly.

"Nawthin'" mumbled Jerry.

"Umph" the pig grunted. "Fill the poipe and hand it over to me, and pay attention for I've something to tell you. You know by this time, I suppose, that it's no ord'nary baste you have ferninst ye; an' I want ye to undherstand," says he, pointing to his pipe, "that tomorrow mornin' whin ye're takin' me to market, you'll be thravellin' in much betther company than I'll be in."

"Well, who and what are ye at all, at all?" demanded Jerry.

The pig leaned over and got a coal for his pipe. "Listen and I'll expatiate," he puffed.

"You must know that I am Killbohgan, the ould ancient Milesian maygician who in an unlucky moment had the comither put on him by Killboggan, an oulder an' a trifle ancienther enchanter; and who to escape from the parsecutions of Killboggan changed himself into a hare."

"Oh, be the powers!" cried Jerry, slapping his knee with his hand. "The first hard worruk ye'll do in the mornin' will be to go out an' change me flock of ducks intil a herd of cows, so it will."

"Oh, you poor man," sighed the magician. "There was a time when such a thrick 'us be only sport and may game for me. But wirrasthrue, that was hundherds of years ago. I once changed a hill of red ants into a dhrove of wild ulephants to plaze one of me sick childher. But Killboggan has dhrawn all the power from me now, an' I used the last spell I had that midnight whin I changed meself into a wee white bonive before your own horse-pittiful dure."

The pig scratched his ear reflectively with the stem of his pipe, and smiled, and shook his head sadly when Jerry remarked: "I aways knew there was something shuperior in your charack-ther, Char-les."

"Be that as it may be," continued Char-les, "as I was sayin': afther I had changed meself intil a hare, what did the bliggard Killboggan do but turn himself intil a hound, and for years and years he hunted me from one end of Ireland ground to the other. One day as we were goin' lickety splicket up the Giant's Causeway the villain nearly had me by the hind leg, and findin' meself in such a duspurate amplush, I quick turned meself intil a herring an' dhropped intil the say.

"Well, anyway, it wasn't a minute till Killboggan had metamurphied himself intil a whale, and, he the mortial man, came sploshing in afther me. And so for hundherds of years we'd been rumagin' and rampagin' from one ind of the everlastin' salt says to the other, till on Chewsday last April, Ned Driscoll, who was out fishing for herrings, caught me in his net. An' as he was passin' your door that same night, I slipped out of his basket an' turned meself into a purty white bonive in the road beyant."

"Well, well, d'ye mind that," exclaimed Jerry, "wondhers'll never sayse. And you can't gainsay, Char-les, but what you've got the best of good thratement."

"It's the truth you're spakin'" nodded the pig. "And now to prove me gratitude, I'll show ye a way to fill your pockets with goold. Whenever you need a little money, just take me to the nearest fair and sell me for the best price ye can get. Then go your ways, and never fear but I'll be back to ye safe an' sound be cockcrow."

In his excitement over this prospect, Jerry lost sight entirely of the sheer dishonesty of the plan. "Oh, be the powers," he exalted, "the goose that laid the goolden egg is a mere flaybite be comparison to you!"

"There's only one thing ye must be careful of," said the magician, raising his pipe warningly to his nose, "and that one thing is this: you are on no account to sell me to a dark, long-faced man with a hump on his back, for that'll be the tarnation schaymer of the worruld, Killboggan. But see, the day is breaking! Tie the rope to me leg, and off to Clonmel with us."

Jerry took the sociable creature at his word, and down the road they put. But the journey was so delayed by wonderful tales of goints and of magicians and by some fine old ballads that Char-les sang as they sat under a hedge to rest, that it was the middle of the forenoon before they found themselves in the busy market place of the fair. At once Jerry was hailed on all sides, and it wasn't long till he was offered two pounds for his fine pig. Almost immediately afthwards, Red Shaun, the drover, raised the bid to two pounds ten.

"No," cried Jerry, "I'll not take a penny less than three pound. And it's ashamed I am to part with him for that. Here you, Wullum!" he called to his first cousin, William Hagen, who stood by. "There's a letther for me in the postoffice beyant; do you hold Char-les here till I go for it."

He slipped the rope into William's hand, and was off like a shot. It wasn't two minutes till he was back again with the letter in his pocket. There stood William, a glad smile on his round red face, and four gold sovereigns shining in his open palm. But the pig was nowhere to be seen.

"Where's Char-les?" shouted Jerry, a cold fear gripping his heart.

"Char-les is gone," chuckled William, "but here's the price of him; and a pound more than you axed for the lazy baste."

"Who bought him?" demanded Jerry, anxiously. "Tell me quick, who bought him?"

"Sorra do I know who the long-faced, black, ould targer was! But he seemed mighty glad to get the pig at four pounds, and was in a great hurry to be away with himself."

Jerry tried to speak, but his voice at first failed him. "Did the schaymer have a hump on his back, I dunno?" he managed at last to gasp.

"No less," answered William, "a hump like a camel's. But what's come over ye, man? You're as white as a ghost."

For answer, Jerry pushed William aside and dashed madly into the surging crowd; and for the rest of that day he searched every nook and corner for some trace of the lost Char-les; but in vain. It was well on to midnight when, footsore and sorry-hearted, the remorseful lad lifted the latch of his own cottage door. As he did, the breath almost left him, for there on the same stool, just as before, sat Char-les. But not altogether the same either, for instead of the usual jolly expression worn by the pig, there was now on his countenance a settled look of hopeless dejection. And Jerry noticed also that although the pig's body was as big as ever, his sides were almost transparent. Indeed, the tongs leaning against the wall, near which the creature sat, were quite visible through the poor fellow's ribs.

As Jerry walked slowly toward the fireplace, the pig addressed him, and the sad tremble in his voice went straight to his master's heart.

"I'm dead now; now I'm dead, Jerry," wailed the pig. "I wrastled with that scoundhrel Killboggan till tin minutes ago, and his spells and charrums have me melted away to a looking-glass image of meself. Oh me, oh my, oh me, oh my! Be accident I got him down at last and managed to

escape and fly to you. But he's comin'. He'll be here in a
minute, and then good-by forever to the raynowned Killbohgan. I can do no more. I'll vanish entirely."

"Och, what a murdherin' pity," mourned Jerry, wringing his hands. "Is there no help for you?"

"There's only one poor chanst in all the worruld,"
moaned Char-les, "but I don't think you'd be ayquil to the
task. If you could manage to stuff a handful of salt into
Killboggan's mouth, that'd put all to his powers and his
parsecutions. I'd soon grow fat ag'in. But sure what's the
use of talkin'—Oh, be this and that, here he is!"

The pig made a jump and a mad scramble for the other
room, and dived under the bed, and Jerry had barely time
to snatch a fistful of salt from a crock oil dresser shelf,
when the kitchen door flew open, and in strode a. tall
humpbacked man with the longest, darkest face Jerry had
ever seen.

"You have that villain Killbohgan here somewhere, an'
you'd bether let me have him at once," croaked the dark
man in a deep harsh voice. He stood wide on legs in the
middle of the floor. "Ha, there he is, skulkin' undher the
bed. Wait till I have him out and finish him here ferninst
ye."

With these words the magician made a bolt for the other
room, but as he did, Jerry, with a courage which has since
become the settled boast of all his descendants, gave a
quick spring and landed fair and square on the ugly
intruder's back. And then began a struggle which for noise
and destruction has never been equaled before or since in
any respectable man's kitchen. With his left arm clasped
tight about the long, bony neck, Jerry strove with his right
hand to thrust the fistful of salt into the villain's mouth.

Round and round spun the magician, as fast as any
top, striving desperately meanwhile to avoid the handful
of salt which Jerry just as desperately was endeavoring to
make him swallow. From one end of the kitchen to the
other they whirled, Jerry's legs flying out behind him like

a couple of flails, and sweeping everything in their way.
Down went the table, up in the air flew the two stools,
crash went the poor old clock, and with one wild sweep
the two dignified brass candlesticks flew madly off the
mantel. And then, saddest of all to relate, swish! crack!
went Jerry's two legs against the churn-dasher, and the
five gallons of fresh sweet buttermilk spread like a white
sheet over the floor.

"Oh, ye murdherin' thafe of the worruld! oh me two
misfortunate legs!" roared Jerry. He gave the magician
such a poke in the back with his knee as to drive for an
instant every whiff of breath out of the rascal's body.

"Huroo! Huroo!" shouted Killbohgan's smothered voice
from under the bed.

At that the frantic enchanter changed his tactics. He
now stood in the middle of the floor bending his body up
and down with the greatest rapidity, so that Jerry fluttered back and forth like a shirt on a clothesline in windy
weather.

The brave man, however, never weakened his hold, and
Killboggan soon found out that this plan was useless, too;
so what does the rapscallion of an enchanter do but begin
backing rapidly toward the fireplace.

"Oh, murdher in Irish, this is where the spalpeen's got
me," groaned poor Jerry, twisting a frightened eye over
his shoulder at the turf fire.

"Keep a firm grip on him whatever happens," encouraged the invisible Killbohgan, "ye're doin' foine."

Whether Killboggan intended to seat the poor lad on
the live coals will never be known. At any rate, if such
was his uncharitable intention the maddened wizard mis-
calculated the direction, and instead of finding the fireplace, he succeeded only in banging the heroic Jerry
against the wall with a terrible thump.

Hard as it was on the poor lad's bones, that same bump
proved to be Jerry's salvation; for the rattling jar of it loosened the big heavy picture of Daniel O'Connell which hung

enshrined on the whitewashed wall above them, and, as though of its own volition, down came Daniel crash on Killboggan's head. The glass was smashed into smithereens, and the heavy frame hung itself round the neck of the bewildered magician like an ox yoke.

And that wasn't the best of it, either, for at this same moment Killboggan's two feet slipped in the buttermilk, and down he went on his back to the floor like a load of turf. The grunt the fallen wizard let out of him could have been heard in the seven corners of the parish. There was an exultant "Hooroo!" from under the bed, and the next instant Jerry, gasping and spluttering, was seated on the black lad's chest striving still with might and main to pry open the long jaws and to crush the handful of salt through the scraggly yellow teeth.

Slowly the great jaws opened and our hayro was making haste to poke in the saving salt, when suddenly a hand caught him from behind, and a familiar voice spoke in his ear.

"Get up out of that. I'm ashamed of ye. What are ye doin' to that stool?" It was his wife, Katie, who spoke.

But Jerry, breathing hard, still clung desperately to Killboggan until looking more closely, what was his surprise and consternation to find that the Wizard had some way changed himself into one of their own three-legged stools.

Jerry rose slowly to his stiffened knees and looked about him in great bewilderment, as well he might; for, wonder of wonders, there was no sign whatever in the room of the late desperate struggle. From his old place on the wall Daniel O'Connell, unharmed, smiled down lofty and serene upon the neatly set kitchen, while upright, and solemn the dark churn stood in its own quiet corner by the dresser. Indeed, there was not an article of furniture out of its place, and Jerry as he knelt looked round in vain for the sign of a single drop of buttermilk on the floor.

"Where's Killboggan?" he gasped, as he struggled to his feet.

"Kill who?" laughed Katie in stitches. "I've seen no Killboggan or Killhoggan, or Kill anybody else, aither. But you and that bliggard Char-les should be half way to Clonmel be this time."

"Char-les, Char-les," Jerry repeated mournfully, wagging his head, "sure Char-les is gone, Katie, an' we'll never see the poor hayro ag'in."

"Won't we, then." laughed Katie. "Quit dhramin', avourneen, an' see who's lookin' in the door at ye."

Jerry looked as he was bidden, and there, with his head poked over the threshold, to his master's infinite amazement, stood Char-les, fat and comfortable looking as ever, with a roguish smile in his eye which said plain as spoken words: "The top o' the mornin' to ye." It was already bright daylight.

"Take ye're bite of breakwus, darlin'" coaxed Katie, "an' the two of yez be off, but mind ye, don't sell the pig for a penny less than three pound."

"Sell him! Katie,—Sell him!—I wouldn't part with Charles for any money." At that he up and told her all that had happened during the wonderful night, and he wound up by saying:

"It may have been a dhrame, an' thin again it may have been a wision, but dhrame or wision, I'll take no chances in having the vartuous Killbohgan murdhered."

"At laste," insisted Katie, "Mrs. Clancey an' the letther is no shupernatural wision, so take the road in your hands an' bring us back worrud of it."

And so, indeed, Jerry did, and toward evening back he came, only the top of his hat visible over the stack of bundles he carried. With dancing feet and clapping hands the children opened wide the door, and Jerry marched proudly in and began to unload. A bonnet box with a bonnet in it that dazzled Katie's eyes; ten yards of calico; eight yards of beautiful red flannel; two pounds of good black tea; three pairs of shoes for the children. "God bless thim," and a great package of tobacco and a fine new pipe for himself.

"Me Uncle Dan in Amerikay isn't dead afther all, Katie," he exulted, "and to prove it he put tin pounds in the letther; an' afther buyin' all ye tould me to and lashins more, I paid the rint, thanks be, and I have still a matther of four pounds tin tucked safe an' deep in the bottom of me breeches pocket."

THE CROCKS O' GOOLD

One June morning on a market day at Fethard, while the sun was as yet winking and blinking a sleepy eye over the top of shadowy Slieve-na-mon, Darby O'Gill, the knowledgeable man, stood upon the threshold of his cottage, impatient to be off to the town.

"In the name of marcy don't ax me to raymimber another thing, Bridget," he complained. "Ye have me bothered and kilt as it is wid yer 'raymimbers', so ye have."

Bridget's voice came soothingly from within. "Ah thin, so ye are kilt, darlint! But sure as eggs is eggs I came near forgettin' to raymimber that we haven't a pinch of tay in the house. Whativer else ye forgit, raymimber to bring me half a pound of the foinest black tay. Oh, wirra, wirra, the medicine for little Eileen's cough! Where's the bottle? I had it in me hand a minute ago." At that Bridget appeared on the threshold as rosy and fresh as the June morning itself.

"And Darby dear, stand still and listen—sure ye have me flusthered wid yer twistin's an' turnin's. The sorra thing I can raymimber—come here till I fix yer neckerchief. Oh, musha, will ye look at him! I want ye to carry careful this dish to Mrs. Malony's. Ah ha, ye'll break it if ye put it in yer pocket with the bottle! Oh, be this an' that, get me two ya-ards of rid flannel to make little Mickey a new petticut; the poor child might as well be without anything, the way he is. An' get two dozen of white chaney buttons an' a packet of black linen thread."

Darby was striving hard to be calm.

Bridget put a coaxing hand on her husband's shoulder. "Shure it's aisy to kape yer moind on it avourneen, if ye'll sthrive not to be thinkin' of an-nything else. An' bring home a little brown sugar, a matther of three pounds say; an' pay attintion, Darby, while that thafe of the worruld, Dugan, is weighin' it out to ye. An' now be off with ye! No, wait a minute! Ye 'd bether get a ya-ard an' a half of corduroy for patches; an' call in to me Aunt Nancy's on yer way back an' get me the settin' of goose eggs she promised me—an' do you—"

In sheer disgust Darby flopped himself down on the threshold. "The duckins a foot I'll stir out of this today," he said desperately. "Go yerself, you an' get yer settin' of eggs!"

It was impossible for anyone to be angry long when Bridget laughed, for she had the merriest, cheeriest laugh with her in all the world. It began with a low thrush's gurgle and then up it trilled and then down again and off into a note, as sweet as a linnet's song in May.

"Don't sit there whinging like little Mickey," she cried, as she pulled the rebellious man to his feet. "Be off now, and God go with ye—an'—Oh, Darby—"

"Don't dare tell me another thing," Darby interrupted fiercely.

"I was only going to say that ye mustn't be stayin' so late at Fethard that ye'll have to be takin' the short cut home through Hagan's meadow afther dark. Ye know they did be sayin' at O'Hara's christening that Norah Sullivan's Dan tould Barney Delany that as he was coming from Jimmy Fogarty's wake and was gallopin' by Hagan's meadow he could almost swear he saw back in the moonlight the shadow of a man pointing a gun at him. The Lord betune us and all harm! Everyone agreed that it must be Black Mulligan's ghost took to walking again."

Faith, now this was disturbing news. All the world knew the story. One night, twenty-five years before that very day, Black Mulligan, the gamekeeper, shot and killed, in

Hagan's meadow, poor, harmless old William Fagan for poaching a rabbit. And though Mulligan died on the scaffold at Clonmel, that wasn't the last of him. From time to time his restless spirit, gun in hand, walked the scene of his red crime to the terror of the countryside. All that terrible story quivered now through Darby's mind.

"They say, too," Bridget warned the now attentive listener, "That any night now ye can see lights movin' 'round in the ruined abbey where the crocks o' goold lie hid."

"What have the crocks o' goold to do with Black Mulligan What put crocks o' goold into yer head?" Darby asked suspiciously.

"Didn't Mrs. O'Hara tell me only last night that ye put the challenge on her Dominic to go hunting for thim?"

"Huh! Dominic O'Hara! We hear ducks talkin'," laughed Darby. "That challenge came out of the bottom of the fourth glass of punch."

He tried to speak carelessly, but that news about Black Mulligan took so much of the pleasure out of the prospects for the day that the bothered man leaned a moment against the cottage door, filling his pipe and ruminating. Maybe he'd better put off the journey. Bridget stood with puckered lips watching every change of his eyebrows. It's a queer way married women have of being able to tell what's in their husbands' minds, especially when it's a thing the wives themselves don't like.

"I'll bring Bill Donahue, the tinker, home with me," he thought to himself.

Instantly Bridget spoke up and a threatening note hardened in her voice, "That wandhering vagabone, Bothered Bill Donohue, will be looking to fasten himself to ye again," she warned. "The last time ye brought him here wasn't I soaping and scrubbing and cleaning for the week afther to get all trace of him out of the house. Now mind this, if ye ever bring that lad streeling again over that doorstep, yerself and himself can have it betwixt ye. I'll take the childher and go to me father's."

Wasn't Bridget with her unreasonable cleanliness enough to heart scald any man? There's such a thing as being too clean for comfort, and Bridget O'Gill, if any woman ever did, suffered from that complaint.

"Why," thought he, "couldn't she let the poor fellow come home with him. True, Bill was not exactly a hawthorne bush in pink blossom! And what if his muddy brogues did leave a few tracks on the kitchen floor? Sure he couldn't help that! However, there is nothing so unreasonable as an over-neat woman," he thought, as he flung himself angrily off the step.

Bridget stood a minute, a smile on her lips and a twinkle in her brown eyes, as she watched him down the road, little dreaming of the wild happenings that lay between her husband and his fateful way back.

The three counties elbowed one another in Fethard by the time Darby reached the old town gate. From that on it was a slap on the shoulder here, and a bone-crushing handshake there, and a "God save ye, Darby, me bouchal" everywhere, so that the pleasant afternoon filled with jokes and news and gossip waned and grew dim before the busy lad could spare a thought for any of Bridget's commissions. Some of them had slipped clean from his mind.

But through all the friendly greetings and pleasantries of the day a constant worry smouldered, for whichever way he turned, the sharp gray eye of Bothered Bill Donohue, the tinker, kept burning a spot in the middle of his back.

"Bad luck to him," muttered Darby ruefully, "if I bring the thieving blaggard home wid me Bridget'll skiver the two of us. None of my blood or breed iver rayfused man or mortial the width of his back for a place to sleep, or a bite an' a sup to ate. I'd' like his company besides, at laste for a bit of the way. Whist! I know what I'll do, I'll slip intil Murphy's stable here an' bide awhile out of sight, an' whin the rover's gone I'll whip over to Dugan's an' intil the back dure with me, buy me wares and off home with me."

No sooner said than done. For a half hour Darby waited, grumbling, in the stable among the cows. No use! When at last he ventured over and poked a cautious head in at the back door of Dugan's shop, a well-known voice hailed him:

"Come in, Darby asthore, I've been waitin' for ye this half hour. I'll be goin' home wid ye the night I'm thinkin', to give ye a hand wid the bundles." And there, sitting calmly on an upturned tub, lolled Bothered Bill Donohue, the tinker. The vagabond's empty pipe was gripped upside down in his teeth—a pathetic hint to the callous Dugan—and he gathering with rambling hand constant mouthfuls of the fragrant contents of the scattered barrels, boxes, and cases.

"We'd betther hurry, me bouchal," he urged, "we've a long road ahead of us. I don't like to kape Bridget waitin'. Whatever hour we'll get home," he confided loudly to all in the shop, "Bridget O'Gill'll be kapin' a foine hot supper fer us."

"Thank ye kindly, Bill," Darby mumbled shamelessly, "an' it's meself that's sore an' sorry that ye can't be comin' with me; but Joey Hooligan was lookin' everywhere for ye. It's a great job of mendin' pots he has for the morrow. Hurry now and you'll be up with him before he gets to the crossroads."

"Huh! to blue tunder with Joey Hooligan an' his stack of ould leaky pots! It's with yerself I'm goin'." Again he took the shopfull of waiting customers into his boisterous confidence. "The rispectablest woman an' the comfortablest house in Tipperary is yer own, Darby O'Gill," he cried. Then coming down from the box and slapping the dust from his trousers he added: "Go on now, dacint man, an' get what yer gettin'. I'll go bail ye forgot half what herself tould ye to bring."

"I haven't forgot," Darby resented a bit spitefully. "Weigh me out one pound of yer foinest black tay, Tom Dugan, an' as much brown sugar as'll go with it; an'—

an'"—he rubbed a perplexed chin,— "Wirra it was something for the childher."

"A pound of tobaccy, a quart of good whiskey, an' a couple of new clay poipes," Bill promptly suggested.

"No, that wasn't it, but now ye mintion it, maybe I nade thim as well! Have ye a good gallon jug, Tom Dugan? It was something for little Mickey's petticut. Was it a yard of corduroy or—" Darby's troubled gaze floundered helplessly from one laden shelf to the other.

"Maybe it was rid flannin," suggested Dugan.

"Or gingerbreads," enticed Bill. "I've always noticed that little Mickey was very fond of gingerbreads, an' I don't wondher; I loike thim meself," he said, beaming his approval on the ring of listening neighbors.

"I think it was the flannin, Dugan. How many ya-ards do I want?" Darby threw himself helplessly on the mercy of the shopkeeper.

Dugan folded his arms judicially, shut one eye and pursed his lips, "Does Mickey take afther yer wife's fambly, the O'Shaughneseys, or is he an O'Gill, I dunno?"

"He's the dead sphlit of me father's brother Wullum," Darby answered, gulping on a note of pride.

"Ah, thin no nade to ax! I'll warrant ye he's a foine soized lad. I should say a matther of five ya-ards'd be lashins for a petticut an' a bit left over for patches." He turned to pull down a bolt of flaming red.

"Patches! That's it," cried Darby, "I want something for patches!"

"Why don't ye take two or three of thim foine smoked mackerel?" urged Bill, unctuously. He lifted one and held it aloft by its dripping tail. "I niver saw fatter," he smacked.

Darby nodded uncertain consent at Dugan; and the three went on till between the urgings of Bill and the suggestions of sympathetic Dugan, Darby and the tinker finally left the shop, their arms filled with bundles as high as their chins. The market was well over. The two strode down an empty road. The twinkling lights in the cottage

windows got farther and farther apart. As they plodded
along through the fast growing twilight, Bill wore a settled
expression of placid contentment, while the knowledgeable man glowered his troubles at the blurring hedges.
The dusk had thickened into murky darkness when the
pair stopped at Nancy Morrissy's for the goose eggs; and,
of course, that good woman wouldn't hear of their leaving
the house till they had finished a few cups of tea with a
potato and a rasher or so of bacon.

"Carry the bashkit in the middle of the handle, Darby
acushla," she cried as the two stepped carefully out again
into the middle of the road, "for if ye so much as joult one
of thim raymarkable eggs ye'll spile a lovely goose. An'
now goodnight and good luck to yez."

It was neither the length nor the loneliness that
weighed heaviest on the mind of Darby. Over and over the
knowledgeable man was asking himself:

"What'll she say to me this night? What excuse can I
give for bringing this blaggard home?"

Suddenly he stopped in the road to laugh. "By the livin'
farmer, I have it!" he chuckled. "I'll tell Bill that I'm goin'
over to the abbey to dig for the goold an' I'll ax him to
come over an' help me. An' whin he refuses me—as of
course he will—I'll sind him on to Bridget, and it's meself
wouldn't be in his brogues thin for tin new shillings."

The eggs rattled in the basket with the dint of Darby's
suppressed chuckling till a sobering realization of his own
risk flared into his mind.

"Oh well, I won't venture but a few steps into the
meadow," the lad finally argued to himself. "It's only needful to climb across the low stile and steal one or two tiptoes into the field. Bill won't be out of my hearing at all.
I'll make him keep whistling or singing. It'd be foine if I
crept along beside him inside the hedge and at the gap in
the corner give one shout. Wouldn't it be sport if it was
only light enough to watch the mad gallop he'll make then!"
The eggs in the basket rattled once more. If Darby could

have foreseen the mad gallop that lay before himself, his laugh might have changed its tune at that.

Bill spoke up, as if vaguely divining what was in his companion's mind. "My but ye're the bould man, Darby O'Gill! They were sayin' all over the market today what a courageous hayro ye wor to be goin' wid Dominic O'Hara afther the crocks o' goold in the ould abbey. Far be it from me to put corrections on ye or the loikes of ye, but I can't help thinkin' that aich one of yez is a pair of two tunderin' fools."

In spite of his bundles the hero's chest swelled. "Well, I tell ye, Bill," he swaggered, "I'm at a loss about takin' that same Dominic O'Hara; he has no more conthrol over his long tongue than if it belonged to yerself, an' the worruld knows that if an-ny wan so much as mintions a pious wurrud while he's diggin' for thim crocks o' goold, in a twinkle he may be turned into a big yellow ox, or into a bit of a starved wran. Now ye know yerself, Bill, that while Dominic is a nice dacint man wid the best of intintions, he has wan big fault; ye niver know whin he's goin' to rip out wid a 'God save ye koindly' or a 'Saints preserve us.' So it's what I wor just thinkin' about yerself, Bill; ye niver said a pious worrud in yer life; an'—"

"Bad luck to me if I'll do it," interrupted Bill promptly.

"It'll be near midnight be the time we reach Hagan's meadow," went on Darby, paying no heed to the refusal, "so we'll lave Dominic O'Hara go diggin' for himself to-morrow night, an' me an' you'll go pardners tonight."

The offer was like sousing Bill with a tub of cold water. He stopped still in the road and shivered. "Hould!" he choked. "There's nayther luck nor grace in even talkin' that kind o' talk!"

He clutched Darby's arm and his voice sank to a whisper. "Listen! As sure as gun is iron, Darby, some mystarious thing is creepin' an' crawlin' on t'other side of the hedge. Whist, they're listenin' now. Oh, millia, murdher, don't ye hear thim kapin' sthill!"

There's nothing so quickly contagious as terror. The tinker's genuine fright sent Darby's own heart with a jump into his mouth. Still and all, it would never do to show the white feather. So he stuttered:

"Ye're right, Bill, me poor fellow, I knew that a half hour ago. There's not one but a dozen of thim beyant in the field. An' oh, be the hokey, (Darby's voice sank to a careless whisper), there's a tall black man standin' just behind the hedge, don't look 'round!"

Bill gave a great lurch forward, as though suddenly kicked. "Wow!" he cried. "If ye don't come on, Darby O'Gill, I'll throw ivery last bundle at yer red head an' run for me loife!"

"Wait a bit, it's the chance of yer life," Darby remonstrated, as he hurried after the tinker. "Come with me to the abbey avic," he called, "an' I'll give you foive thurds of the goold an' we'll allow Bridget, the crathure, four thirds, lavin' only six thurds for meself! I'm making a rich man out of ye."

"Don't be talkin'," shouted Bill with a fresh burst of speed. "I won't sthray a fut off this highroad tonight for all the riches of Crashus."

"Hold a minute! My, but yer a har-rd one at a bargain." Darby caught up with him to lay a detaining hand on his friend's shoulder. "I'll tell ye what I'll do,—you take the six thurds an' that'll lave poor Bridget only the three thurds."

"Will ye niver lave off," hissed Bill, fiercely shaking off the detaining hand. "If ye say wan more wurrud about that onlucky ruin I'll hut ye a kick that ye'll never forget."

Darby slowed up in the road. "If ye didn't want to go why didn't ye say so at once," he expostulated. "Here's Hagan's meadow. There's many a person would give a leg for yer chance this night. Won't ye come? Well, then I must go alone. Tell Bridget I'll be home within the hour. Good luck till ye."

For an instant the two faced each other through the inky blackness. In spite of his attempted heroic air, Darby's voice sounded a bit forced and gasping.

"Man alive, are yez in airnest," cried the tinker.

"I'll cross over the meadow to the abbey," his companion continued, but he shivered as he spoke. "Keep steady
on yer way and look nayther to the right or to the left,
Bill. There's them that will be follying you that's dead an'
gone these hundred years. You won't see them but maybe
ye'll hear them. Pay no attention and yer safe enough. Go
on now!"

The last sentence spent itself on an empty world, for
the tinker had instantly dissolved from hearing as well as
from sight.

The knowledgeable man shouted a quavering warning
from the top of the stile, "An' I say, Bill, ye may as well
whustle as loud as ye can. Thin ye won't be so frightened." He listened an instant but no reassuring sound
drifted back.

If the ground in Hagan's meadow had been covered with
red hot coals instead of being carpeted as it was with cool,
sweet grass, Darby O'Gill's feet would not have shrunk
more from coming in contact with it. However, Bothered
Bill was not to be trusted; he might be watching and listening in the darkness a few feet down the road, so there
was nothing left for it, and Darby, bracing his soul, jumped
off the step, landed in the meadow and ran a few bewildered steps into the haunted field. There he halted, straining his ears. There never was so black or so silent a night
before nor since. In spite of every effort at self-control the
lad's flesh began to creep.

"Why don't that coward whustle?" he complained, bitterly.

Suddenly he stood straining every sense for some kind
of sign from Bill. The uneasy man could have sworn to a
short sigh in his ear and that he felt a quick, cold breath
on his cheek. That was enough! The next second he took
a deer's leap in what he thought was the direction of the
road and sprinted for his life; but murdher in Irish! There
was no stile! Where had it gone? It, too, had disappeared.

He ran a good hundred yards before realizing that he must be running in the wrong direction.

"Oh, blessed day, where's the stile!" he gasped, coming to a dead stop. "I'm in the middle of Hagan's meadow! I've lost me way! The curse of the crows on you, Bill Donohue, for a slinkin' daysarter. Is that a light beyant, I dunno?"

The poor fellow half sank to his knees and was crouched, striving with every vein of his body to make out if that glimmer of light in the distance shone from the old abbey or whether it was only the fitful blink of a friendly star, when faintly pounded toward him through the darkness a sound of terror—nothing less than the quick fall of pursuing footsteps.

"Black Mulligan is after me," he groaned. "I'm a massacreed man!" In the heavy stillness the approaching steps thudded like the footfalls of a giant. A weakness came into the lad's chest so that every bundle and package dropped from his shaking arms; all but the eggs went to the ground. Relieved of the bundles, but still holding to the basket, Darby bolted again into the darkness and ran for his life.

There weren't three men in the barony that could throw a quicker leg before them than Darby O'Gill, and never before that night had he put such speed into his nimble heels. But, fast as he went, the thudding footsteps behind gained on him every second. The breath was leaving him, too, and it seemed only a matter of a few more yards when he'd be nabbed by the neck like a hunted hare. Suddenly a most terrible cry electrified the blackness.

An approaching voice, in a wild, high shriek, called his name:

"Da-arby, Da-arby O'Gill," it wailed.

"The Lord help us, I'm lost," panted Darby. "It's Mulligan himself."

The poor boy's knees failed him then and he had just strength enough left to totter to one side. That proved the lucky move, and not a second too soon, either, for he barely lurched out of the path when a great, black, shapeless blur whirred by in the gloom. So close did it pass that the hunted man might easily have touched the dreadful thing with an outstretched hand. As the shape rushed by, uttering short inarticulate groans and cries, it appeared to be headless and legless and about the height of the new chapel door.

"It's not Mulligan, it's the ghost of William Fagan himself running away from Black Mulligan, the murdhering gamekeeper," thought Darby, "but how did he get me name? He must know I'm here."

All that had happened might have been a nine years' mystery for the seven counties only that just then a bright moon stuck its head through the clouds and took a querulous peep at the night. In the quick wave of light that followed, everything in Hagan's meadow became quite visible, so that Darby was able to make out clearly the form of the flying object. And what the knowledgeable man saw then stiffened every nerve and muscle in his body with angry amazement; for from whom had he been running but from Bothered Bill Donohue.

"Da-arby! Da-arby! Where are ye, Dar-rby?" bleated Bill. Terror had split the tinker's voice into a piping falsetto.

At the sound every shred of Darby's fear turned into white rage. He snatched a big goose egg from the basket and with all the strength of his arm let it fly at the tinker. As a gossoon no lad in the country had a surer aim in shying stones than that same Darby O'Gill.

"Take that!" he yelled. The roar that followed this blow was answered by the startled owls in the ruined abbey at the far end of the field.

Bill stopped to feel his head. "Oh, I'm kilt," he shrieked, "Me head's sphlit into three halves. I feel me wet brains runnin' down be me shoulders. Ow wow! Da-arby, Da-arby, save me!" and again on he plunged forward like a race horse.

"The divil mend ye!" shouted Darby. "Come back till I bate the loife out of ye. Where are yer bundles? What have ye done with the mackeril?"

But Bill, electrified with terror ran on, and Darby followed. The horse that won the Curragh cup would have been proud of their company that night.

"Milhia murdher, the Omadhaun's makin' straight for the fairies' bush," panted Darby. "Come back!" he roared. Then a strange thing happened. Darby saw the tinker throw up both arms and, with a despairing cry, disappear from the face of the earth.

Now in the middle of Hagan's meadow stands an ancient clump of hazel trees, known far and wide as the fairies' bush, and just beside the bush runs a deep, dry ditch. As Bill went galloping past with head thrown back and eyes bulging in terror, a malicious root reached up and caught the tinker's heedless feet, and thump! he was rolling head over heels to the bottom of the ditch.

For a second he lay where he had tumbled; but only a second, for in mind and body the lad moved quick as a cat. Indeed, he was already scrambling to his feet again and had reached the top of the bank when Darby himself came charging along like a mad bull, stumbled on that same malicious root and plunged headfirst into Bill. Saints above, but that was a thump! There was a confused whirl of legs and arms, two series of smothered, rasping cries, and then our astounded heroes, aimlessly clutching and tearing at each other, rolled back, a squirming heap, into the ditch.

The desperate tinker, sure that he was in the grip of Black Mulligan, fought like a tiger. "Ghost or no ghost, yez had no right to break the middle of me back! Take that!" he yelled.

The first blow caught Darby just under the ribs, but the second struck him fair on the chest.

"Ouch! I'm spacheless!" Darby gasped. "I'll have yer loife's blood for this, Bill Donohue."

HERMINIE TEMPLETON KAVANAGH

"Why, thin, is that yerself, Misther O'Gill?" the tinker asked in honest amazement, one hand still gripped in Darby's hair. "I thought ye wor a spurrit."

Freeing himself, Darby rose feebly to his knees and without a word began climbing out of the ditch. The bank was steep and slippery with the dew, so that at first the lad was hard set to get a foothold. He reached the top, however, and was clutching at a bit of a twisted root when, to his unspeakable surprise, the root began to twist and to squirm, and to wriggle in his hand.

Now up to that minute everything that had happened to our bold Tipperary men since they left the fair might have chanced with anyone else going along that same road.

"It's a young rabbit I've caught," Darby thought. He raised the thing for a closer look, when suddenly a little foot flew out like lightning and kicked him squarely on the nose, and a wee, spiteful voice piped up:

"Put me down, ye thunderin' bliggard! Ye've broke the ribs of me side! Pick up me cap ye schoundrel an' put it on me head so I'll have the power to turn you an' that sthreelin' villain behind ye into two yellow tomcats." And there, struggling in Darby's fist raged a bareheaded little old man in a green velvet jacket and brown knee-breeches. His snapping black eyes and weazened face were the angriest Darby had ever seen.

"Man alive, Bill, come here. I think I've got the leprechaun!" shouted Darby.

"Hould him tight. Don't take yer eye off him," puffed Bill as he scrambled to his feet. "We'll make him give us the favors of three grand wishes to buy his freedom."

"Ye lie, ye daytractin' mullet-headed dayrogotory vituperator," raged the little man. "I'm not the leprechaun! I'm Nial the Scold from Slieve-na-mon; an' I've been waitin' here these three nights to help ye whin ye wint diggin' for the crocks o' goold. An' I've lost my cap I've tould ye. This is the thanks I get. Where have ye been? What kep' ye', ye lazy, fiddle-faddling pottherin' dawdlin' polthrooms."

Darby recognized the little lad at once.

Sure as gun is iron no other than Nial himself was in it. Through the six months I have told you of before when Darby himself was a prisoner of the Good People in the heart of their mountain Slieve-na-mon, it's many a chat he shared with that famous Scold. There was no harm in the little fellow, Darby knew that well. But he knew too that Nial had the most spiteful tongue in the world. Unreasonable anger is always the first to follow needless fright.

Darby twisted the fairy upside down, gave him a vicious squeeze and warned:

"Aisy, aisy there, Aist or West, since the day I was borrn, I niver heard yer aquil for bad langwidge. An' I tell ye now, if ye say wan more of thim bliggard wurruds I'll rap the little head of ye again this stone. Tell me, what d'ye mane about waitin' for us to go diggin' for the crocks o' goold?" He gave the fairy a rattling shake.

"Sthop that!" roared the captive. "Do that agin if ye dare! Wait till I get me cap on so I can wurruk me spells! I'll—I'll sussitate the both of yez, so I will."

Bill was the first to recover from this deluge of hard names and, drawing a long breath he blurted:

"Be this an' that, Darby, I'll stan' no more. Hand the lad here till I souse him."

"Oho, is that you, Bill Donohue? I thought it was Dominic O'Hara that was in it. Man alive, Darby O'Gill, what are ye doin' here with that raycreant malyfacthor of a cockathrice of a thinker?"

"Softly now," warned Darby, pushing Bill aside, as the tinker made a thrust at the fairy with his stick. "I'm thinkin' he's here as a friend. Aisy now, what wor ye sayin', little hayro, about the crocks o' goold," and Darby loosened his fingers so that the fairy stood upright in his hand. The tiny lad shook himself and adjusted his cloak.

"Well, as I was sayin'," he sulked, "we got the wurrud that you an' Dominic O'Hara were goin' to dig for the crocks

o' goold an' it's little likin' we Good People have for the
unconjaynial moothorin' spurrits that's guardin' the crocks
these fourteen hundred years, or is it fifteen, I dn' know.
There's nothin' that King Brian Connors and the Good
People of Slieve-na-mon wish for half as much as for some
mortal man to take from them those same crocks o' goold,
and in that way to scatter to the four winds that nest of
shuper-natural nuisances. Have yez the courage? I doubt
yez."

"Look at that now!" exulted Darby. "Shure we thought
ye wor an innimy. To tell the thruth, Nial, yer honor,
Misther Donohue here felt just a trifle afeared of meetin'
up wid thim same ghosts."

The little fairy flung a glance of withering disdain at
the tinker. "What are yez all afeared of? Don't ye know
that one of these days yez'll all be ghosts?"

"I'm not afeared of thim," bragged Darby, "but I don't
loike 'sociating wid the loikes of thim. Ould Mrs. Callahan
had a foine charrum that 'ud kape yer heart lifted on the
loneliest road and the darkest night; she wasn't afeared
of ghost livin' or dead, and she promised to whusper it to
me before she died; but the poor crachure forgot the
wurruds. I wisht now I had them!—maybe ye raymimber
thim?"

"Faix I've heard that charrum of Mrs. Callahan's these
hundherds of years," said the fairy, "but I'll give you a
betther wan. Besides, mine has a grand chune to it."

"I feel," interrupted Bothered Bill pulling out his pipe
and reaching for the tobacco in Darby's pocket, "I feel"
said he, "as if I wor in a dhrame an' I'd wake up an-ny
minute."

"Do ye want to know the char-rum or don't yez?" insisted the wee fellow impatiently.

"We may as well," agreed Darby.

"Who in the worruld will believe us," mused the tinker.

"Thin hould out yer hand straight, Darby, so I can sit
on it," commanded the fairy.

Darby did as he was bid, and Nial seating himself comfortably on Darby's palm, threw back his head. His voice like the tinkle of a little silver bell sprinkled the darkness:

"Oh Phadrig and Phelim and Red Conan More
The Lehras and Lahras are gatherin',
Come out of the mountains, they're weltin' me
    sore,
Bring yer sojers and champeens to lather 'em.

You must larn it. Sing it over with me. Now all together," urged the little fellow earnestly.

Half shamefacedly at first the others took up the tune and sang it over and over, but at last roared it so lustily that "Bring yer sojers and champeens to lather 'em" was heard a good half mile away in her own house by big Mrs. Flaherty, as truthful a woman as lives in the village of Ballinderg.

When they had sung the powerful charm many times the wee man said: "Well, so far so good; now ye're pertected. First and foremost, it's not in the abbey at all that the crocks o' goold are buried, but undher the yew tree in the great court where the monks do be lyin'."

"Come on, Darby, an' bring the fairy man wid ye," cried Bill, starting up. The courage of the charm emboldened him.

"Botheration on ye for a tinker," snapped the fairy, "will ye have patience? Ye must not begin to dig till afther midnight, I warn yez, and ye must ind before cockcrow. After cockrow yez might just as well be diggin' with yer spades in the middle of the ocean for all the goold ye'll find. An' this is the way ye'll go about it. Ye'll find a bran' new pick an' a shovel lyin' snug be the abbot's grave, the grave diggers had thim out this morning; an' ye'll measure foive lengths of the pick handle toward the broken gateway an' there's the identical spot where ye must dig. Ye'll find goold 'nough there to make you and yer ginerations rich for-ever."

Darby gave a great cough into his hand, and Bill Donohue swallowed hard at a big lump that popped into his throat.

"Don't think that the ondertakin' is an aisy wan," warned the fairy, "for there'll be thim watchin' ye the while, an' one in perticular that ye've often heard tell of, that would sthrike the sight from yer eyes an' wither the tongue in yer head if ye'll let him."

"And what's to perwint thim?" asked Darby.

"Ah ha! That's what I'm sent here to tell ye. Until the sthroke of midnight the ghosts beyant are as helpless as a field full of playing childher, and afther cockcrow they're nayther more nor less than a flock of jackdaws roosthin' in the ould rune. Let yez hurry now before midnight and make a ring of holly twunty feet wide around the spot where ye're to dig, the way the rapscallians can't come within hand's rache of ye. The ghost of no deceased per-son can cross a twig of holly."

"Shure the whole worruld knows that," boasted Bill. "If anyone has a ring of holly around him no shupernatural ghost can bother him."

"Ha! Is that so," sneered the wee man. "Well, maybe ye know this, too, Mr. Di-og-gan-ees the pillosopher, that if ayther of the two of ye spake a pious or a rayligious worrud while ye're diggin' in that place, ye'll niver raygret it but wance an' that'll be all the days of yer loife."

"Raymimber that, Bill Donohue," warned Darby, "an' grip yer tongue between yer teeth or I'll make surgents worruk of ye."

Nial lifted a silencing finger.

"Whativer ye see an' whativer ye hear," he cautioned, "stir not a stir outside that ring of holly till cockcrow. All the cajolin' an' all the connivin' that can be larned in foive hundhered ginerations 'll be used this night to frighten ye or to coaxe ye to where they can rache ye. I pity yez if they win. If they can kape yez off the goold till after cockcrow they'll have yez bate."

"How'll we know whin it's midnight?" asked Darby. The little fairy laughed long and low, but something in the sound of that silver laugh raised the hair on their heads.

"Niver moind," he said, "if an-ny human bein' sets foot in the abbey afther midnight lookin' for the crocks o' goold, there'll be lads there an' plinty of thim that'll let him know the toime o' day. And now, Darby O'Gill, raymimber to sing that charrum whin yer afeared. Take up me hat now, an' put it on me head. Good luck go wid yez!" Whisk—he was gone.

By and by the drowsy moon, tossing its heavy blanket of clouds to the top of Slieve-na-mon, slipped higher up into the sky the better to spy out what mischief Bothered Bill Donohue and Darby O'Gill were up to. It grinned its surprise to find the two bold adventurers at the very gateway of the ruined cloister. There the pair waited, their arms bulging with holly and both hesitating and arguing angrily as to which should go in first.

"Oho, will ye look at the moon, Bill! I thought she was dhrownded in the say!" interrupted Darby.

The tinker cast up a disgusted eye. "A fardin' candle'd throw more light," he grumbled. "But man alive what are ye waitin' for? In twunty minutes more it'll be on the sthroke of midnight!"

"Yes, but listen, Bill," confided Darby, "I was thinkin'! Supposin' me watch is twunty minutes slow?—it's always ayther that much slow or that much fast whin it's runnin'—an' just think, if it happened to be past midnight an' I was to go in there now, why—they'd disthroy me from the face of the airth. So do you go in first, me brave fellow, an' don't be afeared, for I'll be standin' here watchin' ye."

"An' wouldn't they disthroy meself as well," snorted the tinker in hurt surprise. "No, no. You own foive thurds of the goold, so you go in first, Darby O'Gill, that's only fair!"

"Oh, that sounds fair enough," conceded Darby, "but ye're not lookin' at it in a sinsible light. Think a bit. If anything happened to me see what a loss entirely it 'ud be to the barony. Ye know well, Bill avourneen, I've a snug bit of a fa-arm, and besides that I'm the father of eight beautiful childher, not mintioning that I'm the husband of a very shuperior woman. I'm a rayspictable, dacint man, an' you are only—You see, Bill, we must all listen to rayson—you are only—Of course you're a *grand* tinker, the worruld knows that, but confaydential betwixt us now, d'ye think ye'd be much missed?"

Bill's answer was merely a splutter.

"Take yer elbow out of me back," suddenly roared Darby. "Stop scroogin' me, or be the powers I'll—" he said no more, for with one tremendous lurch Bill send the knowledgeable man sprawling through the broken arch and stumbling with great strides into the dim, shadowy cloister. He himself stood without the arch a moment, his head peering through. As soon as the tinker made sure that no misfortune had befallen his friend, he followed Darby into the old abbey. As that was no place for a quarrel, the two set silently to furious work and ten minutes later a wide ring of holly encircled the yew tree. Then only the moon and moon shadows and the creeping murmurs of the trees and the mysterious noises of the grass-covered tombs stirred the churchyard. In the corner of this hallowed spot Darby O'Gill and Bothered Bill Donohue, pickax and shovel in hand, stood waiting in shivering suspense the first ghostly sign of the fateful mid-night. The chilling stillness and a quickened sense of lurking invisible beings grew heavier from moment to moment.

"Don't you think, Bill," Darby advised softly,— "this'd be a foine opporchunity for ye to thry that charrum?" The tinker cleared his throat two or three times behind his hand.

"How does it begin, Darby? Isn't it th' Therums or Tharums?" he whispered.

The knowledgeable man started in dismay. "Ye don't mane to tell me ye've forgot the chune?" he asked.

"Oh, I have the chune all right," Bill answered confidently. "It's the worruds that I'm dubersome about. Do you sing the worruds, Darby, an' I'll sing the chune."

"Bad luck to ye for a forgetful tinker," wailed Darby. "Wirra, wirra, I've forgot the worruds too."

"Well, be the powers o' pewther! Everything considhered I think I'd betther make a run for it," Bill quailed. He dropped the pickax. "Look! There's somethin' movin' over there beyant, in the shadows. It's ayther a lion or a goat. Ye may have my four thurds, Darby. I'm goin'."

For answer Darby caught his companion's arm with a grip of iron and fastened him there. As the two stood peering intently into the distant corner, suddenly from the shadows just behind—it seemed almost at their very ears— broke a long sibilant whisper: "Sh-h-h." For an instant, the treasure hunters clung to each other, cowering. Bill was the first to turn and venture a look: and when he did every hair on his head separated like bristles on a brush, for dimly just outside the circle of holly leaves stood what seemed the bent figure of an old woman. She wore a long shimmering cloak that might have been a shroud. The hood was drawn so closely around her head that not one glimpse of the face was visible. Darby couldn't have moved a leg for the County Tipperary. A moment she remained as motionless as one of the slanting tombstones, till slowly raising a stiff, dead hand, she beckoned the speechless men toward her. "Come over!" she hissed. "Come here the both of yez, till I whusper where the crocks o' goold are hid. Ye're far from them." Although Darby's voice came in choking gulps, he made bold to answer:

"Thank ye kindly, ma-am, we're in no nade of yer advice, so if ye'll only go back quiet and dacint where ye're berried we'll think it greatly infatuatin' of ye." It was politeness thrown away. The old woman threw back her head and let a shrieking laugh out of her that curled the leaves on the trees. Now, when an O'Gill grows afraid he grows angry. "An' if ye're not obligatin' enough to do that little fayver," went on Darby, aroused by the disdainful insult, "then be the hokey I'll take one belt at ye wid this shovel, whether or no."

And then, an amazing thing happened. In the snap of a finger the old woman changed into a raging lion the size of a horse before their bewildered eyes; and giving a roar of fury that sent Bill Donohue a foot up into the air, the great yellow beast went charging around and around the hallowed circle until the watchers grew dizzy following it.

"D'ye think I'd betther throw the spade at her?" asked Darby, swinging it above his head. At those words the lion began backing toward the farthest corner of the cloister. Suddenly she stopped; and then after drawing herself together, she made a leap toward the spot where they cowered. The monstrous beast landed with its two front paws almost touching the ring of holly. Then it was that Darby O'Gill by the dint of his high courage made himself forever after the proud boast of the village of Ballinderg. Swiftly stooping, the brave man up with a rock half the size of his head and let fly, striking the snarling creature square between the two blazing eyes.

Maurteen Cavanaugh, the schoolmaster, argues that the welt of a stone couldn't hurt Satan's head because he is a spirit. But Maurteen has no doubt but what the insult must have made Beelzebub dance with fury. At any rate a bellow of rage answered the blow. Then, swish! the lion was gone and the brown old woman flashed into its place. Darby stooped for another stone, but as he did so the frightful old hag with a great swirl of her long cloak and a wild shrieking laugh, vanished into the air.

"Be this an' that," gasped the knowledgeable man, leaning on his shovel, "who'd have thought that an-ny ould woman could be so shuple as that on her two legs? Come, Bill, now's our chance. Let's dig for our lives."

"They'll be thryin' to dayludher us till after cockcrow," whined Bill.

The tinker took the pickax, the other took the spade, and at it they went with a will. Never before had either of them worked so hard. Thud, thud, thud! It wasn't long before a great hole loomed in the soft turf. The treasure hunters burrowed on without speaking; the perspiration poured from their faces; an ache came into the small of their backs, still no sign of the crocks o' goold.

"Well, by the red hemp of Dunleary, if there ain't me two ould friends, Darby O'Gill and Bothered Bill Donohue, the tinker. The top of the avenin' to ye, bhoys! What are ye doin' here?" The tone of the voice was friendly, but when they raised their eyes to see who it was, there in the moonlight stood a terrible figure.

"Darby," gasped Bill, "don't ye know who it is? It's Black Mulligan, the gamekeeper."

Black Mulligan stood not ten feet away, his gun at his shoulder, the threatening blue barrel pointed at Darby's head.

"Stand aside. Get out of the way, bhoys, or I'll have to shoot through yez," he commanded. "William Fagin, the poacher is hidin' there behind yez an' it's him I'm afther. Stand aside or I'll—"

Darby bit his tongue just in time to check the "God save us" that was on his lips, and at the same time he swung Donohue between himself and the point of the leveled gun barrel. As he did that there came a quick flash, an awful shriek, and with it the crashing report of a gun. Our two adventurers dropped to the ground on their faces. Some glint of courage from the fairy's charm must have lingered with them still, for, after a moment or two of stifling silence Darby had spirit enough left to raise his head and exclaim: "Are ye alive, Bill?"

"How could I be alive?" moaned the tinker. "Isn't this the second time I'm kilt tonight?"

"Then up wid ye, man; it'll be cockcrow before we know it." They went at the digging again and Bill had not given five good strokes till his pick struck iron.

"The crocks o' goold!" shouted Darby, and the strength returned to their backs, and the power to their arms. No two badgers ever flung dirt with greater speed than did our heroes. Presently the cover of a great black pot began to show itself ill the bottom of the hole. "My fortune is made," grunted the tinker. And then Bill's pick, glancing to one side, was answered by another metallic ring which told where a second crock was hidden. At the same moment Darby exclaimed:

"I think there's wan over here undher me feet, Bill, an' the duckens take the bit of me if it isn't filled to the top. Oh, blur-an-ages, look who's comin' at us now."

From the farthest black corner of the cloister walls, up almost to the edge of the protecting holly wreath, stretched a broad path of shimmering green light. Down this mysterious gleaming road stalked a gigantic man tall as a tree and breathing fire as he came. He was dressed in slithery black from head to foot, his raven hair stood straight on end, his long face was waxen white and the eyes in his head large as saucepans glowed like living coals. There could be no doubt at all but what Satan himself had come visiting. On he strode to within a hand's breadth of the holly wreath and then he halted with folded arms. All the seething hate and poison malice of the world was crowded into his look.

Darby considered, "I have nothing rale personal agin' him and maybe it's just as well to be civil." The lad pulled off his hat and made a scrape of a bow, but he was too flusthered to think of much to say. "The t-t-top of the a-avenin' to Your Honor. Isn't it a-a-foine night? I, I niver saw yer lordship lookin' so well. I hear," he quavered, nervously twisting his hat, "that Your Honor is havin' gr-reat times wid the Garmin pillosophers these days. At laste Father Cassidy was sayin' so at chapel only last Sunday."

That proved an aggravating remark. Indeed at the sound of Father Cassidy's name a spasm of raging agony convulsed the face of Satan. Sparks of fire spurted from his nostrils and his checks glowed like red hot iron. "Don't mention that name," he roared. "He's the worst enemy I have in Ireland ground."

"Why—why don't ye say somethin', Bill," urged Darby from behind his hat. "The juntleman is lookin' at *you*. I—I think it's *you* he's afther."

"I—I—I'm glad to see ye," put in the tinker, his teeth chattering. "N-n-o—I mane, wor ye havin' much rain this sayson down in, in—"

"Have done!" roared Satan, and the walls of the abbey shook. "Out of this place before I wither you up like a blasted tree. What fool's work brought you here?"

"I'm sure yer Honor don't begrudge us the few dirthy handsful of goold in the crocks below," said Darby.

"Always the gold," answered Satan. "What good does it bring you, you poor insects of the earth? You snails! You worms! You scurrying gnats!"

As all the world knows, from the time a Tipperary lad is the height of your knee he is a poor hand at taking an insult. So now Darby's quick temper got the better of his fears, and he warned hotly:

"Kape a civil tongue in yer head, Mr. Beelzebub, whativer ye do! I niver done an-nything agin you or yours, did I? I'll make a child's bargain wid ye: D'you lave me alone an' I'll lave you alone."

"You rubbish!" roared Satan, "You trembling weeds! You little heaps of dust! You bipeds!"

The last epithet proved too much for the prudence of the knowledgeable man. "Biped yerself!" he retorted. "Ye long-legged, goat-futted, chimbly-pot of a thransgressor! I dare ye to put yer ugly hoof over that holly."

But Darby got no further, for at these words Satan's rage got something fearful to behold. A moment he beat his breast with his hands and it clanked like iron, then flung his arms wide apart. At this last gesture the moon winked out and the night became black as your hat. A mighty wind arose and tore through the old abbey, lashing the yew tree to and fro over their heads. The owls darted this way and that in the sweeping gale, hooting in dismal chorus. In the midst of this whirling confusion exploded the most astonishing wonder of all. The earth cracked open in one wide circle around the now thoroughly subdued men. From this circling crevice an awful crackling sheet of devouring crimson flame shot up into the sky. Satan, serene and triumphant, stood framed in the centre of the blazing cataract.

There is no telling what the end would have been had the tinker kept steadily in his mind the important condition that a person must not utter so much as one pious word while searching for the crocks of gold. It is likely that in ten seconds more Darby O'Gill with Bothered Bill Donohue, as well as their descendants to come for generations, would have rolled in riches. But the endurance was pretty well shaken out of Bill by this time. He could only throw up his hands and exclaim, "God help us!"

Those were the fateful words. That prayer settled the business of the crocks of gold. Immediately a crash of thunder split the whole world. The sky must have fallen; the two men went down into the hole like a couple of rocks; the earth heaved and swayed like a billowy sea, and after that there crashed a deathly silence. Then, clear through the distance from Hooligan's farm shrilled the warning sound of a crowing cock.

It seemed a full minute before either of our stricken and stunned adventurers got control of himself. Darby was the first to open his eyes and look about. He hadn't heard the cockcrow. "The runneygade is gone! Quick, Bill, the crocks o' goold. Huroo, we're not bate yet!" No wonder Ballinderg is proud of the O'Gills.

But Bill was already on his feet, gazing bewildered at the spot where the wide hole had been. Lo and behold, not only had the crocks vanished, but the hole itself was gone; the place was filled to the top. And this was not all: The buttercups and daisies without so much as a broken stem danced nodding and bobbing in the first morning breeze above the spot.

Half an hour after our two heroic but unfortunate treasure hunters, loaded to the chin with bedraggled bundles, hesitated, anxious-faced on the threshold of the O'Gill cottage. Bridget already astir was busying herself above the hearth. She half turned from the steaming breakfast to transfix them with a scornful glare. "What kep' yez?" she flung at her husband. Then from the doorsill where they stood uneasily shuffling, the tired wanderers poured forth together an eloquent account of that night's wonderful adventures. From the beginning to the end of the tangled narrative Bridget never uttered a single word, but waited with tilted chin motionless on the hearthstone, her hands on her hips.

When the two finished their story, Bridget never moved a muscle of her face, but stood with tightly drawn lips, her eye still fixed on them in a wide, unsympathetic stare. At last she spoke, and at the sudden question she asked them, Darby and Bill took a half-step back from the door:

"How much whiskey have yez left in that jug, Misther O'Gill?"

"I—I—believe it's purty near half empty," answered Darby, looking accusingly at Bill.

"I didn't," blustered Bill. "Yer husband fell down an' spilled the jug whin he was runnin' from Nial, the fairy, Misthress O'Gill ma-am; an' he busted a lot of the lovely eggs, too, ma-am. He hut me with one foine egg and spiled a goose."

Bridget didn't say much then. So withering a look settled on her face that one would think that instead of innocent stirabout that was bubbling in the pot it was hot, boiling scorn she was turning into the breakfast bowls.

Bridget was a lady of few words, but many a word concerning that night she afterwards with rare judgment managed to scatter through the remaining days of Darby's life.

How Satan Cheated Sarah Muldowney

Whether it was the onraisonable unscrutableness of Pether Muldowney that first riled up the temper of Sarah Muldowney, or whether it was the high-handed obthrusiveness of Sarah Muldowney that started the accraymonious ambayguity in Pether Muldowney the sorrow one of me knows. Only this is sartin that same provoking question tossed from family to family from day to day at some time or other, started botheratious disputations under every thatched roof in Ballinthubber.

Now isn't it a worruld's wondher how the example of the quarrels and con-tintions of one family will creep sly and unrecognized intil the neighbors' houses lighting up dissinsions when laste expected. Ould Nick himself from their first falling out med a tool and a torch out of the squabbles of the Muldowneys. Look how clever Sattin conthrived the McCarthys intil their first blazing althercation! It was one winther's evenin' afther supper when Faylix McCarthy, a proud although at the same time a sinsible, quiet man, contented with the worruld and filled to the chin with peaceable intentions and butthermilk and oatmale stirabout, sat readying his pipe before the sparkling fire. His wife, Julia, brushed around busy washing up the pots and pans and clacking out a bit of a song the while.

"Isn't it a pity," says Faylix, offhanded, "Isn't it a shame the way Sarah Muldowney harries and haggles the life out of her husband, Pether?"

Why Julia took offense at thim worruds she never afther could explain.

"Isn't it a shame," says Julia, a bit sharp over her shoulder, "isn't it a pity the way she's druv to it? And isn't it a misfortune," she flashed back at him, "that men are the same the worruld over."

Up to that minute, yer honor, there wasn't a ha'porth of hard feelings betwixt them. But pushing Faylix down that way into the same place and pit with Pether Muldowney was like touching a sudden red coal to the back of his neck. So he gives his head a sudden jerk up and then he says, and his hand thrimbled as he put the light into his pipe while he was talking:

"I saw Dominic Flaherty this morning and he dhriving his two pigs with a rope on their legs, and the three of them on their way to the butchers at Fethard. The bastes wor pulling, one ayst and the other west, and dodging up every lane and crossroad and into every hole in the hedge. And I says to Dominic, says I, ''Tis yerself, Dominic, has as tayjus a job as if ye wor striving to manage a headstrong woman.'"

At that Faylix guffawed a little forced and aggravatin'. Julia didn't laugh. She waited a minute, wiping her bare arms with the dishcloth, her lips tight. Thin she says:

"I'll be bound the likeness ye just give is a foine example. For isn't it the poor wives that loike those same condemned bastes are being druv and browbate and parsecuted and disthroyed and kilt intirely all the days of their lives?"

And Faylix answered Julia, but what he said is no matther for the same or something like it was tould be every other husband in Ballinthubber to his wife while they war disputin' about the Muldowneys, and what Julia said agin to Faylix, sure yer own wife has said to yerself maybe time and agin and what she said wives'll kape saying to their husbands till the day of judgment.

But no matther which of the Muldowneys was to blame at the beginnin', sure wasn't the counthryside scandalized

and heart scalded at the way they kep' it up till the ind.
Discontent grows into a habit; happiness is often a bright
habit and ill nature is always just a drab habit. And there's
some people never exhillerayted onless they've just been
slighted or insulted, and there's them agin' that in their
saycret heart of hearts find sport and diversion out of a
quarrel. It was like that with the two Muldowneys. Not
that they ever lifted a hand to aich other or called hard
names outright. As Father Delaney would say the pair war
too scientufic for the loikes of that. There war not two com-
bat-tants in Ireland more ayqual for aich other. It was
Pether Napoleon Bonypart Muldowney against Sarah, the
Juke of Wellington Muldowney.

Pether was the quiet, careful, cowld-eyed kind. It's seldom he'd say a worrud while Sarah was having her full
fing at him. He'd rile the heart in her with his silence.
This was his way of fighting. He'd sit calm and agyravatin'
at the hearth, his right leg trun over the other, his head
slanted to one side, his say gull's icy eyes blinkin' at the
rafters and he humming a bit of a song.

The most cutting, irritaytin' maddening things Sarah's
tongue could manage he'd fence back at her be dhroppin'
the corners of his lips or winking humerous his eyelids or
tossing his shoulders and shutting his eyes. So when she'd
get all heated up and bilin' lika a taykettle and she'd find
that she hadn't raised a hair on him, this is what she'd do
and it inded the quarrel: Sarah would go out into the road
and stand weeping and crying over her gate. If any passing sthranger or neighbor would stop to ask her grief, all
she'd say was, "Go in an' ask himself! I'll not tell on him,
since whatever he's done, he's me wedded husband!"

Ye'll say that Pether was clever and indade he had to
be so for it was a toss-up betwixt them as to which had
the most injaynus tictacks.

The most valuable thing I've learned since ever I was
able to whirl me two fists before me face in a battle is to
beware of an enemy that smiles when he fights and Sarah

was a swate-worded smiler. Though her temper was sharp as a knife and hot as a flame of candle, she'd smile a harmless sounding question at anyone. That same question was dangerous as the jagged razor me own wife cuts the thread with: however careful I shave, I'm sure to put a gash on meself afther. If Pether'd try to answer one of Sarah's questions, whichever way he'd rayply he'd cut himself to the bone.

A woman may trajuce a man about his shortcomings till she's black in the face and he'll maybe hould himself in, but the minute his wife begins trajucing her husband's relaytions it's few husbands can stand that and stay peaceable. Sarah had a jaynus for columniaytion of the breed and brood of the Muldowneys. It's often she bested him that way outrayjous, and when she'd see Pether's face grow scarlet she'd know she'd won.

The way the last quarrel started betwixt them was this away: For a week the two had been cooing and fluthering about aich other like a pair of turtledoves. Of a wet Monday morning afther breakfast they war sitting looking at the lowering clouds and listening to the abusive chilling winds that came hollerin' down the chimney.

"It's a dayspictable thing," he says, "to be shut up in the house on a day like this with no one to talk to."

Of course, he didn't mane it althogether as bad as it sounded, but he didn't say it quite pleasant for all that—just a thrifle peevish. No one could tell be lookin' at Sarah how the woman was bridlin' when she heard that raymark, for she only rocked back and forth a little faster in the rush chair, smiling before she spoke.

Sarah knew that Pether hated to be corrected in his pronownciation, especially when he was feeling a bit sour over something else. It's belittling to anyone at any time. Sarah was altogether too clever for a front attack on Pether, so she kem at him from this wake side. "Don't say dayspictable, Pether avourneen," she smiled, "it sounds so wulger, say dayspictatory!"

"I said dayspicatory, I never said dayspictatable in me loife," answered Pether. Well, the argyment begun and from argyment to battle never amounted to more than a short step.

That last time Sarah got worsted bad so what does the woman do but jump furious from the chair and pack up in a bundle all the clothes she had in the worruld and it wasn't such a killin' big bundle at that, and with her foot on the thrashold and a hand on the latch, it's what she said to her husband:

"To the ructions I pitch you, and all the Muldowneys: and hadn't one of my daycint bringing up the hard lurk to marry into such a family of good-for-nothing tinkers! And I'm off now over the mountains to my sister Peggy who had the luck and the grace to marry into the rayspectable family of the O'Callaghans."

She shut the door quick then, the way she wouldn't be giving him the satisfaction of hearing the answer himself'd make; but she was sorry for that afther, bekase as she wint thrudging up the road she heard Pether back in the house roaring and screechin' with the laughter at some of his jokes an' thin the heart was fair burning out of her to know what owdacious slandher the rapscallion had med up and said about her.

But for all that Sarah never turned her head; she only guv her petticut another hitch an' with her chin up in the air an' her best foot for'rad marched on like a major down the road.

Didn't I meself heard Father Cassidy say from the alter only last Sunday that there wasn't a lazy bone in Sattin's body. That night and day the Ould Boy never slept but conthrivin' against and temptin' everyone in the world and particular the Irish. And as Mrs. Murtaugh and meself were walkin' down the lane from the chapel that day my wife says to me—(your honor knows that Mrs. Murtaugh was an O'Grady and that the O'Gradys the world over are faymous for their wise cogitaytions and wonderful concatinaytions) she says: "Isn't it a pity and a scandal, Jerry Murtaugh, that whin the Satalites are be night and be day lepping and limber and ayger afther yer own immortal sowl, and you to be using the bad langwidge ye did yestherday whin the pony kicked ye in the knee?"

With that she turned facing me in the lane and pinted a warnin' finger at me chist. "Jerry Murtaugh," she says, "ye're gettin' as free and careless about yere precious sowl as if it only belonged to a common Far Down or a Connaught man." And be that she put a seriousness on me that I feel in me bones this minute.

Faix, when I've finished aylucidating to ye what happened to the Muldowneys yer honor'll say, too, "Ah, thin, isn't Father Cassidy the larned man, and isn't Mrs. Jerry Murtaugh the deep rayligious woman!"

Well, as I was telling you: it wasn't her prayers that Sarah was sayin' ayther, as she wint whirling along, though she might betther have been doing that same (for the road before her was wild and lonesome enough and many's the turrible tale was told about it), but instid of doing that, every har-rd word and scorching wish she could lay her tongue to Sarah was pelting at the image in her mind of her husband, Pether.

"Oh, wasn't I the bostheen of a fool to be wastin' me chanst on him an' the loikes of him; I that had ivery boy in the parish afther me. But I'm done with him now. And I wish I was Sayzer's wife, so I do, so I could turn him into a pillow of salt, the big lazy sturk, I'd—I'd sell him to Sattin for six-pince this minnit, so I would."

The words were no sooner out of her mouth than, Pop! a wondherful thing happened. Believe me or believe me not, but it's no lie I'm tellin' ye; the road in front of her sphlit in two halfs accrass, and the ground opened before her and up through the crack sprung a tall, dark, slim, illigant lookin' juntleman, an' the bow that he med there in the middle of the road was ayquil to the curtchy of a Dublin dancin' masther.

For a minute Mrs. Muldowney could do nothin' but ketch her breath an' stare at him with every eye in her head, an' she said aftherwards that he was the foinest lookin' mortial man she iver set her two livin' eyes on, barrin' her own first cousin, Tim Conners.

He was dhressed from head to foot in glossy black. His knee breeches were of satin an' his swallow-tail coat an' low weskit were of shiny broadcloth. There would be no manner of doubt in the mind of any sinsible person who it was. Sattin himself stood ferninst her. But Sarah Muldowney came and sprung from the proud conquering race of the Fogartys on her mother's side, and the world can tell the Fogartys know no fear.

Clicking his heels together again the juntleman med a second polite bow and then spoke in a deep solemn voice:

"The top of the day to ye, Mrs. Muldowney, ma-a-m," says he, "I didn't hear quite plain the price you was settin' on your husband, Pether. I'll pay you any raysonable sum for him, an' it'll be cash on the nail ma-am. So spake up!"

To be sure while you'd be giving two winks of your eye, Mrs. Muldowney was flusthrated.

But it's she was the woman that was quick at a bargain, and handy at turning a penny. And now was her chanst.

"I was just sayin' that I'd sell him to Sattin for one pound tin this minute. An' be the same token, who are you sir, that comes poppin' up out of the lonesome road like a jack-in-the-box, frightenin' daycint women out of their siven wits. I said two pounds tin, that's what I said."

"It's little matther what me name is, Sarah Muldowney," spoke up the juntleman. "You'll be introjuced to me proper enough afther awhile. For the prisint it's satisfied yez'll have to be to know that I'll buy Pether from ye an' I'll pay ye the two pound tin in goold suverings the succont ye hand him into me power. Are ye satisfied?"

Now the good woman, seeing how aisy Sattin was with his money, felt the heart inside of her scorching up with vexation to think she'd named so small a sum, so shaking her head slow and sorrowful it's what she said:

"Throth thin, I'm not satisfied. You have no idee how lonesome I'd be without Pether an' what I'll do at all at all the sorrow one of me knows. An' will ye hurry up now with your answer for if anyone of the neighbors were to see the both of us collogueing out here together I wouldn't give a button for me repitation. So if ye 're willin' to give the three pounds tin—"

"What!" shrieked the dark man, an' he guve a lep up intil the air. "Three pound tin, ye schaymer of the worruld, ye said one pound tin at first."

"Tin fiddle-sthicks!—Three pound tin and not a fardin less. An' how dare the loikes of you be callin' a daycint woman loike me a schaymer," she shouted, clapping one hand in the other undher the nose of the sthranger, an' she follyin' him as he backed step by step from her in the road. "Kape a civil tongue in yer head while yer talking to a lady or I'll malevogue ye, so I will."

"Hould where ye are, Mrs. Muldowney," said the flustherayted man, and he backed up agin a rock. "I'll own I was a thrifle quick tempered but I meant no offence ma'am, an' if you'll bring Pether to this spot on the morning of the morrow and hand him over to me here I'll guv ye the three pounds tin down on the nail."

So Sarah waited for no more but off she skelped and without stopping to ketch her breath hurried by every short path till she came in sight of her own door. Then the clever woman slackened her pace the way she would be thinking and planning out some nate, cunning schame to deludher her husband into going with her on the morrow.

Just as Sarah left Pether in the mornin' that's the way she found him whin she opened the door; with his two feet upon the fender and his hands deep in his breeches pockets.

"Pether avourneen," she says, and you'd think butther wouldn' melt in her mouth, her worruds were that swate.

"Pether," says she, "it's a foine job of worruk I have for ye up the mountainy way."

"Have ye now," grunted Pether without lookin' round. "Well, I wouldn't be puttin' it past ye: It'll rain tomorrow or maybe even snow, so kape the foine job for yerself. Think shame on ye, woman, to be sendin' yer own husband out into the cowld an' the wet to be ketchin' his death from the dampeness."

"Oh no, wait till ye hear what it is," chuckled Sarah, as she untied her cloak and hung it careful on a peg behind the dure. "It's dhry as a bone an' snug and warrum as a roasted petatie ye'd be."

Pether cocked his ear in lazy curiosity. "I wondher!" was all he said.

"But maybe I'd betther not tell ye what it is," Sarah wint on, "bekase it's a job for a sober, daycint man; there's such a temptation for the dhrink in it, so I think I'll he givin' it to Ned Hanrahan."

Pether straightened his back at that an' took his hands out of his pockets. "Tut, tut, what's that yer sayin'?"

"I was sayin'" herself answered careless, readying the pot for the petaties, "that little Michael Callahan will be movin' his still from Chartre's wood to a foine cave up in the mountain, an' he wanted the two of us to help him. He has two cart loads of kegs and one of bottles and jugs and all of them filled with the foinest of mountain dew. But of course you wouldn't want to be doing the loikes of that."

Pether was on his two feet in an instant ivery hair on his head brustlin'.

"Death alive, woman!" he cried, "you'll be the ind of me one of these days. Sthop that hugger muggerin' and hurry the supper an' hurry on with me now or he'll have some one else in our places." From the minute he got Sattin's message a raymarkable change kem over the lad; he lost every tinge of his onscrutableness.

It took all the wit and injaynuitv of Sarah Muldowney to kape her husband Pether in the house till the mornin' of the morrow. And thin at the first shriek of day they were off together, he flyin' up the road with all the strength in his legs, an' she pelthin' afther him. The two of them nayther sthopped nor stayed till they came within sight of the Devil's Pool, and there be the powers, standin' in the middle of the road, straight as a ramrod, with his arrums fowlded, stood the polite dark juntleman.

Whin our two hayros came up to him, Sarah took Pether be the arrum the way she would be houldin' him back, an' it's what she said to him:

"Pether darlint, this is the juntleman I was tellin' ye about who has the foine daycint job of worruk for ye to do."

Pether glowered, dumbfounded, from one to the other.

"Michael Callaghan, ye said! Well the divil himself is in it if this long-legged rapparee is little Michael Callaghan!"

At those worruds the dark man put his hand on his dust and bowed:

"I don't blame ye, Misther Muldowney, for bein' a thrifle surprised," he said, with a sootherin' smile like a peddler's, "but to tell ye the truth, your good wife and meself med a pleasant little bargain about ye."

The next minute Pether was rubbing his eyes, thinkin' he was in a dhrame, for what did he see but his own wife Sarah go smirking up to the dark sthranger, an' whin she did that he saw that same juntleman houlding out half the full of his hat of silver shilling to her, and whin she'd dhropped the last one of thim into her petticut pocket, it's what she said:

"Yes, Pether asthore, the kind juntleman offered me three pounds tin for ye, an' I tuck it. An' he wouldn't give a penny more for ye, an' I wouldn't take a penny less."

"An' now, Misther Muldowney," says the juntleman, "since yer paid and settled for, fair and honest, will ye plaze put on that shuit of clothes that's lyin' there on the ground beside ye, an' we'll be off together."

Looking to where Sattin pointed, Pether an Sarah spied a shuit of clothes made of iron an' it sizzling red hot in the grass with the flamin' sparks coming out of the arm holes of the weskit.

Oh thin wasn't Muldowney indignant. "So this is the foine, dhry, warrum job yez have for me, is it?" he says, nodding sarcastic towards the shuit. "Well, before I put on thim clothes will some wan plaze expatiate to me whereabouts in the bounds of mathrimony it says that the faymale partner has the mortial right to sell her husband's four bones to Beelzebub?"

That pint of law sthruck Mrs. Muldowney and Sattin flat; an' for a minute they could only stand gawpin' at aich other.

"Would ye be goin' back on the bargin your wife med, shameless man? Would ye be makin' little of her givin worrud? Are ye a man or a mouse, I dunno!" he says.

"It'd be just like him to be makin' little of me," snuffled Mrs. Muldowney.

"An' if it comes to that," blustered Sattin, "if anyone was goin' to sell ye will ye tell us who had a betther right to do it than yer own wife? You an' your pints of law! Didn't Joseph's brothers put sivin coats on him an' sell him for a mess of porridge to the Aygyptians? Answer me that," Sattin cried triumphant.

At that he swelled out his chist an' took a deep proud breath till the stomachs of him glowed red like a furnace.

"Oh hasn't he the larning!" cried Sarah. "Why don't ye spake up, Pether Muldowney,—haven't ye the face to say that Lanty and Cornalious, thim two bagabones of brothers of yours have more right to sell ye than I have?"

"How d'ye know they were goin' to sell me?" cried poor Pether. "An' I don't know anything about Joseph an' his sivin coats of colors an' his mess of porridge, but I do know that the price of three pounds tin on me head is belittlin' an' insultin' to a Muldowney. Ye shouldn't have taken a penny less nor six pounds for me, so ye shouldn't,"

he says, turnin' hot on Sarah. "You an' your little three
pounds tin! Sure didn't Teddy Nolan only yisterday get
foive pound eight for the fractious red cow that used to be
jumpin' the hedges, an' ateing the cabbages. To think that
a Muldowney wouldn't bring as much as an ould cow," he
said, half cryin' with wexation.

While Pether was saying thim things, a new idee came
to Sarah, an' it's what she said:

"There's rayson in what he says, Sattin. Pether may not
be worth six pounds tin, but you might well have guve it."

"He that has all the riches of the say at his disposhial,"
chimed in Pether, raysentful.

Sattin stood look-in' from one til the other his eyes
bulgin' and his jaws dhroppin'.

"Thrue for ye, Pether," spoke up Sarah, bridlin'. "I'm
beginning to think that the schaymer has chayted us."

"I'll not stir a foot with him," says Pether dayfiant,
claspin' his two hands behind his back. Sarah sidled over
to her husband.

"Small blame to ye if ye don't," says she, "afther the
way he's thrated us. Will ye give us the six pounds?" says
she. "Don't go with him Pether, if he belittles ye," she says.

"Why," says Sattin, "you owdacious ringleader of a
woman!" an' the eyes of him were blazing with angry as-
tonishment, "ye offered to sell him to me for sixpence. I
heard ye well though I purtended not to."

"I didn't!" shouted Mrs. Muldowney, her two fists on
her hips.

"Ye did, ye runnygade," roared Sattin, an' the breath
came puffing out of him in blue smoke.

"Oh, vo! vo! will ye listen to what he's afther callin' me!
Oh thin, Pether Muldowney," she says, turning bitter on
her husband, "aren't ye the foine figure of a man to he
standin' there in the middle of the road like a block of
wood listening to this sheepstalin', undherhanded, thin-
shanked, antherntarian thrajucing yer own wedded wife,
and you not lifting a finger till him. If ye wor worth two

338   HERMINIE TEMPLETON KAVANAGH

knots of sthraw ye'd break ivery bone in his body!" says she, beginning to shumper.

I know the saying is that to be quick in a quarrel is to be slow in a fight. One who is clever with his fists isn't handy with his tongue. Such a one is like cantankerous little Manus Hannigan who makes the boast that he has started more fights and fought less himself than any other man in the Province of Munster. But it wasn't that way at all with Pether. Such a rayproach of backwardness never darkened the honor of any of the Muldowneys. The lad was ready with his fists and as proud of them as is the juty of every Tipperary man to be. So at the taunting of his wife every drop of blood in Pether's body flared up intil his face and what does he do but rowl up the wrist-bands of his jacket an' go squaring off at Sattin in the middle of the road.

"Before we begin," says Beelzebub,—an' there was an anxious shadow came intil his eyes, for the Muldowneys as far back as anyone can raymember were renowned gladiathors— "before we attack aich other," says he quick, side-steppin' an' backing away from Pether, "do you bear in mind that she thried to sell ye to me for sixpence."

Sarah hid her face in her apron an' she wailed: "Oh murdher asthore, will ye listen to that! I didn't Pether! An' what's his repitation for voracity agin' my repitation?"

At the mintion of his repitation it was plain to be seen that Sattin winched.

"Will ye guv me back me three pounds tin, ye robber of the worruld?" says he, thrimbling with anger.

"Tut tut!" cried Sarah, tossin' her head. "We hear ducks talkin'. Didn't I kape me part of the bargain," says she. "Isn't Pether there in the road ferninst ye? Why don't ye take him?"

Beelzebub had no time for rayply bekase Pether, with his two big fists flying around and round aich other, was dancing forward and back, and circling from the right to the left, and this way and that whichever way Sattin twisted himself, an' all the time makin' false lunges at the middle of the black lad's chist.

"Howld still, Pether Muldowney, unfortunate man!" cried Sattin all out of breath. "Do ye see Father Delaney comin' down the road behind ye?"

At that Pether and Sarah turned to look, and as they did—Crack!—they heard the ground open, an' before they could twist their heads round again Sattin was gone.

The two hayros stood a minute gaping at the spot where the innimy of mankind had disappeared. Sarah was the first to speak, an' it's what she said, taking hould of Pether by the arrum: "Come on home avic! Did ye see how the conniving villyun thried to chate us? Oh, but yer the brave lad! Give me yerself yit!"

With that the two of them, arrum in arrum as loving as a couple of turtledoves, wint down the road together, an' they never sthopped till they came to the big flat stone by O'Hanrahan's spring; thin a sudden fear took the breath out of Sarah.

"I niver counted the shillings whin the ould targer handed thim to me," she says, "and how do I know whether he counted thim right. It'd be just loike one of his thricks not to."

"We'll sit right down here on the rock an' we'll reckon thim together before we go a step furder," says Pether, anxious.

And so they did. And Sarah made a wide lap to hould the money, but with her hand over her pocket she hesitated a moment, for her mind misgave her that something was wrong. An' sure enough, the two poor crachures got a bad turn, for whin Sarah pulled out a handful of the money it wasn't money at all at all that was in it, but only a fist full of bits of broken glass. An' whin she had her pocket emptied, the sorra thing was there but a lap full of broken bottles.

While the pair of thim, blazin' with anger, sat staring at aich other with faces red as a couple of thrumpeters, far down the road split the wild screech of a laugh.

"D'ye heard him there," whuspered Sarah. "Oh, the dasayver of the worruld! D'ye think if ye were to slip back ye might ketch him, Pether?"

Pether shook his head, and a throubled frown wrinkled his forehead.

"I misdoubt it," says he, "an' besides, I was just thinkin' what'll become of us all at all whin he ketches the both of us on the day of judgment. I hate to be thinkin' of it," he says.

"Oh ho, have no fear, Pether avic," says Sarah, soothin. "I've hit on a jewel of a schayme that'll brake the black heart of him, an' it's this: Do you Pether asthore, lave off the onscrutableness an' answer me back once in a while, an' as for meself, you'll niver hear anither crass worrud out of me two lips till the day I'm buried onless ye dayserve it. An' now, Mr. Sattin, what d'ye think of that?" says she shakin' her fist down the road.

Pether gave his knee a thraymendous slap. "Oh, ye phaynix of a woman!" says he. Wid that he laned over an' guv her a kiss on the lips that might have been heard three fields away.

"That's the first in fufteen years," says he, "but it'll not be the last by any manner of manes; bekase I think the divil niver comes betwixt a man an' his wife tell they lave off kissin' aich other."

"Arrah, go on ye rogue!" says Sarah, smilin' an' givin' him a poke wid her elbow. "Come along home now; I'll put on the kettle an' we'll begin all over again from this day out."

And they riz up then and started for home but afther a step or two Pether turned and shook his fist down the road.

"Oh, aren't ye the outraygeous chaytin' dispectable villyun," he shouted. "No, I mane dayspictory," he corrected himself.

"Ye never said dayspictable at all," soothed his wife, "ye said dayspictatory the first time ye mintioned it," she says.

There's many a couple believe that when they've had a bad quarrel they're ruined and kilt forever. Only yestherday morning Bridget Cronin, twistin' up her hair with thremblin' fingers, rushes over to me own wife and she says, savage:

"I'm going over to me own mother's house and take the childher. I'll not live another day undher the same roof with Marty," she rages.

"Why thin, what murthering thransaction has poor Marty done?" asks me wife, wondhersthruck, for Marty is the broth of a lad.

"Why this avening the baby was peevish, and be accident I let the stirabout scorch in the pot and the petatie cake burn a bit in the ashes. An' what do ye think he says to me at last? Why, that he'd betther be bringing his own mother over to tache me how to manage. He said that, Mrs. Murtaugh, an' all I've done for that man! Do ye think I ought to lave two of the childher with him? He's so fond of Eileen, and he'll be that lonesome avenins," she says, beginning to cry. "I wisht I was dead, thin he'd see," she sobbed.

And Marty stood inside the byre leaning on his arrums over the stone wall glooming down intil the road with a face on him as if he wor looking at thim shoveling clay down on his own coffin, whin ould Mordacai Cannon hobbling up, axed him:

"Is there anyone sick in the house, Marty?"

"No, its a dale worse nor sickness," mourned Marty. "Sickness can be cured," he says, lifting open jaws up to the sky. "Bridget has just tould me she didn't love me, an' would hate the ground I'd walk on till she died. If it warn't for the childher I wouldn't care a rap what happened to me."

And Mordacai caught him be the sleeve and led him, shamefaced, intil the house and thin hobbled over and led Bridget crying intil the house, an' he waited a minute till he saw the two of them standing houlding aich other tight in the middle of the kitchen, and he went down the lane on his shaky legs chucklin' to himself. "They wor wantin' to die!" he crowed.

Whin Marty, fifteen minutes afther, went out into the fields light as a skylark, two long tear sthreaks ran the one on ayther side of his nose the length of his face.

Sure, isn't it the rain that sweetens the green-growing world, and that's the way it is, yer honor. Sure, afther a quarrel all the couple nade do is to raymimber that love is more worth than pride. I meself heard a middle-aged, sinsible looking man sitting in this same jaunting car boasting that he and his wife never had a cross word in all their lives. "God pity ye," says I. For I knew it's little happiness two could have living together all their lives who had as little deep feeling one for the other as never to touch a sensitive narve.

So, although the Muldowneys rayformed entirely, still and all they had their fallin's out. Only Sarah never scolded Pother afther that day except when she thought he dayserved it, and undher them sarcumstances all sensible wives should do that same, and whin she did begin on her husband she rated him in a hot tempered, outspoke tongue-lashin' way as was her natural ordinary jooty.

As for Pether, whether he dayserved the lambasting he got or not he never again met it with smirks and smilings and shrugs and onscrutableness, but with beggings off and excuses and barefaced daynials as any level-headed, sinsible wife-fearing husband is expected to do, and if they didn't live peaceable all the days of their lives afther, at any rate they lived happy and continted.

PATRICK OF THE BELLS

It's many's the fine tale concerning the stormy disputes that raged between great Patrick of the Bells and Ossian, the mighty son of Finn MacCumhull, that the learned clerics of Ireland used to be writing down in their thick leather books; and it's many's the account of the wonderful deeds wrought by Patrick that these same ancient clerics used to be putting there, too—for it's given up by everyone that Patrick of the Bells was the greatest saint that ever lived in the whole world for the working of miracles.

Wasn't it he that, by the ringing of his bell, drove the seventy-times-seven demons from the bald top of Cruachmaa and put them prisoners in the bottom of the Well of the End of the World? And wasn't it he that banished into the depths of the green, shuddering ocean the writhing serpents, and crawling vipers, and every kind of venomous thing that infested the pleasant land of Ireland? And wasn't it he, as well, that stopped the black famine there, by making the grass to grow again in the blighted fields, by putting the swift gleaming fish into the gray, silent streams, and by filling with sweet milk the dried udders of the kine? But greater than all these marvels, I think, was the miracle Patrick wrought upon the pagan chieftain Ossian, and that is what I am going to tell you about now.

Hundreds of years before Saint Patrick first came to Ireland—and it's hundreds and hundreds of years ago entirely that was—Finn MacCumhull and the warriors of

343

the Fianna ruled from their king's dun at Almhuin, over the pleasant province of Leinster. Three score captains there were of the Fianna and five score champions followed every captain when he went to the wars; and the like of them for heroes the world has never seen before nor since.

There was among them there Gaol, the hundred-wounder, who, from the rising to the setting of the sun, on each one of five days fought with the giant Cathaeir of the speckled ships, and killed him after; and there was Faolan, the manly, who slew in one combat the seven brave sons of Lochlin; and Goll, the mighty; and Diarmuid, the brown-haired, beloved of women; and mighty Oscar of the strokes, son of Ossian, who slew the king of Munster, and Cairbre of the silken standard on the same day.

There were among the captains, too, Glas; and Gobha the generous; and Caolite of the flaming hair, whose feet could outrun the west wind; and Conan Moal, the giver of curses, whose words were more biting than the east wind in winter; and Feargus the nimble; and Conn of the sharp green spears; and Ronan, who with his well-tempered blade could pierce an oak tree; and there were many others, too, of renown, of whom I have not time to be telling you. But the like of them all for heroes the world never saw before nor since. Seven feet tall was Minne, the smallest of them all, and the handle of his spear was just a young ash tree. By that you may know what the others were like. Many's the grand song has been made up about them by the ancient bards of Ireland.

For grace and courtesy, for strength in battle, for swiftness in hunting, for skill in making melodious music, there was not the like of the Fianna in all Ireland, and if not in Ireland, why then, of course, never by any chance at all in any other country of the world.

And as it's one above the others there must always be whenever three men come together, so among the Fianna, next in favor and in merit to the great chief Finn there was always standing comely Ossian of the strong hand.

Son of Finn MacCumhull himself is he, and his mother was the goddess, Sadb, daughter of Rodb, the Red. Great was the beauty of Ossian and his fame was over the four kingdoms of Ireland. He could jump over a branch as high as his forehead, and stoop under one as low as his knee, and he running at full speed; and he could pluck a thorn out of the heel of his foot at the same time without hindrance to his flight.

On a day at the court of Teamhair, in the presence of the five Kings and the five Queens of Ireland, the three caskets of honor were given without lessening to Ossian by Cormac, the high king. The first casket held the five silver lilies of courtesy, which meant: mercy to the conquered, hospitality to the stranger, charity for the poor and distressed, gentleness to old men and children, and white homage to women. The second casket contained the five bronze nuts of learning, which signified: skill in fighting, sleight in wrestling, swiftness in hunting, caution in chess-playing, and sweet cunning in the making of melodious songs. The third casket held three golden apples, which denoted courage in danger, faith in friendship, and truth in speaking. And no other man before or since ever got these three caskets at one time without lessening.

So no wonder it was at all that Niahm of the golden hair, who was the daughter of the King of the Country of the Young, fell into conceit with the great fame of Ossian, and journeyed all the way to Ireland for love of him; and no sooner did Ossian set his eyes on Niahm of the golden hair than he loved her with every vein of his body, and it's what he said to her:

"From this day out I will have neither ease of mind nor peace of heart until your life is the same as my life; and for me there's no other woman in the world but you, O woman of the deep-shining eyes!"

For answer, Niahm bent down from the white horse on which she rode, and kissed him on the forehead and on the eyes, and this is what she said:

"There is many a king's son has paid court to me, O Ossian of the comely brow, but it's to you I give my heart and to no other. And it's to take you back with me to my father's country I have come, bringing the white horse of magic for our journey."

And it's what he said, lifting her white hand and pressing it hard to his breast:

"All the sorrows of my life are gathered and crushed into what I must tell you now. At the coming of the new moon, Muirdris, the giant King of Serpents will trail his heavy way through the hundreds of miles of bogs and fens from his den in the west to work destruction on the men and on the sheep and the kine of the pleasant land of Ireland. Every year he comes and goes, and seven champions of the Fianna has he destroyed. It is I that am under the bonds of a warrior now to go and meet him on his way, and it is a sorrow bitterer than death itself that I must part with you here, maybe to never hear your thrush's voice again."

But Niahm only smiled and tossed her golden head. "Let that be no hindrance, my brave Ossian, but rather a reason for a journey to the Land of the Young. As every one knows there is not a sword made by mortal hands that can pierce the enchanted scales on the sides of the King of the Serpents. But there hangs on my father's walls a shining blade of power against serpents. It's the white horse of magic will bring you back at your own wish and bidding, and if you love me as you say, you will come up now and sit behind me here."

So he did that, and the great white horse turned his face to the western sea. And when Finn saw this, he raised three shouts of sorrow: "My woe and my grief! O Ossian, my son, to be going away from me this way! for I know you will never return."

But the white steed never stayed nor stopped, but rose to meet the green combing waves and leaped into them, and the people of the Fianna saw them no more. And

Niahm and the warrior went their way together on the horse of magic over the high-tossing sea and under the dark-running waves toward the Country of the Young.

And as they were going along that way in the shining afternoon of the day, a hornless fawn leaped suddenly up on top of the waves before them, and a red-eared white hound was chasing it. And straightway Ossian, the great hunter, was eager to follow in the chase; but it's what Niahm told him, that these forms running before them were only the creatures of the Sidh, and what they were trying was to lure him from her, the way he would be destroyed in the strong green waves. So, hearing that, Ossian turned his eyes away. Presently, again, a young maid came riding by on a brown steed, and oh, it's she that was beautiful! Her chalk-white skin was like the swan's breast as he plumes himself on the clear waves of Loch Dearg; her lips were the color of the rowanberries; and her hair was just a golden cloud on her shoulders. In her right hand she held an apple of green gold; and it was fast she rode, throwing many a look of terror behind the while. Close after her a youth came riding on a slim white steed; from his shoulders floated a mantle of crimson-red satin, and he was holding a naked sword in his hand.

At that Ossian's hand was on the bridle-rein and his sword was almost from its scabbard, when Niahm quickly warned the champion to pay no heed, for no danger at all was on the maid, but it was she who was no other than the hornless fawn that went past them a minute before, and the youth with the naked sword was that same white hound with the red ear.

As Niahm was saying this, the maid with the golden apple turned, laughed mockingly, and then she and the youth sank together into the sea.

Many other things of wonder Ossian saw on that journey; but the white steed never changed his course nor stayed nor halted till at length and at last it reached the shores of the Country of the Young. There, in the great palace of that land, the King and the Queen gave to their daughter Niahm, and to comely Ossian of the sword, a hundred thousand welcomes.

Some of the poets were saying that it was three hundred years that Ossian lived with his beautiful wife Niahm and their children, and other poets used to be saying that it was five hundred years that he remained there. But, however, long it was, one thing is sure: that he didn't feel the time passing, nor did he dream how long he had been away from his own land. And as there can never be thought of trouble or of danger or of cruel deeds in the Country of the Young, so any thought of Muirdris or of his warrior's bond to fight with the King of the Serpent, never entered into his mind. Neither in the Country of the Young is there age nor sickness nor wasting nor dying, but always feasting and music and hunting and friendly warriors contending one with the other.

And so it was presently that all the recollections of green Erin and of the old life there were driven from his memory by the magic of his beautiful queen, and he was going on forever after, happy and contented with the feasting of today and the hunting of tomorrow. But, if Ossian had forgotten the house of his father, the fame of the warrior still lingered on the misty hills and in the wide valleys of his own country; for the bards of Ireland never left off singing of the brave deeds of the exile and of his comeliness and of his high honor.

And this is the way it was with them when Patrick of the Bells came over to Ireland to preach the truth to the people. And after awhile it came about that Patrick loved to be listening to these old songs of brave deeds; for in his heart of hearts a great saint is neither more nor less than a warrior, only that it is against himself his arms are turned.

And one evening as Patrick sat listening to Cinnfaela, son of Oilill, and he singing the lay of "The Battle of Cnoc-an-Air", a strange wish crept into the saint's mind, and then it grew into his yearning heart; and the wish was no less than that he might bring Ossian back across the western sea from the Country of the Young and baptize him, and so save the hero's soul for heaven. For wasn't it a terrible pity that a hero so lovable and courteous and brave must spend all the ages of time down in the burning pit because there was no one to baptize him or to show him the way to get his many sins forgiven.

And so, for many a day, the saint prayed for this return at matins and at vespers. But whether what happened was in answer to the prayer will never be rightly known; be that as it may, one thing is certain: On a day when Ossian and his young men were coming home from the hunt, a great red cloud of Druid mist settled on the side of the hill before, them, and out of the middle of the cloud a sweet-sounding harp began playing, and the heart of Ossian stood still for he knew it to be Suanach, Son of Senshenn, who was in it playing, and the song that Suanach sang was the lament for the death of Oscar.

And straightway a sudden famishing for a sight of the wide green hills of Ireland, and a hungry yearning for the sound of the long-forgotten voices took the strength from Ossian's limbs, and the enchantment fell from his eyes. When he came up to Niahm it's what he said:

"O Niahm, queen with the sweet voice, my breast is like an empty plover's nest, for the heart that was in it has flown over the seas to Ireland, and I think I shall die now of the lonesome sickness that is on me for the sight of my people. And my warrior's bond is broken and my honor is destroyed and the bitterness of death is sweeter than the loss of a warrior's honor."

And she answered him, and she said: "Ah, then, it's the sorrowful word you're bringing to me this day, husband of my heart, going away that way, and it's maybe never coming back to me."

"Haven't we still the white horse of magic?" he said, "to bring me back safe again to you? The thought of my people is like a burning coal in the middle of my brain."

And it's what Niahm said: "There is grief before you where you are going, comely Ossian, for not one you ever cared for is alive this day to welcome you back to green Ireland. Great Finn and his champions are lying under the heavy stones these hundreds of years. Even the old gods have gone from there. A stranger from Rome with book and bell has banished them, and the faces of the hills are cold and strange. And Muirdris, too, he was driven from Ireland to lie forever chained in the bottom of the farthest of the seven seas. But I give you leave to go, for when the home longing comes into a man's heart all the waters of the world will not quench its burning."

And Ossian could not believe that the great Finn was dead, nor that Muirdris was banished, and it's what he thought, that it was only the tenderness and the love that was in the heart of Niahm for him that made her, after the way of women, speak what was not true. But it's what he did: he took Niahm, his queen, up in his arms, and strove to comfort her, and it's she that cried her fill. By and by she spoke, and this is the warning she gave to him then:

"Remember, O Ossian, what I'm telling you now: If you but touch your foot to level ground you will never come back to me, for the enchantment will be broken by one touch of mortal earth. And I say to you again—and hearken with every vein of your body, my husband: it's danger there is for you in every blade of grass and in every leaf on the bough when once you leave the Country of the Young. And a third time I warn you: if once you leave the horses's back or touch hand or foot to the ground of Ireland, from that moment out your magic youth will fall from you, and you will be old and shrunken and sightless, and there will he no strength in your limbs, and the blood in your veins will turn to water, and death's hand will be on your shoulder. Ochone, mavrone, my grief and my woe, it's well I know you will never come back to us!"

He comforted her as best he could with all manner of promises while he held her there, but when Ossian fronted the white horse of magic to the sea, Niahm gave a great cry of sorrow; and when he leaped into the waves, it is kneeling on the white desolate sand she was, beating the palms of her hands and keening bitterly, like one crying over the face of the dead. And that is how it happened that a mortal brought the first sorrow into the Country of the Young.

Ossian never looked back, but rode as swift as the wind over the high-tossing sea and under the dark-running waves till he came to his own fair country of Ireland. And when he came into the land there was great wonder on him, for the duns of the kings and of the chiefs had disappeared altogether, and the people had dwindled in size till the tallest man of them could walk upright under Ossian's arm. And they stared at him with round eyes, and the women gathered their children and ran from him as if he were a god and it were from Tuatha de Danaan he was coming. And he asked a man of them: "Where is Finn MacCumhull hunting the day?"

And it's what the man said, he stammering with his wonder: "There is no such man in Ireland now, but hundreds of years ago there was a great champion named Finn MacCumhull, and he was the head chief of the Fianna; and the poets have songs about him, and they do be saying that he was the greatest hero that ever lived in Ireland."

And a cold dread came on Ossian, and it's what he said: "And had he a son named Ossian?"

"And the poets do be singing of him, too," the man said, "of how he went with Niahm, the golden-haired, across the seas to the Country of the Young, and how he never came back. But I don't be giving much heed to those old pishrogues, for I don't think they can be true."

Then Ossian asked about Caolite, and Diarmuid, and Goll, and Lugaidh's son, but the man only stared and made a swift crossing sign on his forehead and walked quickly away, and after that the people fled, every one, leaving the great strange man and the white horse standing alone on the roadside.

And a blast of loneliness, fierce as a sweep of a winter storm from the ocean, smote Ossian so that for a time he had no care to live. But presently from the moor a curlew began calling, and the bird's note put a thought into him of the great marsh about the dun at Almhuin, and it's to himself he said:

"I will go up into Leinster; I will go up to the dun of my father at Almhuin."

With that, he lifted the bridle-rein over the neck of the white horse of magic, and they went like the wind, without stopping, until they came to Leinster and to the hill of Almhuin. And when they came to the hill of Almhuin it was a sorrowful, woeful sight that lay before him; for the broad hillside was bare and the walls of the great dun had been leveled to the ground, and the tall weeds were blowing and nodding above the scattered stones. That is how he found the home of his people. But it's when he came to the wide bare spot where the feasting-hall used to be standing, and to the great black hearthstones, long grown cold, that the wildness of grief overwhelmed him, and he struck himself on the breast with clenched fists, and it's what he said:

"Oh, isn't it the sorrowful day, Finn of the open hand, for your own son to be this way a stranger above your empty hearthstones! And you, Goll, and Caolite, and Diarmuid of the fair women, and my own son Oscar, is there never one of you will rise up to bid me welcome? Oh, where shall I turn my face, and who will cover me in my wide grave!"

And as he sat there mourning his head dropped so low that the long yellow hair of him streamed upon the white mane of the horse, two red foxes came out of a hole and began fighting, one with the other, before him. So when Ossian saw that—the great sign of loneliness and desolation in the house of his father—the weakness of sorrow melted his bones and he sank from the top of the horse, and it's how he lay with his lips to the ground, his arms stretched wide, and he was the same as the dead.

Now it chanced that hour that Patrick of the Bells, son of Calphrun, with two of his clerics, was on his way to Ath Cliath to preach the new faith to the people. And some one told Patrick of the strange beautiful man who looked like a god of the Tuatha de Danaan, and who had just gone riding on a wonderful horse up the hill of Almhuin, and who was now lying as one dead upon the ground.

But when Patrick went to that place he saw no wonderful horse, and there was in it no god of the Tuatha de Danaan, but only a tall old man and he lying moaning and mourning among the stones. For, as Niahm had foretold, the instant Ossian's foot touched the ground, the horse vanished and the chill of the ages crept into the warrior's bones and into his heart, and he was a withered old man! Even the mind in him was old.

After Ossian had told his wonderful story to the clerics, Patrick took him by the hand and led him the ways to Ath Cliath, where for three days Ossian listened to Patrick of the Bells preaching to the princes and to the people. And every night, through the long hours till between the crowing of the cock and the full light of day, Ossian would be telling Patrick and his clerics in the monastery the story of the Fianna and of the wonderful Country of the Young. And they would never be tired listening to him.

At first a sorrowful wonder sometimes troubled the heart of the saint, seeing the great warrior so changed and shrunken and old. Maybe it would have been better to have left him in the land of love and forgetfulness and happiness. But Patrick would realize afterward that such thoughts were only subtle temptations from below, for sure wasn't the joy of Heaven a thousand times better than any other sort of happiness.

On the fourth day of the preaching, when Patrick was getting ready to baptize the people, it's what he said to Ossian:

"Come now with the others, son of Finn, till I baptize you and save you from the torments of hell; for if you are not baptized you can never enter heaven."

"But tell me first, Patrick of the white book, where are the Fianna—my son, Oscar of the strokes, Art Garriada, the victorious Caolite son of Ronan, and Finn, my father—are they in your heaven?"

"No," answered Patrick, taken much aback, "their likes would not be let into heaven; you understand they died unbaptized; they are prisoners in deep hell, suffering the torments of fire."

A spot of red anger burned on either cheek of Ossian, and it's what he answered:

"Then keep your heaven for yourself, O Patrick of the crooked staff, and for the likes of these ill-singing clerics! As for myself, I want none of it. I will go to this hell you speak about, to be with Finn, my father, and my son Oscar, and the friends of my youth."

And Patrick was sore sorry to hear this, for he loved greatly the high loyalty and the white honor of the old Fenian; still, he could not keep back a quick surge of wrath, so he said:

"O witless old man, if you had been given but the short peep of one eye into the place where the Fianna are confined, it is a different sort of wish that you would be speaking, and it's humble and frightened enough you would be at the same time!"

Then Ossian, striving hard to keep back the anger, asked coolly of Patrick:

"But how big is this hell of which you all are so much afraid, O son of Calphrum?"

And Patrick was obliged to answer him: "I do not know how big the place is; but, be content, it is wide enough and deep enough, and strong enough to hold forever the sinful Fianna of Ireland."

Then Ossian burst forth: "Well, let me tell you, O stranger in the country, if hell were half the size of Ireland, my

Finn and his champions would cut their way with their swords from one end of it to the other. And know, too, if it were heaven they were wanting to go into, it isn't the likes of your God that would be keeping them out. It's little knowledge you have of Finn, son of Cumhull, to be saying things like that. On the plain of Gabhra, Finn with his own hand slew two hundred fighting men."

"It isn't hundreds that Finn has againt him now, O boastful old man, but thousands, and tens of thousands, and hundreds of thousands."

"If there were as many against him as there are drops of water in Loch Dearg, O Patrick, who belittles the champions of Ireland, my Finn and his heroes would not leave a head on a neck from one end of hell to the other."

And Ossian was not baptized that day. And neither on the next, nor for seven days after that day, did Patrick even speak to the rough old warrior of heaven or of repentance or of any pious thing; but every night of the seven the two were together its only kindness and the deep flattery of long-reaching questions that the pagan got from Patrick. And the saint noticed with great grief that every day the old chief was fainter of voice and weaker than he was the day before, and the fear grew heavy on Patrick that Ossian would die upbaptized. And if the son of Calphrum grew fond of Ossian, it was fonder of the saint that Ossian himself became; and it's what he said at last:

"O Patrick of the long prayers, it's little liking I have for your clerics and their fasting and their singing and their sour faces; but you, O strange man with the pleasant word, it's great the warmth that's in my heart for you, and it's loath I'd be to part with you when we die. Maybe it's not much enjoyment you'll be having in heaven, I'm thinking, with all these wearisome persons fretting and keening from morning till night around you about their souls. Whisper! Do you, Patrick, give up heaven and come with me to the Fianna in hell, where I promise there is plenty of eating and drinking, and singing, and hunting, beautiful women and courting, and chess-playing, and warriors contending one with another. I'll speak the good word for you to Finn, my father, and it's a hundred thousand welcomes will lie before you."

But Patrick answered him sadly: "O foolish man of the sword, it's little of those pleasures are allowed to the enemies of heaven."

On another day Ossian said: "It's what I'm thinking sometimes, Patrick of the white cloak, that if Finn and the King of saints are enemies now, it must be the way that some other king is carrying jealous lies between the two of them. Couldn't you send word to your King that Finn was always the true-hearted man with the open hand?"

"Finn and the Fianna are overthrown; they are in the bonds of pain, being punished for their pride, their boasting, and their misdeeds."

Then Ossian burst forth again: "It's easy for you to say that to me now, when the strength has gone from me, O soft-handed priest; but if Minne, the least of the Fianna, were here, it's few psalms your clerics would he singing in this house the night. And it's many's the sore head would be running about Ath Cliath looking for a place to hide itself. And now, don't be talking to me that way any more, O Patrick of the crooked staves, for it's little heed I'll be giving you from this out!"

"O witless old man!" cried Patrick in great distress, "it's a bed of fire you are making for yourself this day, when you should be striving for the delights and pleasures of heaven!"

"Tell me, Patrick of the golden vestments," the son of Finn asked again, "will Meargach of the green spears, who fought against us with his hosts of Cnoc-an-Air, enter heaven?"

And it's what Patrick answered then: "The unbaptized are enemies of my King; they can never enter heaven!"

And it's then that Ossian said: "it wasn't that way at all with my king, for the whole world might come to his door and get meat and shelter there; and they'd find a smith at a forge, too, that would be mending their arms while they stood boasting, maybe, that those same arms would be reddening the ground with our blood on the morning of the morrow. But tell me another thing, O Patrick: would my horse or my hound be allowed with me in that city?"

"Neither your horse nor your hound nor any soulless thing may enter that place."

"Well then, take my last answer, Patrick of the wheedling tongue: If in heaven you can never hear the song of the blackbird nor the linnet on the bough, nor the cry of the hounds on a, frosty morning, nor the bellow of the stag as he comes leaping down the mountain, it's not the kind of a place I'd like to be spending the rest of my days in. No, no, Patrick of the Bells, don't be throwing up your hands that way, for, whatever happens to me, where I'd be is with my father and his people."

And after that it's how Patrick marveled that while he and Ossian might be talking pleasantly forever about battles and adventures and wonders, still and all, if the two of them began speaking about religious things, then before one could walk five spear-lengths the saint would be losing his temper and the hot anger would drive all convincing arguments and all good discourse to the four winds. So Patrick made up his mind that 'twas an evil spirit that was coming between the two of them, and that for the future the old warrior might say what he liked and Patrick would keep his temper.

Always toward the end of the day, Ossian used to be climbing with his staff up the green slope of Slieve Carman, and it's there he would stay, his chin sunk in his two hands, and he gazing sadly out to where the red sun was sinking into the western sea.

On a day, the son of Calphrun followed him to where he was sitting that way on the hillside, and the two of them remained there awhile without talking together, until Patrick spoke up and said:

"I'm wondering, O Ossian of the brooding mind, what is the secret worry and long fretting that's on you. By virtue of our friendship tell me what trouble it is that you are keeping hidden and covered."

At that the old warrior shifted uneasily and turned away his face. "This is the trouble that's on me," he said at last. "Here I am among strangers, without bread and without any pleasant food. Look you, my breast is beginning to slant inward like a nesting curlew's breast, and soon enough, I am thinking, the two legs of me will be sunk to the size of a robin's legs. My grief and my woe! I, that was used to living in such great plenty, to be spending my days now among a houseful of stingy, fasting clerics!"

"It isn't true at all, what you are saying," the son of Calphrun replied. "Two score round wheaten cakes, with their share of wine and flesh are what is given you every day except the fast days. No, no, it isn't starvation at all that is on you, ungrateful man."

But Ossian wagged his gray head and spoke stubbornly: "It's little liking I have for these same fast days, O priest of the contending tongue, and it's few other kinds of days are coming into your house, and it for my sorrow filled at the same time with praying and doleful singing. It's well I know that if generous Finn and my brave son Oscar were here today we would not be without plenty of meat this night and we now at the command of the bell of the seven tolls."

And it's what Patrick, smiling, answered: "Have done, fond old man! Well I know that it's neither the fasting nor the prayers nor the chanting of the clerics that is on you, but only a long deep yearning for the unblessed woman of magic in that far country, and for your children. And don't I know, too, why you come here day after day, staring across the white-ridged water?"

When Ossian heard that he was silent for awhile, but his two eyes dimmed with the tears that afterward came creeping hot down upon his face, and when he answered it's what he said:

"Well I know what a deep shame it is for a great warrior to be mourning for the sight of a woman, or to be ochoning and sorrowing after little children. But I promised her and she took my promise. And over there beyond that measureless sea, on the white shore of the Country of the Young, Niahm, my beautiful queen without blemish, is every day standing waiting for me, and that is why I sit here from the red of the evening till the black of the night. O Patrick, the heart inside of me is dry and empty as a withered nut with the lonesomeness and the age and the longing for sight of her."

And Patrick spoke, comforting him: "Surely it is, as you say, a shame for a great warrior like yourself to be mourning and fretting, and she unblessed—a woman of magic and not human at all. And you'll quit thinking of her now."

And it's what Ossian said then: "O Patrick, who has traveled the world over, it is yourself has not seen, East or West, nor yet have any of your clerics seen the equal of that woman for beauty or goodness. Her voice was softer than the blackbirds of Derrycarn when she spoke my name; a gold ring was always hanging from each curl of her shining hair; and the kisses of her lips were sweeter than honey mingled through red wine."

And Patrick said then: "Isn't it a pitiful thing to hear a withered old man with such silly words in his mouth? Isn't it fitter that you should be crying those hot tears for fear of the anger of God?"

And Ossian spoke from behind wet hands: "I will cry my fill of scalding tears, O Patrick of the white staves, though not for God, but for her and for Firm, and for my lost people."

But Patrick put down his anger and he said: "It is a sin for you to be crying that way after the like of any woman, and I will tell you now of how a woman first brought all the sin and trouble into the world."

And with that the saint began telling Ossian the true story of Adam and Eve. But when Patrick got to that part

of the story where Adam was telling God that it was all
Eve's fault, and that she had tempted him to eat, Ossian
impatiently waved the saint to silence and wouldn't be
listening any further, and it's what he said:

"Don't be telling me any more about your saints or of
their doings! If I had Adam before me now, it's little breath
I'd leave in his body to be carrying tales again that way on
any poor woman!"

It was hard for Patrick to control himself then, but he
put down his just wrath and said: "Will you ever leave off
with your empty words, O hoary old man? Shameful it is
for me to be listening, and you always talking in sinful
mockery of the great saints."

And Ossian answered: "It isn't mockery. Were my own
Oscar and your three greatest saints hand to hand on
Cnocha-bh-Fiann, and if I saw my son down, I would say
that your saints were strong men. Patrick, ask of God if
he remembers when Finn fought with the king of the speckled ships, and if He has seen East or West or in His own
country, a man who was equal to my Finn."

And Patrick strove in vain to answer with a soft tongue,
but he cried:

"O wicked old man, it's little you know of God, to be
speaking such wild words. It was He who made the sun
and the moon and the stars; it is He that gives blossoms
to the trees and makes the grass and the flowers to grow in
the fields."

And Ossian spoke slowly and with scorn then:

"It wasn't in making grass and birds and little flowers
that my king took delight, but in spreading his banner in
front of the fight, and in hacking at bones, and in leading
his warriors where the danger was greatest, and in courting and swimming and hunting, and in beholding all in
the house drinking. It was in such things as these, O son
of Calphrun, that my king took delight. Now, Patrick, by
virtue of the white book and the crozier that is lying there
at its side, relate to me any great feat of strength or any

great deed of fighting that was ever done by your King of saints; I haven't heard that He ever reddened His hands."

At that Patrick rose hastily from the rock, and took his crozier and his white book from the ground, and he was very wroth. Twice he tried to speak, and twice he held his words. Then it's what he said:

"Cease your blasphemies, O withered old man! It is your ignorance and want of knowledge that saves you from the present anger of God. Your time of grace is dwindling into hours; before they have slipped away entirely, submit to Him who does all things well. Stoop your head and strike your breast and shed your tears."

And it's what the warrior answered: "I will strike my breast, indeed, and shed my fill of tears, but not for God or for His saints, but for my Finn and the heroes." And the next second Ossian was alone on the side of the bleak hill.

But that night Patrick brought his own share of wheaten cakes and gave them to Ossian.

And on another day Patrick was speaking of the day of judgment, when all the dead would rise, when all who fell in battles and all who were drowned in the waves, as well as those who died in their beds, would be coming together in one place for judgment. And the son of Finn asked of Patrick:

"Oh, tell me, priest of the pleasant speech, is it sure that Finn and my son Oscar will be there, and Luanan of the heavy spears, and Cruagan the mighty, and Mualan of the exploits?"

And Patrick answered: "Finn and all his host will stand before the judgment-seat on that day to take sentence for their sins."

And Ossian asked again: "Do you think will Cairbre, the high king, with the hosts of the Clanna Moirne, be let within sight of the Fianna?"

And Patrick answered, as before, that all men that were ever born of woman must stand before the judgment-seat that day.

And it's what Ossian said: "Well then, I'm thinking, Patrick, that if all Finn's champions come together again that morning with the hosts of King Cairbre, who fought against us at Gabhra, you may tell your God that since the world began He never saw, East or West, nor between heaven and the grass, such grand fighting as He will see that day."

And Patrick answered him sharply: "It's little fighting the Fianna will be doing there, and it's little they'll be thinking of battles, but it's mourning and weeping they'll be, and gnashing their teeth as they are being driven away into the burning pit."

And it's what Ossian answered: "O stranger in the country, isn't it the great spite you have against the champions of Ireland, who never did you any harm, to be putting the heavy lies on them that way! But let me tell you that it isn't mourning or weeping at all we will go from that place, but free and unhindered marching proudly together, one breast even with another breast, our slanted spears shining, our silken banners spread, our bards chanting the noble war-songs, and the soldiers of heaven running frightened and scattered before us."

At that Patrick was in great trouble; and he went out of the house then, and shut himself up in the chapel, and it's there praying he was until evening; and he never stirred while the vespers were being read, and even long after the cloisters were still with the sleep Patrick was kneeling, with bowed head, like a statue of stone. But at the turn of midnight he arose and went to the cell where Ossian was sleeping, and it's what he said:

"Awake, O Ossian of the stubborn heart! Arise, for my God has taken pity on your unbelief."

Then Ossian, without a word, rose wondering, and the two went into the darkness and the silence of the night. It's by every short way they went over the hills and through the valleys until, by dusk of the evening of the morrow, they came to the ford of the river that flowed through the

wide plain of Gabhra. And when Ossian saw that place a
great weakness came on him, and he leaned his full weight
on the shoulder of the saint, and it's what he said:

"My grief and my woe, O Patrick of the helping arm!
it's well I know this sorrowful spot. It is the battlefield of
Gabhra, where the bravest and the comeliest lie buried. I
saw that stream before us run crimson red with the best
blood of Ireland. Och, ochone, my grief! There at the hill's
foot fell my son Oscar of the strokes, and just here sank
down together the seven brave Sons of Caolite, and there
died Lugaidh's son; and never in this world before was
there such loss of fighting-men. Why have you brought
us to this sad place, O Patrick?"

And it's how the saint answered him: "It's because the
dust of the Fianna lies buried all about us here that we
came. Tell me, Ossian of the long years, if Finn and the
Fianna were at peace with God, would you also be baptized, and so be prepared for the city of saints?"

"It's little use to be striving to hide it from you, Patrick;
it's hard it is to be at odds with you, and gladly I'd be
friends with God just for your sake. Besides, if there be
need of fighting-men in heaven, the King of saints cannot
do a wiser thing than to send for Goll and the mighty Oscar
of the strokes and the soldiers of the Fianna."

And Ossian could not understand at all the tears in
Patrick's eyes nor the tremble in his voice as the saint
answered him:

"The mercy of God is more wonderful than all His works;
He has answered the prayers of the humblest of His ser-
vants. So, Ossian, this night you will be christened with
Finn, your father, and with your loved comrades of the
Fianna; your high loyalty to them has conquered heaven.
Come with me now to the ford."

At that he led the old pagan's faltering steps into the
shallow stream and baptized him as he stood leaning on
his staff in the full sweep of the moon. When that was
done he bade Ossian return to the water's edge and wait

for him there. But Patrick remained in the water praying, and it's what it seemed, that his figure grew taller and his face glowed with a white light. Three times he raised his arms toward heaven, then bowed his head again and waited. And the wind hushed into sudden silence, and the dark rushes on the bank ceased to sway and to whisper, and from the old battlefield around them came a low swelling murmur of many deep voices.

While he, Patrick, waited there, a heavy, luminous mist settled on either bank of the stream. Presently the figure of a giant warrior with shield and sword, and two spears of ancient make, stood at the river's edge, outlined against the mist; and Patrick knew by the noble face and the king's crown that was upon the warrior's forehead that it could be no other than the great Finn, son of Cumhull himself, that was in it. And proudly the warrior figure strode into the stream and stately bent his knees before Patrick, and the saint baptized him there. When that was done the mighty son of Cumhull arose and passed on into the mist of the shore opposite whence he had come. Then followed Oscar of the strokes, and Carrioll of the white skin, and Faolan the liberal, and Conan of the sharp tongue, and Caolite of the flaming hair, and his seven sons. And as each passed he bent his knee in the flood, and Patrick sprinkled the water on his forehead and spoke the words that changed him into a child of God. Thus captain followed captain, and host followed host, until the warriors came no more.

When the last figure melted away into the haze, Patrick knew that his task was ended. But as he turned to regain the bank a resplendent figure stepped forth to meet him. Of all the men Patrick had ever seen in the world, this one was the stateliest and comeliest. It's more than seven feet tall he was, and the hair of his proud head fell like burnished gold to his shoulders. Upon his brow was a golden fillet, and a collar of red gold encircled his neck. In spite of the youthful beauty of the man's face, Patrick knew that it was Ossian and no other that stood before him. As the saint gazed, the apparition raised its right hand high above its head, with the open palm toward Patrick. And it's how it stood there smiling a little minute, and then disappeared through the cloud, the way the others had gone.

As that happened the mists lifted, and Patrick went out to the shore where the figure of the old man was lying, and it's how he lay with his forehead to the ground, and he cold and dead.

And the great saint, silent from troubled thinking, knelt a little while over him there, and then it's a strange enough prayer for a Christian saint to make that he offered to God and this is what he prayed: "Oh Father, of the mortal and of the immortal—Lover of the lands of life and of the lands of fairie! among all your countless creatures, where was there one life worn with braver honor or in such deep agony of loyalty. Thou whose Omnipotence canst join the real to the invisible, take pity on the fevered longing of his soul; somewhere in your unseen Universe let the two faithful hearts join once more and forever. I ask this prayer to be granted not out of Thy mercy but from Thine Infinite Justice. Grant him peace and rest and happiness, Oh Lord!"

Some learned clerics do be arguing that the saint meant this and others do be contending that he asked that by this strange prayer. However, all agree that a Christian saint couldn't have asked that the soul of an unbaptized person should be joined through all eternity with a woman of the Sidh who was an unbaptized person as well. It isn't for the likes of us who have little knowledge of pious ways to contradict them. But a poor puzzled hope comes into my own mind sometimes. Anyhow sure God understood.

At any rate, after asking God those things the saint arose with a lightened heart and journeyed till he brought back five holy monks for the burial.

Then Patrick made a wide grave of stones over against the hill's foot where Oscar fell, and he buried Ossian there, and while they said the prayers for the dead over the new grave they wept for him.

Now that was the greatest miracle of Saint Patrick—bringing the Fianna of Ireland from the grave the way they would be baptized and saved for heaven.

Coachwhip Publications

CoachwhipBooks.com

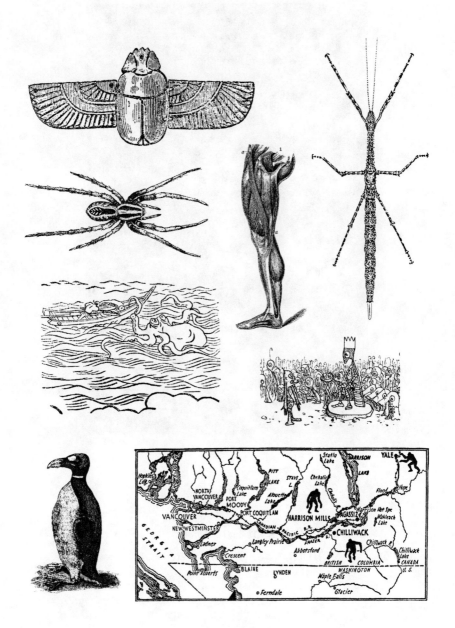

Shadows from a Veiled Creation

Classic Tales of Supernatural Fiction
in the Christian Tradition

ALSO AVAILABLE

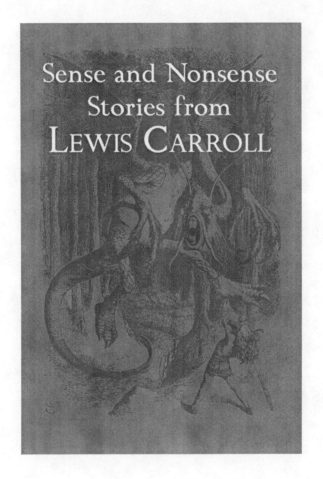

Sense and Nonsense Stories
from Lewis Carroll

Alice, Sylvie and Bruno, and More...

ALSO AVAILABLE

The Wit, Whimsy, and Wisdom of
G. K. Chesterton

VOL. I
THE NAPOLEON OF NOTTING HILL
THE FLYING INN
THE TREES OF PRIDE

The Wit, Whimsy, and Wisdom
of G. K. Chesterton
Volumes 1-6

The Man Who Was Thursday, Manalive,
The Ball and the Cross, Heretics,
Orthodoxy, and Much More...

ALSO AVAILABLE

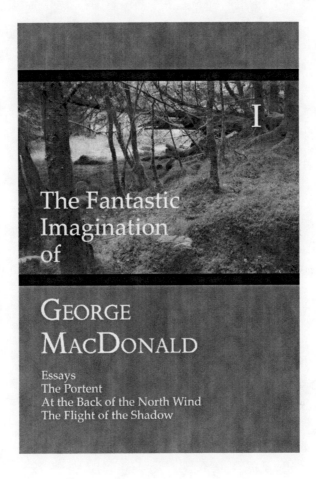

The Fantastic Imagination
of George MacDonald
Volumes 1-3

Phantastes, Lilith, The Princess and the Goblin,
and Many More...

LaVergne, TN USA
01 April 2010
177918LV00001B/254/P